TRY ME

BY

FARAH DAMJI

Try Me is a powerful biography of migration – a tale of displacement, sex, betrayal and the moral and intellectual struggle on the edges of contemporary culture. This is a modern woman's journey to define herself and reclaim her life.

Farah's journey begins in Africa and traverses three continents. She leaves several identities, that of the only 'brown girl in her school', that of the editor of a revolutionary style magazine, that of one of the glitterati in New York, to become an addict and a quasi-criminal.

This is a fascinating, confessional and defiant glimpse of that life. What happens when money, sex and power just aren't enough? This is a riveting behind-the-scenes glimpse at the lives of the rich and the privileged. What made a socialite from a fortunate background, who was on her way to becoming an important voice in British media become a quasi-criminal?

Friends and family become enemies, enemies become allies and lovers; nothing in life or in the version of her story, which was followed by the international media, is what it seems.

Through this retelling Farah contends that nothing is what it seems:

"The truth," she says, "is just an agreed upon set of lies."

ISBN 978-1-907-18804-6

Credits:

Book design and layout by Marina Maskovsky
www.coroflot.com/maskovsky

Cover Concept by Big Fanta
www.bigfanta.com

Cover Photography by Paul Soso
paulsoso@hotmail.com

Printed by CPI Antony Rowe

Published by: The Ark Press Ltd
www.thearkpress.com

Dedication

This book was written for my son and my moon, Imran and Marina.

With thanks for the unconditional love and broad shoulders of my Rockin' Rabbi, Isaac Sinwani whose screaming scanning and prayers in unlikely places work.

With gratitude to Rabbi Yacob Leib HaKohain who teaches me that he doesn't teach but that I learn when I stop talking. And listen.

With thanks to Farrukh Dhondy, David Molyneux and Imran Khan who stuck like glue through sick and sin.

For Jim, Raj, Clive, Anna, to all the people along the way, you were the angels on my path.

Dedication

There is no greater agony than bearing an untold story inside you.
Maya Angelou

The world is what it is; men who are nothing,
who allow themselves to become nothing, have no place in it.
Sir V. S. Naipaul

This book was written as an antidote to:
The worldwide monopolies that sweep all before them with exuberant
contempt for people's rights, their property and their past.
Henry Porter

The times they are a-changin'

Farah Damji was born in Uganda in 1966 to South Asian parents.

In 1970 she moved to London, where she did most of her growing up. In 1985, as soon as she was legal, she left for New York, promising to take up a place at UCL. Alas that never happened.

Farah has seen and done many things: from art dealer, to interior designer, magazine publisher, to mistress and socialite. In all things she excelled, until the irresistible urge to self annihilate – instilled in her by her loving parents – kicked in. Drugs, sex and drama didn't fill the " guest shaped" hole at the core of Farah's being. So she rebelled against all the things she was supposed to be by trying crime, the way someone else might try on a new pair of shoes.

Today, she describes herself as a work-in-progress on the way to becoming a human being, rather than just a human doing. She is the mother of two adorable children, a writer and an ethical fashion designer. She lives in London and dreams of Tuscany.

Raising Malawi

Fifteen per cent of the author's royalties are being donated to Raising Malawi.

Since 2006, Raising Malawi has been dedicated to bringing an end to the extreme poverty and hardship endured by Malawi's one million orphans. Co-founded by Madonna and Michael Berg, Raising Malawi uses a community-based approach to provide immediate direct physical assistance, create long-term sustainability, support education and psycho-social programs, and build global awareness through multi-media and worldwide volunteer efforts.

To find out more please visit www.raisingmalawi.org

Prologue

It took a second of distraction, a quick look back to ensure that no one was watching, and then a series of those moments, separated by months or years, for a life to come undone.

London, February 2005.

I am bored with the relentless police investigation into me, which has lasted three years. I can't move, I'm caught up in my actions and I'm hogtied for fear of what the pigs will come up with next. My bail conditions specify that I must spend each night at home in Chelsea which means that I can't go to my sanctuary in Hampshire for the weekends.

The bail conditions don't stop me, I go anyway, speeding down the A3 in my silver sports Mercedes, and I enjoy living dangerously and not getting caught. Stupid rules were made to be broken. But now, I want this to end. A zealous policewoman from Fulham Police Station watches over my every move; she is more down-sized Columbo than the slick sharpness of CSI. She has found mail belonging to other people who live in the same block of mansion flats, during a recent search.

I am being charged with stealing from Royal Mail. She gets little or no co-operation from the so-called victims. The whole building's post is dumped into the slot in the front door of whichever flat the temporary postman feels like, we have no post-boxes in the entrance hall and other people's post is often delivered to me accidentally, as mine is to them. She is floundering to find something to stick and send me to prison. I am the resident evil in my part of Chelsea as far as she is concerned.

She is calling contacts in my cell phone and her latest gas is to tell my friends, as she makes her way through the address book, that I am dangerous and that I might have links to "suspected terrorists." This image of me as the dark Nikita designer terrorist with a mortar grenade strapped inside my Chanel jacket makes me smile. Indulge me; I can still joke about this, the London bombings haven't happened yet.

They are a good five months away. The cockroach – DC Sophie Roche – comes to my flat on Kings Road in the early morning, almost weekly, to arrest me and to drag me to the cop-shop; she does not have much sway with the Crown Prosecution Service.

They told her, most recently that they would not be bringing a witness intimidation charge against me for sending an e-mail to an ex-tenant who had left my flat in a frenzy and smashed up the boiler.

The main indictment concerns me stealing a nanny's credit card to buy a laptop. For now, let's just say I needed it.

Knightsbridge Crown Court is in Southwark. True to the Byzantine organization of the Criminal Justice System, it is the local Crown Court to Chelsea. The papers for the Crown's case are in disarray, the court has lost its bundle and the Prosecution hasn't managed to assemble a coherent set of indictments. As surely as the minute hand on the clock face moves with stifling regularity, the case is postponed, again.

We go back to court, again, in two weeks and there is a technical error, which means that they are still not ready. It doesn't help that I am committing more crimes whilst I am out on bail. My mother reluctantly coughed up the £10 000 cash imposed upon my freedom. My parents have been good for nothing, except money. The Judge has told the Prosecutor to go away and come back with the correct sheet of indictments.

The dopey, half-smiling Judge, who is out of touch with life in the real world, is a lot further removed than the few feet of height his podium lends him. He is the Queen in the courtroom, I remind myself, and I must try not to sneer.

It's a weekday afternoon and I am in my office. Boredom is my anathema. I call the chambers of the black prosecution barrister. It is easy enough to find out which set he belongs to and what level of experience he has, I say I am calling from the CPS. I have a natural ability to impersonate or personify, in order to glean information that I need. "Social engineering" or a journalist's bloodhound resilience, call it what you like.

These skills grease the way to get his home and mobile numbers from the eager clerk on the other end of the phone, who I imagine is also bored, in an office with no air and no windows, faraway on the other side of London. Information is power. It is easy to access; it comes down to how it is requested. If you ask nicely, you'll get it.

The phone rings a couple of times and the small and barely audible voice of my conscience thinks I should hang up now; this is a fool's game. But I don't feel any danger; there is no thought as to what the consequences of this conversation might be.

I haven't planned a conversation; I'm going to play it by ear. This is how I live, by the seat of my La Perlas. His eagerness makes the game too easy. He is dead pleased to find himself in a case important enough that it warrants him being called at home by his employers and masters. He begins to talk and the words trip off his tongue, wadges of words. Soon he has volunteered more information than he should have.

He never asks me to verify who I am; I have given him a made-up name and restricted my number. I know enough about the case and the flaws in it to lure him into a false sense of security. I reveal just enough to ease his mind and trick his confidence.

He tells me that he won't be able to attend the first day of the trial, as he is a witness in a burglary case. I draw him out about it, there's nothing small people love more, than to talk about themselves. He appears to have a chaotic personal life and a pretentious double-barrelled surname.

Our man is a fine tribute to Uncle Tom; he has recast himself in a favourable light to please the eyes of the master race. There's enough of the anti-black in this refashioned version to make him palatable. He has decided, on the advice of the police insect that I, Farah Damji, am guilty as charged.

There is very little I can say, overtly, in my defence, without giving the game away, but I want to chuck a spanner in the works. I throw a little power trip his way. I have spent half a lifetime still standing, in spite of not thinking that I know or am enough, but I do know my way around a person's ego. I have spent tens of thousands of pounds on analysis so I know the rudiments of psychology. "I" am speaking as someone in authority.

I patiently test the evidence and I put holes in his swaggering confidence; I ask him if he knows that Stuart Riley, who is one of the victims in the postal theft case, had been a tenant of Farah Damji and left her with £8 000 worth of damage to her half million pound flat, with no forwarding address? That he is a yuppie trader at Goldman Sachs with whom the jury is unlikely to sympathize?

Is he aware that the policewoman knows these details and I helpfully suggest that maybe she isn't giving him all the salient facts of the case? Does he know that the CPS has received a phone call from David Blunkett's office asking us to review the case carefully; Ms. Damji is a personal friend of the Home Secretary.

David Blunkett's unusual domestic arrangements have made front page news recently: the country is drowning in the swilling backwash of the Kimberley Quinn Nannygate affair and the Home Office has been turned upside down. The first fine thread has been pulled which will eventually unravel the Sadie and Dave regime. But this is not unusual; such things are known to happen in this government. There have been many acts of deceit, cover up and nepotism. Labour has already laid the deep foundations for its legacy of sleaze.

I tell him I will send a file, with new statements the policewoman has kept from him, and some more evidence, which he can collect from the reception of Knightsbridge Crown Court the following morning. I haven't thought this one through; now the words have taken over, they are tripping off my tongue.

The next morning.

We have just come out of court, he has asked for an adjournment to meet with my counsel. He is clearly flustered. His white powdered barrister's wig is set askew, revealing his tightly-curled head. His brow glistens like sweating chocolate. He flaps his long poly-cotton black wings and bursts in without knocking.

I am sitting at the table of the life-sucking grey cubicle, waiting for my own barrister to find me after he has finished speaking to a witness. It is obvious political pandering to have a black barrister act as the lead prosecutor in the case against the wayward Asian socialite; no one can later level charges of racism. After all, we are all shades of foreign, just different variations of beige.

"Is Mr. Wrack here?"

He is nervous and edgy; he stands in the doorway, which frames his bulking, lumpy mass but he doesn't quite step over the threshold. Good, I think. I don't turn around to look at him.

He speaks to my back. "No idea. It's not my day to watch him."

"I need to speak to him. Ask him to come and find me, I'll be along here in one of the small meeting rooms."

"Go and look for him yourself. I am not a messenger."

I turn only my head to address him, so he knows when I turn away from him, that he is dismissed. I have no rising anxiety about the potentially messy and inexplicable situation I have created.

This is the day before my trial is meant to start. The prosecution's case is still shambolic. The weary, leering Judge, His Honour John Samuels has told the CPS to set its case straight several times. As the files mount up, as I continue to commit more and more crime while I am out on bail, the CPS ties itself in pretty knots made of the same pink cotton tape that holds their towering, crumbling bundles of evidence together.

He, my racially profiled and politically correct black prosecutor-persecutor has not been able to attend that day's hearing; he has his own case, remember. He, the hunter has become the prey. The rumour round the building is that he's been rolled on his way home from a pub and club crawl. Stand-in counsel has just briefed him.

When Nick comes back, he asks me directly if I know anything about a call to the prosecutor. He tells me that strange allegations are being made. It is easy enough to convince him I don't know anything with a flippant flick of my long black hair and a shrug of Chanel cashmere-covered shoulders.

He has been selected to represent me by my solicitor, Imran Khan and is a tenant in Michael Mansfield's Tooks Chambers. I lie to Imran too, I lie to everyone.

He believes me, for the chaos on their side is like the courtroom scene from *Alice in Wonderland*. The Judge struggles to maintain decorum. The promised file, the lethal document that will slay the she-dragon hasn't materialized.

The black barrister made some nasty comments about the investigating officer to me, during that fake phone call. He was complaining that she was too eager to get the conviction, that there appeared to be something personal about the case which was unprofessional and that she was constantly pushing him but unwilling to do any work, such as evidence checking. Clearly he doesn't like or respect her. And he told me as much.

In the cold, colourless light of the courtroom corridor the realization that he was stung begins to dawn on him. Shame creeps into the edges of his fingertips. Then anger courses through his veins.

I smile to myself as Nick Wrack shrugs his broad shoulders and sighs to the Judge, with the patience of Saul, how he wishes that the other side would get their act together. He asserts to the court that he will not accept any more delays.

Back in the grey conference box: we pull our chairs closer and we begin pouring over the files and statements that he has been handed most recently. A delicious sense of wickedness, of doing something naughty and daring settles over me like afterglow. Finally, I have handed them shit which can stick.

There was no art in my deception; I knew I was going to get caught. I wanted it, to end the mess of my life which I had made so far, but I didn't know how to stop. I was hardly the greatest criminal mastermind the world has ever seen. No, I was more the wicked witch of West London, and the fabrication of everything you wanted me to be, the reflection of fantasy and evil. You created this monster.

In the beginning...

Another Life

The morning scratches her claws across the blackboard of the night. Streaky scratches of light open a little wider and turn milky. Clouds and colours are revealed. The sky is slung low in Africa, if you could stretch your arms just a little further, your fingertips might graze something soft and black and enter into the layer of dreams. Slowly, the eyelids of morning open, still heavy with sleep and day raises her arms. Another day, time for the fuzzy remnants of our dreams to take flight. The hemlines of night's gown rise slowly and are folded away.

We live in a squat, sprawling house, in Kampala, 17 Acacia Avenue. It nestles in the shade of thorn trees and a vanilla and raspberry ripple swirl of a magnolia tree dominates the front lawn. Every morning, the grass is carpeted with waxy, smile-shaped petals and I can hear the gardener sweep them aside with a broom made of twigs as it scrapes the footpaths which meander between his manicured flowerbeds.

That sound, the crackle of dry branches, the swift whisk of his wrist as he flicks, is the sound that percolates through my half-sleeping state. I am four and barefoot by choice. I don't wear shoes or socks. It takes much wrangling and cajoling by Teresa, my *ayah* to make me wear more than the orange, cotton-lawn print dress which reaches above my knees and a straw boater with a trailing, cream ribbon, which my father has brought me back from his travels somewhere west. This is the uniform of my childhood.

Ours is a stuttering, cluttering house, filled with noise and newly whitewashed. It's stuffed with the latest gadgets such as Hoovers and record players. This is the late 60s and my parents lie at the heart of beautiful, bright, brown things that inhabit this play-play paradise.

My grandparents made Uganda their home; they had been brought here by the British in India to supervise the network of railways that was required to connect the far-flung corners of this dark-hearted continent. But Africa never loved us or reached out to take us in; we were unwanted guests who overstayed our welcome, sucking out all that was good and rich and leaving resentment and dry bones in our wake. We claimed it anyway; we staked out our homesteads with tall fences and razor wire and pretended everything was just fine. "This is now mine," we asserted.

This is now mine.

My ancestors glare angrily from fading sepia toned photographs at the mess we have made, they look stern, in their military uniforms with their MBE's shining; they look so British with their stiff, swarthy Asian upper lips. They were more British than the white boys from home.

The Asians, who came from India, are the proud, fair-skinned Farsi's from Iran with their lilting language and the Hindus and Muslims from Northern India and Pakistan. They had no predilection for going native; that was a mad dogs and Englishmen affliction, only for the white sahibs – those other, affectedly barefoot, Home Counties ex-pats who called Keeh-nyah "home."

My ancestors on my mother's side were honoured by having streets named after them across East Africa that were changed after the uprisings and eventually, independence. Alidina Visram Street became Daniel Arap Moi Avenue. Like specks of dirt in the tropical rain, our heritage in that part of the world was washed away, swirling, down, down into history's forgotten sewers.

We had no right to belong. That was removed by the swift stroke of an unforgiving pen, the same one that rewrites history over the centuries. What would they say to that, those khaki-camouflaged proud forebearers of mine? But for now, this is my kingdom, and it stretches as far as I can see.

The house is enclosed by a high wire fence, around the perimeter and there's an *askari* at the gate. He stands up straight and tall when guests or delivery boys arrive; he is proud to have a purpose and that he can commit his respect with action, in the smallest task. He towers over me like the black knight in a pack of cards but he doesn't frighten me; Teresa and Askari are my playmates. I call him Askari. Askari is the Swahili word for guard, I hear my parents address him in this way so I call him by his function. I never knew his name. In my play world Askari is the hunter, he chases lions and tigers through the wilderness of the garden, shouting to me if he catches sight of one, which only he and I can see. Teresa shakes her head, convinced he is wasting time when he should be working. She tells me in vain, that there are no tigers in Africa.

These are the people that populate my games of pretend, they willingly take on the roles I give them; Teresa will stand still for me as I tie her with lengths of string, which she uses to hang up the laundry. We pretend she has been captured and all the while she only smiles and sweats sweetly, letting off the fragrance of carbolic soap and cocoa butter.

While I play under her feet, she shakes out the wet clothes from her straining reed basket and hangs them up to dry so they flutter, making mute, dazzling prayer flags which smack the white, midday sunshine.

The consequences of other people's actions make my life what it is. That much is clear, life was what they made for me, and mine was stable and predictable.

Teresa goes to the market most mornings to buy fresh vegetables for soup at lunchtime. Sometimes, a stream of *mbogha mamas* forms a shuffling queue, outside the gate to our compound. They wait in a silent, restless queue for her to come out and see what they are selling. They pray that today she doesn't feel like treading the melting tarmac under the sweltering African sun, which floats amidst Disney-like animated clouds.

At this tiny age I understand rank, and Teresa pulls it with the corner of her mouth or the flick of an eye, a cold stare and the vegetable ladies straighten up like a ragamuffin regiment. In this scorching equatorial inequality, I learn about the relationship between the buyer and the seller, she has the power: she chooses our lunch and that choice will decide which of the vendors will have money. Then they can feed their own, all hungry like baby cuckoos. The crumpled, dirty banknotes she takes from her apron pockets, which look dead and dull to me, confirm her place at the top of their supply chain.

The skin on Teresa's balloon face is shiny and almost indigo, like an aubergine. She leans her huge bosom over the basket for shucking peas, which she lifts with calibrated precision, then she lowers herself down, flat-footed in the same way that small children and yogis do, but her massive behind balances her out so she doesn't topple over.

Carefully, she drapes her starched apron over her knees, and it makes snowy peaks of their mounds, and there she sits over the peas in their pods and she nips their long green talons. She inspects each one. Those that pass muster she gently places into a pan of cold water, next to her swollen and cracked ankles. She arraigns the rejected peas, cursing under hissing breath, as if they are deliberately trying to cheat her, with her flinty eyes shining and her flat nose flaring. They will be dealt with later.

After the labour of the morning, the aroma of freshly made bread and steaming soup curls from the kitchen into the garden, and she calls me,

"Farah, *toto kidogo*, come to eat."

I pretend not to hear and she calls again. This is part of our ritual. She waddles, out of the house, carrying the glass bowl of clear vegetable soup, which she holds in a corner of her apron. On the edge of the bowl she has balanced slices of bread. The bread is warm and steam rises from the soup, but Teresa seems to feel no pain. She can walk barefoot like a stoic on the footpath with a basket of vegetables or laundry perched on her head, an exotic jungle cat.

I sputter behind her, jumping up and down, if the soles of my feet hit the ground for more than a second, I am like hot oil off a heated frying pan. All the time, she walks serenely, unaffected, as if she is in a deportment class, but balancing a basket and not books on her head.

The skin on her soles and her heels are as cracked and dry as the clay seams in the earth, but I am fascinated with her hands; where they turn pink and fleshy. Her hands tell a life-story; the ridges on the sides of her fingers where dark meets light skin form an almost straight line. It's the same way in which night falls on the horizon, a parallel line against the fading sun softened landscape.

I hold my tiny, brown hands against her arm, broad, hairless and muscular. Her skin is as taut as a drum, she is wrinkle free. I love the contrast, of my light and her darkness, there is something familiar and comforting in her deep, burnished colour, and I look uncooked beside her. I love her warm hands, they feel safe. But best of all I love her voice.

She tells stories of magical animals and warrior men that talk to them, who fall asleep under open, starry skies, in the dusky shadow of a lion's mane. Her tales tell of man and beast sharing the earth, living side by side. At night she sings to me, her voice is as soft and sweet, as full as the moonlight's sanctuary which covers our house under its midnight veil.

In Africa I live close to the earth and I feel the nuances of her moods in the shapes of the seasons; the rain falls like clockwork, at noon. It pours down like the unleashed notes of a symphony from the sky, freed from the order of any music. Rain loosens frenzies of invisible chains, which whip the ground the colour of dried blood, into a foamy copper fury. Plants and buds grow before my eyes; seasons change in minutes and as fast as the rain comes down the sun scorches all signs of the downpour away.

Life has Kodak-chrome intensity; colours breathe alive like fire and jostle for space. Scents unfold, laying their trails to tempt honeybees, and butterflies as large as my hands quiver by, they shimmy to a tune I can't make out. Life teems at three feet high.

I remember almost falling, so many times but his pale hands with long, tapered fingers would always catch me. I remember grazing my knees, falling out of trees or into bushes and he was always there with a clean handkerchief and a kind smile in his grey eyes. He is my Bapaji, my father's father, handsome with heavy lidded, almond eyes, which are set deep within his slim, almost gaunt face. His were the engulfing hugs that comforted me when I couldn't understand the excitement over the arrival of a new baby brother, who was the apple of everyone's eyes except his and mine.

His were the arms that broke my skating falls as I slided and glided along polished parquet floors that marked out the flattened boundaries of my early years. He is more of a secret ally than a grandparent. His deep voice caresses my troubles away with the softness of a fingertip over velvet.

He is electric and enigmatic; he doesn't care what anyone thinks. He isn't like the other grownups that crowd my world.

4

Whilst my father who was the prototype yuppie was busy recreating himself in the shape of his God, my grandfather was a hippy before it was chic. He held a continued interest in all things from the sub-continent, which his peers had shunned as soon as they touched African shores. They shook the dried dust of the Mother country off the soles of their *chappals* and never looked back. But such gestures of disavowal weren't for Kassam, he was a living alchemist; he changed everyone around him.

He was born in Karachi and met Jena, my Maa in Dar-es-Salaam, but he sent my grandma, his new bride, to his family in Karachi, which was still in pre-partition India, after my dad was born. The First World War had broken out. He was a pacifist but he fought in the war because he wanted to secure a future for his newborn son and his young bride. The war promised the protection of the empire; it was a passport to citizenship in 1939.

All the stories that were told about my grandpa after he died, all the bitterness and the twisting of history into contorted shapes to suit my family's dysfunction, they carry the clear hallmark of lies. He was the gentlest man, who named me after Farah Diba, the wife of the Shah; he must have seen the star that anticipated the way my life would twist and turn.

There's so much in a name, he told me. My name is a wish. In Arabic it means specifically the communal joy and happiness such as that elicited by a wedding. Perhaps he thought an inspirational name, for it was the Chardonnay, Bianca or Apple of the times. Maybe he thought it would guarantee success in my life. If I could have chosen my name, I would have chosen the same one. It fits me.

"Farah," he says it in barely a whisper, but still his voice is filled with meaning, which is what I brought to his cynical world. I unwittingly lent him a fresh pair of eyes through which he could refocus, through the gaze of a child. I didn't mind, he was my Merlin.

My parents are blurs, they are studies in motion; there are pictures of my father, he looks dashing in his suit trousers and tie. He is holding me and smiling. There are other pictures of me as a baby with my mother in short skirts and beehives. I look grumpy and I have kohl around my eyes, which is an old Indian tradition for keeping the bad spirits at bay. I remember wearing it, panda-eyed. From the time I can remember having a sense of my memory; I have felt the world around me through all my senses. I was constantly sucking up and soaking in colours and smells, the textures of things. I saw not just with my eyes.

The earliest 3-D memory is of the dentist. After a bad reaction to antibiotics, I remember the mask being pulled over my face and screaming and then nothing, as the nitrous oxide coursed through my veins. I woke, hours later without my milk teeth. I was ugly, bleeding and frightened in the pitch black; my parents were trying to comfort me. I was wrestling them, outside a tall office block in downtown Kampala, refusing to go with them. I wanted him.

They had to take me to his flat, though it was late and then I was comforted. He glared at them when he saw me. He made them responsible for my pain. Only he could do that and they hated him for it. It made me love him more; he forced them to be accountable for how much they failed their child.

Every birthday we sit in his balcony which overlooks the main square the start of the procession route; my birthday falls on the same day, in the same year as Uganda's Independence Day. I am another child of midnight, whose birth is meant to symbolize crossing into freedom, but I am still bonded to that other continent. Every birthday is filled with marching bands and shiny, brass trumpets and generals with faces like plums. They have bulbous lips and shifty eyes. He tells me the bands and the parades are for me, I am a princess and foolish child that I was, when I still believed in fairies and happily ever after, I believed in him and that we would be together forever.

He couldn't stand shoes; he never made me wear them. There's a family legend that he gave away my father's expensive handmade English leather shoes to Dawoody, the houseboy because he had none. My father, who was thirteen and who had acquired airs, was in full dandy mode because he was fresh back from boarding school in Stroud. He had left a pair of leather brogues outside the front door to be polished.

When my father screamed outrage later, my grandfather looked at him with even eyes and asked him what the problem was, he had other pairs of shoes, and Dawoody did not. My father cleaned his own shoes after that.

When I was a small child the clinic was part of my routine for some vaccination or another and I allowed myself to be taken only by him. He was stern with the men in white coats who seemed intent on bruising and puncturing my arms and he took me to Snow-Queen afterwards.

Together we would sit in his old banger, perched at the peak of the hills which circle Kampala. The sun melted the ice-cream and flushed away the hue of the city and one-by-one the lights below us flickered, hesitantly for a second and then they lit up like a big smile with white teeth in a dark African face.

Still, I long for the sparkling fairy lights of the magical city in the valley, slung like a diamond pendant on the collarbones of twilight. We sit in silence, eating our cones, watching the day fall into night. Silently, the city slinks into her sparkly, spangled, midnight blue cocktail dress of streetlights, which reflects the stars shining and my desire to belong.

Stealing Me

On a large projection screen we see a three year old child, sitting in the back of a sedan car. Her tricycle is perched precariously on the rear shelf. The car is black, German. Her mother is in the driver's seat and together they are singing the Doris Day song, Que sera sera her mother seems anxious and often checks the rear view mirror. She pulls up and parks outside an office building in downtown Kampala. It's a dusty afternoon but the air is still and sombre.

Zarin: I'm going to leave this with your daddy. I'll be back in two minutes.

She waves a large white envelope in the direction of the child and opens her door to step out of the car. At the same moment a large black hand reaches in and snatches the car keys from her hand. He pulls her out and she is thrown to the floor. He is wearing a red Polo shirt. Another man in a blue T shirt takes the passenger seat. They attempt to take off but Zarin is still holding onto the driver's side door. She is dragged along besides the car, her shins scrape the street and the tires and the imprint of tread marks is smeared in blood in the road. A few seconds later, she is thrown off and lies in a heap on the road

Switch to a close up of Farah in the car, silent but frightened.

Farah: I want to get out! Where are you taking me? My mummy's taking me to the lake, get out of my car!

The blue-shirted man tries to push her back into the seat; she takes his hand and bites down on it hard. The car swerves dangerously as he retracts his hand with some force and shouts, startling his colleague who is driving. The sound of screeching brakes followed by police sirens

Blackout

The scene gradually lights up to reveal a small round dining table, where Kassam is seated on a wooden straight-back chair, holding his head in his hands. A half-empty bottle of Scotch is next to him and there is a tumbler filled with scotch and ice in front of him on the table. Jena sits sobbing on the sofa, uncontrollably and Yasmin, Amir's youngest sister tries to console her. Amir paces the length of the room, her mother stands very still, frozen as if in shock. Her legs are freshly bandaged from her knees to her ankles.

Sound of a Radio Broadcast: The three-year-old daughter of the Asian businessman Amir Damji has been taken by insurgents against the government, in Kampala.

The female child is called Farah is the grand-daughter of Kassam Damji, an advisor to the ex-Obote government. The family is most anxious. Anyone with information about the perpetrators of this nefarious misdeed against a child should get in touch with Kampala CID. Road blocks have been set up around the perimeter of the city and police are working with security forces to ensure the child's safe return. There is a reward being offered, if anyone has any information, please contact...."

The radio fades. Kassam who had been still until now, slams his fist on the table, making the bottle and the glass shake

Kassam: It's my fault. These bastards have taken her to teach me a lesson. I must keep my mouth shut.

Phone rings. Amir Answers

Amir: Yes, hello? Oh Brian, it's you…yes, you have heard the news then. They've locked down the city, the General's own security are going into the trouble spots where these people live. The flying squad are out…No, there's no need, not at the moment, Papa called in a favour from an old friend, and they have been on the phone to the Old Man He's alright, holding up, liquid courage, he blames himself – he's not eaten all day. They say the first forty-eight hours are the most important, that's when she is likely to be released without being hurt…the golden hours…listen Brian, don't speak on the phone, I'll meet you later at the club. Six o'clock? Fine, thanks …yes, if there's anything I need I will call you. *Stares at the receiver in his hand before he can replace it there is a loud noise, the doorbell which makes them all jump. The sound of rapping on the door with a stick*

Amir: Now what?

(Answers the door, stands in the frame, not letting anyone through) Yes?

Voice: Are you Mr Damji? Mr Amir Damji?

Amir: *(Stepping aside)* Yes, what is it? Have you found her? What's happened…? *Two men step into the room, both are policemen*

First Detective: You must come with us sir.

Amir: Why, what's happened to my daughter, you can tell me.

Detective: Sir, you must come with us, you are under arrest.

Amir: You must be kidding. I'm not going anywhere; my daughter has been kidnapped, look at the state of my family.

Second Detective: We have a warrant for your arrest sir. If you do not come to

8

the police station we shall be forced to take you.

Amir: What have I done?

First Detective: Allegations have been made about illegal activities concerning currency trading violations and contraventions of the Foreign Exchange Act.

Amir: *(To his wife)* Call Anil Korda and tell him to meet at the police station, then call Brian at the Consular Residence and tell him what's happened. Tell him to get there as soon as he can.

Kassam*: (Stands up, furiously, his chair crashes backwards, Jena is more inconsolable)* You bloody bastards. First you have taken my grandchild now you want to take my son? Why don't you take me, that's what you want after all, isn't it? *(Begins to put on his jacket. Anger overcomes him and he raises an arm to hit the first policeman. They restrain him, gently)*

First detective: Mzee, we can see you are upset…

Amir: *(To his father)* don't make things any worse, you stay here, I'll be back in a few hours.

Sound of a prison cell door being shut and a key turning in the lock. Lights out

An urban police station, Amir Damji is in a cell, the door is left open, he is sitting on the bed, his feet up, reading a newspaper. A scuffle and some commotion, he lowers the paper and looks up as his daughter is brought in, startled and frightened by the bright lights of the police station. She sees her father and releases herself from the hand of the female police officer she is with.

Farah: Daddy!

Amir: Over here… *(They hug, and then he holds her some distance from himself, looking at her)* Are you all right? Did they hurt you?

Farah: I want to go home. Where's my Bapaji?

Amir: He's going to be so happy to see you; they're all at home waiting for you.

A high ranking army official enters in a military uniform, covered in medals. He circles the father and daughter. He sits on the wooden chair in the cell and takes a soft cloth out of his pocket. He takes his rimless glasses off and starts to polish them, solicitously, as if there is some speck which only he can see and must remove.

Cop: I see you two have found each other. She was left by the side of the road, outside Kisumu. My men picked her up a little over an hour ago. She is unharmed but we shall call the doctor to see her at once. You are free to go. The

General has intervened personally; the charges against you must be dropped. You have suffered enough. But you should think about leaving Kampala. Your people are no longer wanted or safe here. Just look at your beautiful young girl, so innocent, it would be terrible indeed if anything happened to her…

Amir: *(defensively but quietly)* my people made this country; we built it up from the dirt. We have given our lives to make this our home. There's no need to call a doctor, she can see our doctor when she gets home.

Cop: A father's love for his daughter, is there anything we wouldn't do to protect them? See how you are her whole world, how everything she sees is reflected in your eyes? She looks to you for protection; can you still give her that? Once they are broken, these tiny hearts, they are not easily mended. Look after your daughter. *(Gets up to go)* Good night sir, bye-bye little girl.

Amir: Are you threatening us? *Brian and Anil Korda arrive*

Anil: We came as soon as we could; they've thrown up a cordon, all around the city… *(Stops when he sees Farah)*

Amir: I'm free to go; all the charges have been dropped.

Anil: Well, you must thank Brian and the High Commissioner for that…

Amir: It was all a set up, don't you see? They staged the whole thing to scare the life out of a child and an old man and to frighten us into leaving.

Brian: That's a bit speculative old chap…

Amir: That's what I've just been told by that goon. "We are no longer safe here." Let's go home.

Anil: Do you think they would really take a three-year-old to terrorize your family? You have lived here all your life, you are as African as they are and you have as much right to be here as the next man. I am going to file harassment charges, we'll ask for an internal investigation, find out who did this…

Amir: *(Quietly)* it came from the top, Anil… leave your Oxbridge presumptions of *habeas corpus* where you learned them. You can bring as many cases as you want against them, they don't want us here anymore. We are out of time, case closed and no right to appeal.

Brian: How can you say that? Your father fought in the British Army, you are being paranoid, and you are a pillar of society…

Amir: *(Tired and resigned)* Let me get this child out of here, come home, we'll talk about it there.

He begins to put his belongings into a leather overnight bag, Brian takes it from him

Brian: Planning to stay a while where you? *(Trying to be light-hearted)*

Amir: I was planning to stay for the rest of my life, to see my grandchildren grow up here. But that's over now. God knows, with these people, I think we are lucky to get out alive.

They exit; the Chief of Police is left alone, polishing the unseen speck on his glasses.

Seeing in Black and White

We left Uganda, soon afterwards. We were ghosts in a graveyard who slipped into the light of dawn, before it could pin us down into being. We couldn't afford to be anything more than ephemeral. It wasn't only our comfortable lives we left behind; it was the history of who we were and the blueprint of all that we were meant to be. Fruit crates and cardboard boxes stored whatever we thought we needed to bring with us. Then the skies parted and our own Exodus began on chartered Boeing 747's.

We, the dispossessed, abandoned our identities when we surrendered our passports at the airport. We left behind more than empty spaces in the little house called home on Acacia Avenue. Yasmin, my father's youngest sister had left a year earlier to study on an Aga Khan bursary at Oxford with her mistake of a first husband, Sky. We parted in the nick of time. It was the spring of 1970; my brother was still a baby. Two years later, Idi Amin would rout out all the remaining Asian vermin.

England was a shock to the Mowgli child I had become, this strange and foreign place where I was forced into not only shoes but also knee high scratchy socks and a winter coat. The pictures of me salvaged from Jena's antiquarium (she was like a magpie, my grandma, school reports, buttons, every photograph that commemorated a landmark in the Damji family's history, they were all to be found somewhere in her collection of old biscuit tins) show a small, grey child in a black and white picture. I have reed straight black hair which is half-hiding my face, and sad eyes. Like many of her generation who owned so little, Jena was a hoarder of objects and emotions. She collected everything.

There were few other Asians in my world then, just as there had been only a few in Uganda. The Mother country, which had reluctantly taken us in, had yet to bear the weight of dependency which would come with the prodigal foreign progeny, the offspring of ill-conceived flirtations in far-flung places when we came clamouring to the Sovereign Nation in our hour of need.

The ugly bartering between Governments as to who could claim the right of residence and the ultimate honour, of being recognized as being a British Subject with the right of domicile, didn't begin for another two years. We missed that indignation.

London woke up one morning and Civil Servants' eyebrows shot up in feigned disbelief over china cups of Darjeeling. They were feeling disgruntled by the grumbling of the despot's tirades. Stories of ethnic cleansing and cannibalism came to these mandarins of the machinery. They chose to ignore the missives that came across the wires in the still night of disbelief. The clattering message bearing telegraph machines cracked like sniper shots across the marble corridors of Whitehall. Still they wouldn't acknowledge the dot matrix messages, commemorating another bloody night of unrest, which were splattered across their desks in the morning, in the form of daily briefings.

Armageddon happened while they looked the other way. The dark thoughts the Africans harboured, those natives whose lives we had restricted so they were little more than indentured slaves, those thoughts took shape and became deeds. The sound was of fury and revolution, the fledging movement of Pan Africanism was born. The anger of the Freedom Fighters sought the scent of blood and Asian blood would do.

The second generation, whose grandparents had been forcibly brought from India, were easy targets. The ruse of the railway building was a deceit; we were the comfortably padded cushion like an interfacing between the indigenous population and the white masters. Like ants in an enclave, the Asians worked hard and prospered. We were aspiring, ostentatious with our wealth and family and values were sacrificed for the hope of a fortune in the future.

Soon many achieved positions of power and prestige, and whilst on the surface there was the display of congeniality and friendship between the African and Asian population, the reality was the two tribes had no choice but to co-exist. In the same putrefying way a parasite needs its host, we needed each other, for exploitation and survival.

The ideas which were once only whispered, now fomented revolution. Ideas became massacres which blew over oceans in the breath of the Scirocco, which were retold in hushed voices at parties, tales of how the monster had taken an Asian bride. This was the ultimate desecration of our own rotten lie that we were different from them. He hadn't only taken our land and the reddish tinged 24 carat Indian gold our women wore in their wedding jewellery. He hadn't just taken the showy cars and the neat, fenced-in bungalows; he sucked out the marrow from our grandparents' bones and licked them dry so they rattled around like hollow people, barely strung together.

They shouldn't have had to face the prospect of becoming refugees in another hemisphere. They had been cast out into a world that didn't fit the shapes of their dreams.

But how did we dare to feign surprise and betrayal? We had lived like make-believe Maharajas in a land we couldn't call our own; we were the uninvited

13

guests who never left. My wise grandpa saw it coming, he read the writing on the wall and bowed by the inevitability of what was going to happen, he caved in and we left as a family.

The murmurings I heard later about my parents having to leave because my father had been involved in exchanging foreign currency were never confirmed by anyone I trust. The final nail in the coffin of shame was when the spiritual leader, the Aga Khan undertook the responsibility to resettle his followers, the Shia Imami Ismailis. He had to negotiate with Governments so his flock could proceed unhindered to Canada or Britain. We became human pawns, bartering chips in this enforced geopolitical displacement. We were given value by Lloyds Bank, in a wave of soft loans to ease the burden on these developed economies. It helped to lessen the strain of having to take us in.

It was cold when we deplaned in this unfamiliar grey country, not grey by a trick of photography but grey everywhere. And soon the grey shrouded us, grey people in grey suits, grey roads lined with slightly lighter grey houses; it was a continuum, this endless gradation of grey. My first snapshot of England was the view from our Everest, at the top of the moveable staircase hastily fastened to the mouth of the airplane which was vomiting its cargo of baffled people; everything was flat and colourless.

The first tragic act started with the host country stealing away my Bapaji. We settled in a mid-terrace semi, on Fordhook Avenue in Ealing Common which was grim but close to a tube station. On the corner of our street was a Ford dealership with a prized Cortina up on a raised platform and brightly coloured bunting and loud signs, which looked out of place in the gloomy corner of West London which we inhabited. It was a nothing house; I have no particular memories of it. Bapaji went in for a check-up, which was part of the tangled bureaucracy, another regulatory hurdle for him to clear before he could enroll with a local doctor.

My whisky-swilling, chain-smoking grandpa who held my faith in his unwavering gaze fell ill. He never came out of the hospital. I remember him, ashen against the snowy hospital issue pillow case, eyes closed in defiance but not sleeping. He strained to sit up and greet me and I could feel the painful spikes of his shoulder blades, which poked rudely under thin pyjama cotton.

Hospital killed him, and grief settled on me with the stealth of the sun slipping behind banks of clouds on a bright afternoon. It shouldn't have happened. The sense in my nonsense childhood was gone; the glue that held the bits of me together was wiped clean.

Poor Jena, my grandma became undone. She descended further into quiet hysteria and slowly, insanity. As much as she complained about him when he had been alive, she needed him like air. When someone who has loomed as strong and as tangible as my Bapaji disappears, in a minute, life ceases to hold any prospects. The future is laid bare and vast.

We were blind-sighted by the stark realization that this is all there is, that now is a moment already gone. There's no getting rid of this listless useless feeling, it sticks like a stain. Jena started her life-long dalliance with prescription drugs; pills to stop her epilepsy, Mogadon for sleeping, Valium to calm her shredded nerves, pills to make her eat and others to make her go to the bathroom. She ate lots of little pills, in pretty Smartie colours and shapes.

Jena wore her hair in a plait, a great thick welt of a snake braid, unless she was going to the mosque. On Friday evening, she made a neat round bun. A fistful of curly pins and a gossamer fishnet kept her hair tidy and secure. She didn't wear make-up; she didn't need it though she slathered her face frequently with Ponds Cold Cream. She developed an allergy to the sun one year, quite suddenly and flaky white patches began to appear on her brow and jaw. It was another rejection of light and life from her tiny body. In the summer these areas of white skin became angry and red and they'd glisten with lashings of Betnovate, a steroid cream. Her mouth was permanently turned downwards, in the way a child depicts a curve to draw sadness. Her deep eyes were often covered over with mist and sorrow, but that could have been the endless march of chemicals, which were constantly coursing their way through her body. They dictated her demeanour.

She seemed to bear all of our pain and even that of our ancestors' on her slight, stooping shoulders. I noticed as I grew taller she seemed to shrink and recede into herself. My Jena looked like the Bollywood tragedienne Nargis. She deteriorated rapidly, she became laden with sighs and impotence, and her eyes drooped into sunken pits overnight.

Every morning she would un-braid her plait with her bony fingers, in the way evocative of women all over India. This was a ritual that bound women in posh apartment blocks on Malabar Hill in Mumbai and women who lived in tents in Rajasthan. It locked her into another place, Jena loved India. Her hair fell way below her waist and she'd comb it through, rhythmically with a fine-toothed, wooden comb, sleeking down the stray tresses, with coconut oil. A few times she had tried to do my hair but I resisted, I didn't like the smell or the slippery feeling. When she had finished this morning sacrament, she heaved a sigh and stood up. She reached into her huge bosom where she kept a jangle of keys that had nestled there forever or for at least for as long as I could remember.

All day, from the moment she woke up she'd sit cross-legged on her bed with heavy velvet curtains drawn behind her. She would worry away her rosary beads on the fragile silk thread that still held her belief together, while she supplicated long prayers to the God who had made her life stormy with grief. After praying for the first few hours of light, she would make her way over to one of the three cupboards, the one she always kept locked.

15

The moment she turned the tiny key in the circumference of the lock, between her first finger and her thumb, the aroma of Aladdin's cave filled her musky bedroom. Rows of beautiful, perfectly folded silk saris on plastic hangers jostled for space next to Marks and Sparks synthetic sweaters Jena was convinced she was allergic to wool. They drew the battle lines for the textile wars of the future. But they weren't what she was looking for. She sought the tiny, brown, glass headstones on an eye-level shelf. The scents crowded each other, expensive perfumes my father had brought her back from his trips overseas and her own favourite, the sharp, cheap sting of Charlie. Then there was the almost human scent, which was exhaled by warm acres of breathing silk. Permeating all of it was the chemical stench given off by the contents of the medicine bottles that kept her sort of alive. She'd count out pills with the astuteness of a moneylender in the temple, bedazzled by her loot, and then she'd replace the lids, twisting them till she heard the childproof click in her hands. Reassured, she would carefully place them back where they belonged. Until another day, the chemical army could return to its somnolence, it had given her just enough courage to continue, for now.

Slowly life shifted, the monochrome sickness seeped from the sky into my lungs and I had a perma-cold. England became home. We moved into bigger house in Harrow and Jena still lived with us.

There were some happy weekends with Yassi and Sky in Oxford. They had a basic marriage ceremony at the registry office in North Harrow but she looked happy, the Indian bride in her heavily embroidered white sari and her mother's wedding jewellery. There are pictures of me in a white *broiderie anglaise* long dress that she made for me, with a marigold coloured ribbon at the waist, she's leaning down and I'm tilting my face upwards to reach her cheek.

What happened to that love? Mine and theirs? It was a day of perfect deception. Sky wore his wide tie and blue-tinted prescription glasses, we all thought we knew him and we loved him. He played tennis in white shorts, who did we think he was, this brutal stranger, tall and handsome, who claimed to love my precious aunt? Later his lies would destroy her but her complexion on that day, the bloom which radiated through the camera lens, seemed as if it might last forever and a day.

Those were innocent days, which were not complicated with expectations. We had a limited perspective, for that was all we knew back then. We only aspired to the status of invited guests. Yassi and Sky set out to live the great big white life; freed from the shackles of family and their past through the initiation of life at Oxford. They wore their anticipation like new clothes, carefully, not brimming over or spilling too much excitement.

I spent sunny Sunday afternoons, punting with Yassi's friend the illustrator turned author, Jonathan Kingdom and another young Oxford grad, Simon who only had eyes for Rekha. She was one of Yassi's beautiful Indian friends from Kampala, an exotic flower amongst the neo-hippie leftovers of the late 70s.

Crowds of students in their billowing flares and Liberty-printed Biba dresses craned to catch a glimpse of the deity descended. At the age of ten I could begin to discern the draw of her power, she exuded something else with a tiger-lily in her hair and liquid kohl which drew lines on her eyelids and everyone around into her spell.

Yassi lived a quasi-Bohemian lifestyle in inexpensive lodgings in Somers Town. She was subsidized by my father's growing wallet and she seemed happy. Life's rainbows sheltered her from the gloom and shadows other ordinary mortals had to suffer. How sad then to watch that dream as it came undone.

Another new house heralded the birth of another baby, my mother in Yassi's wedding pictures looks beautiful, fecund, and her rounded belly protrudes from beneath layers of an antique bronze sari.

Zarah is six years younger, and as the last born has never forgiven me for being born first. She was born early and wired to a heating pad and an incubator; she had tubes running though her nose and her mouth that made her look like a baby mouse entangled in an unfortunate laboratory experiment.

My mother is from a big army family, hers is the Parsi side, so they are fair-skinned and fine featured. There were seventeen siblings but only thirteen survived childhood. She's one of five surviving sisters and they are still claustrophobically close. I have dozens of cousins, scattered like pollen across the world but there's a pernicious quality to my mother's devotion to her family, it excludes anyone else, even her own children. When we were younger heaps of aunts and cousins would come and visit for weeks at a time, especially in the holidays so we couldn't even have that time with her. I was frequently ousted from my own room and had to share with Jena, sleeping in one of the twin beds that occupied her room.

I resented my mother's family, in my eyes; she clearly loved them more than she loved her own children.

On my father's side were the Ramjis. They were Dallas-like in their aspirations and the depths of their deviancy. The oldest son, Sadru, was a reasonable copy of JR Ewing from Dallas.

They lived in a gigantic house in Ealing. One or other of the younger brothers was embroiled in some semi-criminal shenanigans. We didn't have much to do with the Ramjis when we first came to England, there had been a rift because the four brothers had ganged up against my father in a business venture and ripped off a lot of money. A million pounds was a lot of money in the early 70s. Sadru was the great patriarch, the benevolent despot of Park View Road and he was kind to me. French cologne and hair pomade coiled off him but in his prime, he was elegant. I still remember all four brothers and my parents in their prime, at the Golden Age of forty. I was his Tun-Tun and he was a safe and predictable father figure for me.

Maami Ramji (*Maami* means sister-in-law, the wife of the oldest brother in a family) was wrinkled like a porpoise and moved slowly, with great deliberation, like an old Empress. She wore the stale smell of sour milk in the folds of her Kashmiri embroidered shawls.

Her skin was soft and pale, as fragile as a petal from a Himalayan poppy. On her face, furrows and crevices had been sketched by age and tears. She was selectively deaf like many other older, wiser people. She'd raised four boys and a girl on her own but she was closest to my Jena, who had lost her birth parents when she was still young.

Behind the house was a rolling lawn where the children played. It was a children's garden with paths that wound off to shaded areas and a greenhouse where we tried to grow plants but which we forgot to water and left to shrivel and die.

Sadru had married his first cousin, Malek who was thin and edgy like a nervous sparrow but that was at a time when it was still common for Asian families to intermarry, better the devil you know. My dad used to joke about me marrying one of my first cousins.

The lawn was lined with tall rose bushes which drew blood, pleasure and tears. The first lessons of beauty and pain nestled in the cool shadows of the garden at number 53.

Maami elicited fascination and fear, the way old people do in small children. There had been another sibling between my brother and me but I hadn't known him. He lay in the margins of my memory, another unspoken episode, like my kidnapping. His ghost commanded our silence. I had forgotten him. He was revived in a hushed conversation between Maami and Jena, sitting on the bench as they sheltered below the overhead embrace of the hundred-year-old oak tree.

The afternoon's heat had melted their guards and the memories of other hot days on another continent were unlocked. The sun has a way of extracting secrets which were told under her former self. Old ghosts stirred and took shape in the forms of words spoken, they came out to create mischief in the revised versions of history harboured by these two old ladies. Myths which they had kept secured in the archives of their minds were unleashed.

"What a shame about the other boy. He was so fair."

Fairness was a prerequisite for the favourite child. In my youth, fairness was prized; we were kept out of the sun. Skin was scrubbed at the hint of the sun's stain. She was looking at me as she said it but I was a sun-worshipping pre-teen. I had recently rediscovered the pleasure of being barefoot again; I was, at that moment, savouring the damp, alive feeling of the grass on my soles, tickling the spaces between my toes.

My ears pricked up, what other boy? I knew those frozen moments well; when adult conversations dropped off as I entered a room, when laughter suddenly sank to the bottom of wine glasses and glances were exchanged, furtively. It was as if I could make sound stop in mid-flight. There were so many secrets but they weren't buried deep enough in the bones of the family's cadaver and sometimes, like hands reaching out of sealed coffins they'd seize one of the adults, these haunting demons, and draw them into the mad dance of denial and un-forgetting.

"What baby boy?" I wanted to know and I looked up from the game I was playing, an afternoon game of trying to catch my hand's shadow.

Jena let out a sigh that lasted a year. She was a bad liar my grandma, and that afternoon I learned another sad tale in my mother's life. He had died of cot death when he was just a few months old. No mother, they say, should have to bury her own child. The wound is too big to live in, for the rest of a lifetime. A part of her goes with her child.

There was no explanation for his death; he just slipped away in the same way he came into the world, without a fuss. I have only watery recollections of him, I try and remember his name but it's like speaking while I am drowning, I can barely let out the sounds and I can't make out his face. My fingers reach out to him but they don't connect to what I want to know. The baby sounds and smells have been erased; he wasn't here for long enough to make any more than a tiny mark. I don't remember his name, nothing of him. It is as if he never lived or drew a breath. Everything about him, his own awareness was muted. His is the rotten flesh at the core of the woman who called herself my mother.

Yet still he populates my dreams, he's the unborn child I gave up, he washes up on the shores of my grief as he dissolves in a sea of souls and spirits that won't say goodbye and go. He is one of those who are reluctant to give themselves up to the folds of their own other world. And still he haunts me.

Great White Lies

My father was away a lot. When he was at home, he wasn't there. He occupied space but he was emptiness. I couldn't reach him. Our parents were the first generation of shape-shifters. They had stepped out of the traditional, extended network and the safety of the family. They tried to fit as congruently as they could, to the west's notion of how East African Asians should live.

I felt several times removed from India, but not only by continents and oceans, India horrified me. Frequent images of floods and famine flashed on black and white TV sets were something to deny we were any part of; we were the gentrified Diaspora, not the great unwashed. Back home was a black hole of non-being. We had discovered our true selves in the western hemisphere. Everything before that was wiped off the slate.

They were both young, good-looking, smiling, back then, the parents. He cut a fine figure in his smart, hand-stitched suits and his pointed Bally Suisse shoes. My father's presence was double-edged; I feared and adored him. I wanted him around me all the time, because only daddy can reflect the glory of a little girl's dreams, but too often his presence was accompanied by stony silences, as the gloom settled like nuclear dust after another marital argument. We three kids learned to dance fast to avoid the splinters their rage left hanging in the air after frequent outbursts that often led to physical violence.

Soon after Zarah was born in 1972, his mania for building started. It was a desire to create monuments to his growing fortune, which was bigger than him. As much as Kassam had shunned possessions, Amir hoarded them. He started working at fourteen, pumping petrol at a gas station to provide for his mother and his two sisters, while Kassam was off on another adventure. He wasn't for the day-to-day of this world, my grandpa.

The exiled want to accumulate because we understand the impermanence of belonging but we crave belongings as if their solid structure might make us more tangible. Yet we build in the knowledge that it is all in vain.

Our modest detached house was in a suburb of Harrow. It started to grow, organically, sprouting new rooms; sometimes whole extensions would grow, as if from magic beans out of nothing. That house, with an apple tree in the front garden was refurbished and renovated *in extremis*. He thought he could trick time by creating constant flux. By constantly changing the boundaries of his kingdom, my father felt as if he still had some control, that he could buy belonging or build it around him. He thought he could deny the inevitable, rejection and decay.

We learned to live, at a young age with wheezing coughs and dust in our hair. Plastic sheets divided half-finished rooms but my dad was in his element arguing with his architect and builder, Kalsi, a patient Sikh. They knew each other from Kampala.

This house was close to Harrow-on-the-Hill tube station, on the outer limbs of the sprawling Metropolitan line and near the A40. It was convenient for my dad to get to his office on Great Marlborough Street, where he had acquired the second floor of Number 40 and started a travel agency. The building was well-placed, on the edges of Soho, which was seedy but the office was safely in the shadow of Liberty, the department store which sold Westernised Oriental Glamour to Londoners.

He employed me, during holidays and half terms, as a Girl Friday, and I'd go and collect tickets from plush airline offices or lunch from the spicy-smelling donor kebab shop a few doors down. I enjoyed answering the phones; I was pleased to show off my un-inflected English accent.

Being in London and working was an intensive education for a little brown girl who wanted to get away as fast as I could from anything remotely Asian. Twiggy-thin white women with panda bear, kohl-lined eyes floated by in paisley dresses. They were wrapped like sweets in cloying clouds of incense; their clothes were printed with fanciful foliage and psychedelic paisley.

These were the colours that formed the backdrop against the Georgian limestone architecture of my early double digit years. I couldn't see the beauty in it and I wanted no part of this white sahib, William Morris peacock parade of Eastern paraphernalia. I had invested myself, lock, stock and lunchbox into the great, white hope of another life. I didn't see myself as brown, or white or anything. I was blessed with colour myopia and was blissfully unaware of the difference that I represented until I met Caroline.

Next door at Number 23 there was an English family. They were a middle-class Irish Catholic family, normal, but they answered my prayers: fur boys and a girl, who was two weeks younger than me.

They felt at home with who they were and how they lived, in their chaos. She was as white as I was brown, with thin straight hair and pale blue eyes. We managed to lose our front teeth at the same time so we are simultaneously gap-toothed and grinning in the photographs of us. She had metal braces installed and that stole away her smile.

There we are in these fading photos, squinting up at whoever was taking the photo, she has pigtails. I look like an outsider. For the first time, I felt envy, I wanted to be something else – to be blonde and have blue eyes, to have skin that was pale and bloomed with invisible capillaries which rose and made blushes on my cheeks.

I was the only Asian or black child at both my primary and secondary school for the first few years and that was difficult. There was a girl from India, Asha, but she stayed invisible. No one noticed her, except for the first two fingers on her left hand were fused together. She was a novelty for reasons of biology not race.

All I wanted was to look like Barbie and I came home and cried to my mother to make me white and golden-haired. I wanted a rosebud pout and although I was a pretty child, the doubts and fears of pre-adolescence started to creep into the corners of my eyes. There had been talk of braces to try and amend my extended overbite but I was having none of it, the earlier adventure which had resulted in all my baby teeth falling out prematurely, had cured any residual oral vanity left in me.

I have another aunt, besides Yasmin. She is the middle child, Zarina, but we have always called her Julie. She's always been "artistic" which is the worst insult my mother, the purist dispenser of reason, could deliver. She lived in Bath and through her; I tried to escape the inevitable track my life was destined to follow.

She had to see hosts of Harley Street specialists because she had a nervous disposition, the Victorians would have called her melancholic. She would grind her teeth so hard in the night while she slept she would wake up with bleeding gums. There are terrible tales of what her first husband did to her, but no one will talk about it. My father blames himself for her particular madness; maybe he shouldn't have let her go, maybe he should have found her better doctors. My father loves to self-flagellate. Pity and guilt make him feel better. She too, took potions and pills to maintain the illusion of being alive.

She was slight and taller than her siblings, built more like her father, angular rather than rotund; she didn't have Jena's body. Her face is a study of planes and sadness, like Picasso's pictures of weeping women. She is a Demoiselle of Avon, with dark, brown eyes framed with dark brown circles and fine silky hair with which she fidgeted in her long, tobacco-stained fingers. When the tobacco tins were emptied, she would paint intricate flowers and miniature fairies on them in oil paints. When I visited her with Jena it was like travelling to another country.

She discovered Caroline. She had lived in England long enough to know that our polite, white neighbours wouldn't dream of introducing themselves and there would be no more exchange that the perfunctory hello but she'd spied Caroline from the window upstairs, playing in the garden and decided that I should know her.

As a child, observing Julie was fascinating. She revelled in extreme Bohemia, she'd long rejected our new culture revolution and she loved anything Indian, from the scent of incense to the cotton printed clothes. She was Flora's daughter, crisped by the sun, and from hours spent tending her allotment. She wore layers of antique, printed chiffon, and silver jewellery but not in that fake Biba way. She was like an empress in my eyes. But she was elusive, no one could know her, being around her was as fascinating and infuriating as trying to catch a butterfly.

One Easter, I had gone to stay with her and she enlightened me to my father's affairs. She told me how he had always cheated on my mother, even within the family. She told me in great detail of a long affair with Mary, his first cousin. I didn't understand any of it but it rankled in my head. She lived with her long-term partner, who was more like a caretaker, Mick.

From my cloistered world of Church of England Schools, of yet another move further along the tentacle-like veins of the Metropolitan line to Northwood, the higgledy-piggledy mosaic of a life Mick and Julie had created from bits of junk found at Oxfam shops and left-over's from my parents' homes, was romantic. I envied their cobbled together existence, in which all the rough seams, borrowed and traded from their experiences and those of the people they cared about, were still visible.

She would take me down to Devon by train and we'd play in the sand or walk quietly along the coast. I felt valued in her life for who I was, not some version of what she would like me to be. She had inherited some of my grandfather's ability to sit in non-judgment. But also for mischief.

The words they used were different, she called Mick "lover". In my home, my mother had a problem with the word "dear" and if she called you "darling", you knew you were in for some phony, cloying sentimentalism, which had been inspired by guilt or alcohol. Both parents drank, socially but it was at that time that I began to notice my father's drinking. It must have been then that the fights became louder, or maybe the noises echoed further as the rooms were bigger and emptier, in that sad house on Nicholas Way.

The sound of furniture dragging on parquet floors and doors being slammed so hard that their wooden frames quivered and made my heart stop. I learned to dread the sound of a whisky bottle as it was unscrewed, the slow viscous trickle of liquid being poured into a glass, cracking the ice cubes which would then float and make a tinkling sound, like the top notes on the far reaches of the piano. Then the sharp warm smell of the unseen toxin wafted through our home on currents of centrally heated air, as the spirit filled my father's veins and every crevice in the house. I could feel its potential for unpredictability.

There was much ritual instilled in my father's drinking, in those days when he still had all his stomach and could drink scotch. He drank from pretty lead crystal glasses; I would carry the water jug, the ice-cubes in a cooler and an empty glass to him. Then, like an alchemist he would mix his drink and summon the concentration needed to invoke a spell. He'd let it sit for a while and then he would wait for the transforming fire to appear.

None came.

Those were the first shoots of the disease; its green, nimble tendrils were taking hold of him. I was afraid to face the sickness, which made him choose it over us. It's still bigger and more frightening than I can manage. I tried to justify it. It was a new life, and he suffered peer pressure. It was his escape from a life he didn't know how he had got himself into. Sometimes, they told me it was my fault; he drank because I made him sad and angry. If only I would do or not do something or the other then he would stop. I must have believed them.

I felt my chest tighten, as if something there was being clenched in a fist and my breath stopped flowing easy. I was entering into a volatile time; this altered golden-hued state when rules and boundaries changed with no notice, and a smile could shift to a smack in the time it took for an ice-cube to melt just a fraction of a millimetre. A sense of foreboding and fear loomed and I waited, huddled and hiding in my room. I became the prisoner of his disease, waiting for morning light along with my mother's shrieks from downstairs to get out of bed. It might as well have been the rattling sound of the warder's chain that let in the new day.

That day was particularly important to my mother; my father had taken to staying away for whole weekends quite often so this wasn't unusual. I don't know why it mattered, or why the shouting and the spitting fury into the telephone fragmented into anger more than ever. We three tip-toed to our beds, scarcely daring to breathe for fear of making any noise which might set her off again. With sleep came relief, an exhalation into a place where adults and their dramas couldn't reach me.

It was pitch black, but the need to go to the toilet was pressing me out of my dream. I opened my bedroom door to make my way down the darkened corridor a few steps but I was caught by her figure, sitting hunched, halfway down the stairs, by a window, which faced the front garden. She was lit up in the fluorescent shock of the moon that seemed to be jostling in the corner of the window frame, to come into the house. I stood stock still, not knowing whether I should flee back to the safety of my bed or descend those few steps and comfort her. I had never seen my mother cry, she is not prone to displays of emotions, and they seem fake, emanating from her stiffness. Frustration and anger made their way out of her with a sharp pinch or a smack to the side of a bare leg, usually mine.

Nicholas Way was a gloomy shell of a house. It was too big, even when we first moved in but my father had insisted on making it even bigger. The last owner, the sour-faced widow Mrs. Majereus, had recently buried her husband and needed to leave his memory behind. When I saw her, the first and only time; she seemed middle-aged but could have been forty. She wore a mid-calf length skirt and she was standing in front of the window in what was later our "big" lounge. She was patiently cross-examining my father, with the simple language she might have used for a half-wit or a child. We were the first brown family to push through the North-Western frontier, though hundreds followed soon after. I suppose that is what she was afraid of; she was asking where he was from, what he did, how many of us there were and how many would be living in the house. Her face betrayed her concerns. We were foreign. So was she but at least she was white.

The house shuddered as she made a fist and slammed it straight into the lead paned window. She snatched a shard of glass that was loose and still barely attached to the frame and started to cut herself, over and over again, slicing in the same place, till blood started to pour from her wrist. She didn't stop, she was in pain, but she could control this pain. I didn't understand till much later that she needed to feel pain or to cause it, in order to feel alive. She needed it to distract her from the greater pain in which she lived.

The moonlight unravelled black and white movie reels of the horror which was unfolding below me. The only colour was red where it stained the wooden treads and her flimsy nightie, which was growing stains.

It didn't feel real. I closed my bedroom door and cowered back into bed. All desire to go to the toilet had left me. The steps to reach her were too difficult for me to negotiate; I could have managed K2 with greater ease.

The next morning he still wasn't home.

It wasn't a school day but breakfast was quiet and hurried. She wanted us out of the house and delivered us to a friend. My mother's hand was bandaged where she had injured herself. A piece of cardboard was sellotaped over the empty space where the window should have been. The blood which had spilled onto the pale wooden treads had been mopped up, not a drop remained. There was no evidence of last night's episode. When I asked her what had happened she said the wind must have blown the window in and when I looked quizzically at her bandaged wrist, she maintained that she had cut herself, accidentally with a knife.

When we came home later that same day, the smashed pane had been expertly replaced. New putty was holding the new pane in place. The lead borders were neatly polished. They were a different colour to the others in the mock-Tudor window, that was the only clue which gave her away. For a moment it felt as if I might have imagined the whole incident. I must have dreamt it.

But then I remembered her bandaged hand, and the swollen hurt in her puffy eyes. Earlier that morning and I knew it had happened. Like the scaly dragon-skin on her shins, where the tyres had skidded against her when she didn't let go, those marks were real and still visible. She didn't know how to come out of her expensive, loveless marriage, so she bore it; she donned the invisible hijab, over designer clothes, of shame and suffering.

She retreated further from me and though she never said anything about it, she knew I had seen her in a moment of weakness. The distance between us grew, imperceptibly at first, but then it was noticeable. She could no longer reach me. I lost respect for her, it was hard to feel any compassion for a woman who would put up with abuse and infidelity in exchange for a comfortable life. I swore I would never do that.

She said to me once, that she had lost me a long time ago, when I was still young, to my father's family, to Jena and Yassi. But she didn't lose me, she never had me. She couldn't protect herself from him, I never trusted her to protect me.

Interlude

The thought of that part of a man's body in my mouth makes me feel sick. Boys are different. I have many boy cousins who are like my older brothers; they come and stay with us often, especially the two from Nairobi, Karim and Aziz. My dad teases me and says I am going to marry Aziz, the younger one. They have grown up with us; we see so much of them. They are part of our family. Most long holidays, if we do not go to Kenya, they come here.

This summer, my mum and dad have decided that I should go and visit the oldest one, with his brother. He is three years older than I am but he looks after me. We have a lot of aunts, uncles and cousins we haven't seen for a long time and I am excited, it's the first time I am going overseas without my family. There are lots of short plane rides, between the big cities across Canada and America where different parts of the family live.

He has lifted the armrest so I can doze with my head resting on his shoulder. I like to fall asleep on planes. I am half asleep, listening to the music on the headphones when he takes my hand and puts it on his lap. The scratchy blanket hides my hand, which he presses on the bulge in his jeans. He fumbles to unzip his flies and slides his thing out of the slit in his Y-fronts. Immediately, I try to pull my hand away. It is like being burned but he takes it again, harder this time, he keeps his grip and he slides my hand over the swollen bump.

The lights are off and just the two of us are seated in that row of the plane, with him in the window seat. He rubs my hand up and down against it, hard, it hurts and then there's a sticky mess, his warmth shudders over my fingers. I wipe it on his jeans and pull my arm away, I am upset. What has he just done? I get up and head towards the toilet cubicle. He has done this to me before but never so that it made a mess. He has come to my bed since I was nine. That summer I was fifteen.

"Do you need anything, dearie?" The smiling air hostess looks down from her high heels, kindly.

"No. Thanks." What I need is that bucket of ice from her trolley to pour over his head and bring him back to his senses.

I am sick in the toilet, until she knocks on the door. She is worried and asks if something I have eaten has given me an upset tummy. I tell her I am all right but she can see I have been crying. She bends down, from her waist and she hugs me, she doesn't mind the sick in my hair and helps me wash it out. She tells me we will be landing soon, that I will be home in a few hours. But home feels a long way away; we are only halfway through our trip. This went on the whole summer, when we were staying with our mums' brothers and sisters.

He would put it inside me, between my legs, just a little bit so I could feel it there, half in me and half out. I would lay perfectly still not daring to move and praying for the moment when his sticky mess would erupt between my legs and this could all be over. I prayed each time would be the last. I would ask myself why he was doing it and how he could, he had a girlfriend, his own age in Nairobi, I wondered if this is what they did together. Perhaps he missed her. But I didn't like him in that way, I wanted it to stop.

He'd kiss me on the mouth and he would lick me down there, from where I went to the toilet. He asked me if I liked what he was doing and I said no, but that didn't make him stop. I hated it; it felt dirty. He was kissing me down there and I'd plead with him to stop. I felt like I was falling into a pit of grime and I felt dirty, horrible. He said I was enjoying it, that this is what men and women did, but I was not ready to become a woman at nine. He told me they would be angry with me if I told anyone, that he would say I had started it. He was my mum and dad's favourite, the oldest son that they never had. I didn't say anything about what he was doing to me.

I started to withdraw into my own world. I didn't like to lie on the grass in the front garden anymore, the way I had done before him. I used to lie there for hours, flat on my back, skirt hitched up, bare legs in the sun, and make myself happy and dizzy as I watched the clouds whirl in the sky. I didn't like the loud parties my parents had anymore, this happy clappy world of Indian music and cocktails served in pretty glasses. I didn't like the way the men looked at me.

They didn't say much when I retreated into my room and refused to come out, they put it down to the oncoming of adolescence. My dad would say I was soon going to be a teenager and that this is what my mum should expect. They never asked me what was wrong, they just told me I was being difficult.

He did it to me at home, in my own bed. He slept in my little brother's room, next door to mine, which he would take over so that my brother was turfed out and had to sleep elsewhere in the house. It was convenient because then he could come to me when it was late and dark. I used to lie awake at night, scared but not able to sleep, knowing he would come but not knowing when. He always knocked, gently. I would pretend to be sleeping and curl myself into a tight ball with my long nightie firmly held down, tucked below my feet but he would unfold me and make me lie there. He wanted me to lie still, to pretend I was sleeping. It was so easy for him.

This went on for years until finally I told him I would tell my mum and that I didn't care if she was angry. I was less frightened of her than I was sick of myself for what he was doing to me. I didn't want him to come into my room, I didn't want him to touch me or put that thing in my mouth. I didn't have a name for it then but I knew I hated it. I must have scared him because he stopped.

Faith and First Kisses

St Helen's School was an independent girls' school. It's not natural, this excess of estrogen leaking out of every adolescent pore. Breasts sprouted as if overnight. Like clockwork, every one of us, in the same regimented fashion as inmates in a prison, started to ovulate together. Suddenly the skimpy bikini panties which we had opted to wear, sneakily, instead of the uniform knickers we were required to wear, were put away and the baggy green ones pulled out of bottom drawers and put on to accommodate oversized sanitary napkins. We had to learn to wear sanitary belts, medieval contraptions with hooks and straps to keep these female nappies in place.

The stench of sweat and stale blood in the gymnasium was as tangible as the spongy gym mats by the end of the forty-minute lesson. It was the smell of girls becoming women. St Helen's was fine, not strict and not soft. It was stable. Every year we had the same teachers for PE and more than a week out of every month, we recycled the same excuses for not being able to participate in swimming lessons – periods.

The school grew. It went from having a few international borders, the wealthy daughters of rich African families, to building whole houses with names like The Gables, dedicated to the schooling of young women from the old Empire. First generation savvy parents anticipated the priceless return on the capital investment outlaid for the acquisition of the right schooling and an Anglicized accent for their progeny, so much better for their ratings in the marriage stakes. Girls flooded in from India, Nigeria, with parents who were eager to learn the secret rites of passage that would make us one of them. There was more than monetary value in making the right connections. The potential was vast, a handful of private schools provided the right social status and an access-all-areas pass into the upper echelons of English Society.

There were two significant boys' public schools nearby, Merchant Taylor's and Harrow. Jude Taor, a sometimes-best friend, had brothers at Harrow, and lived in a narrow house opposite the school's chapel. Around the school, Harrow had bred a village for its self-sufficiency, which comprised of a delicate doily of shops that sold tuck and the essentials of the school uniform. Harrods was the official purveyor of school kit. Harrow represented another world; it still waned nostalgic, of Brideshead days and afternoons spent playing gentle games of cricket. The school courted the fashion for Orientalism by educating students who were the sons of Arab Royalty and Jordanian Princes. For good measure there were Nawabs and Maharajas-in-waiting, who learned to play polo and speak Latin, in order to play the game of ruling when they went back home, thus continuing the traditions of Empire through the Establishment. School dances were orchestrated by both boys' schools and we were chaperoned by squadrons of teachers doing overtime. There was no alcohol, officially.

My parents got religion when I was twelve; I had been born into the Shia Ismailia sect of Islam, we are followers of the Aga Khan. He's a thoroughly modern spiritual leader who raises thoroughbreds at his stud farm in Ireland and buys diamonds the size of Gibraltar for his wives. He is allegedly directly descended from the Prophet (we are not from that sect who worship the one that went behind the curtain, ours is the tangible, fistfuls-of-cash-deity, none of that Wahabi separation and esoteric nonsense for us), and with much fancy footwork, like a New Age Nataraj, he dances a fine fandango between east and west.

The Aga Khan, or K, as he is known to his jet-set friends, lives on an estate outside Geneva. When the bloom had faded from his English rose of a first wife, he traded her in for a German Princess, a botoxed and buxom Eurotrash, surgically enhanced vision of minor royalty. That didn't last long; she fast-tracked her grievances to the High Court in London and sued him for divorce and billions.

The second Begum counts wily Bill Gates amongst her close friends, so K was divested of much of the wealth that wasn't his in the first place. Sarah Crocker Poole, the first Begum had the right idea, she sold her fabulous collection of finery at Christies' to fund a children's charity. How many diamond earrings can I wear at a time, she sighed, divesting herself of the glittery baubles of his love, as hungry bidders raised their paddles in a frenzy. We mortals all want to own a piece of the goddess' embellishment.

It was harder than I realized, then. Trying to reconcile going to an English school, learning history from a Eurocentric perspective during the week-days (we never touched on Ghandi or Independence, let alone Africa in our history lessons), then sitting cross-legged and barefoot on the floor in the school and community halls where the Ismaili prayers took place on Friday evenings. It was beyond incongruous.

I couldn't deliver my doubts about the living god at the door when I handed over my shoes and went into the school / prayer hall. We used to go to a small community hall in North Harrow, which was before the Aga Khan bought the chunk of land in the middle of Cromwell Road opposite the V&A. There, he built the existing Ismaili Centre with its meditation pools and its baguette-cut roof.

The women, my mother's friends, were magnificent, like diamond-bedecked birds of prey, carefully plumed and sprayed. Their heads hung like unmoving relics, spritzed with perfume and *Dynasty*-inspired shoulder pads. They wore heavy make-up, designed for a skin colour far paler than their own.

One of them, Mary Lalji, who had been a lowly schoolteacher in Kampala, had become a teacher in England and her husband opened a takeaway. From the Acton corner shop stinking of grease and chips, they cooked up a chain of hotels that belied their humble beginnings. Soon after they opened the first hotel in a dingy part of West London, which hangs perilously onto the farthest edges of the Royal Borough, Mary's coiffeur - very Sue Ellen Ewing - rose in height, directly reflecting the ostentation displayed in her new fleet of cars. Hotels sprouted like mushrooms. As a young girl it was gripping to watch this transmutation of her identity, the negation of being an attractive thirty-something Asian woman to a parody of herself, a *Splitting Image* puppet with big, bouffant hair and a slash of red where her mouth should have been. It was better than television.

The assimilation into a society that neither wanted nor understood us was uglier than we might have you believe. My parent's generation edged precariously between the portal of their own culture, which we had dragged along with us from India, via Africa and a new one, yet they still didn't belong anywhere. Where was their home?

The Ismailis recite a shortened version of the traditional Arabic prayers. Our take on Islam is the cut-and-paste, easy version, Mossie 101, split into five byte-size pieces and the whole *d'ua* takes less than five minutes. I spent weeks, sitting on Jena's bed, learning it parrot fashion, by rote because it wasn't in my heart. With the help of a small booklet and Jena's careful patience I finally knew it and my time had come. This had been the preparation for the biggest test of my little life so far.

It was a Friday evening; every one of my Asian girlfriends was there. We had initiated the mass exodus to the Northwest with my father's acquisition of the house on Nicholas Way, but an alphabet of suffixes, with other -ji's, had followed, the Nanjis the Shamjis and even a Shah who lived at Number 2 and whose boy, Saquib attended Harrow.

The first four parts tripped off my tongue. Jena radiated proud confidence as she sat cross-legged facing me. She was far from her usual perch with the other old crones, where they sat on folding metal chairs in rows, and formed a hooded margin with their sari *pullahs* drawn tightly over their heads around the edges of the hall. Their eyes were closed, they were fixed in rapture and prayer and their hunched little bodies rocked back and forth, following the incantation of my words.

The local priest and priestesses sat on the floor, either side of me, women on one side, facing the female congregation and men on the other. Low tables were placed before them, which were covered with white cloths and silver trays ready to receive the tithing money that was to be given over by the flock after the prayers. Ten percent of a substantial congregation has built up a large empire of chateaux, hospitals and hotels.

My father didn't have much time for my mother's newfound zealotry or this highly ritualised religion, but he left his office early to come and hear my recitation that evening. Then I stopped and started to stutter. A switch had gone off in my head and all I could draw on was a blank space, no words came. I was stuck at the part where the forty-eight preceding Imam's names are mentioned in a wholesale invocation, for fear of offending one of the mighty by omission, but I stopped dead at number forty.

The congregation murmured the next name, in a low communal moan and I stuttered on. It wasn't unusual for a young child to lose her nerve, the first time, but then I faltered again. The priestess looked kindly at me and helped but now I was becoming unraveled. I could feel two hundred pairs of eyes boring holes in me. I looked down; tying my fingers into knots, praying the exertion would strike a memory. I tugged at my cuticles, willing the words to come out of the pain. I couldn't bear to look up at the concerned faces.

The main priestess must have felt my distress because without skipping a beat, she simply continued. By now I was stricken with stage fright and I had to sit there till the ordeal was over, my eyes and cheeks burning. But I didn't cry.

As soon as it was over, my father strode over and reached out a hand to help me up. I took it and immediately, I felt safe. I wouldn't die of embarrassment. My Maa and mum fussed about me.   Jena was the picture of consternation,

"She knew it all perfectly. How did she get it so wrong?"

"Farah, shall we go for a walk?" He asked as he extracted me from the milling crowd, away from the people anxious to catch a glimpse of the tongue-tied child. He headed straight for the exit, my small, clammy hand enclosed in his dry, firm grip.

We walked around the little building, which was set off a busy road. I was silent. Maybe I had known I didn't know it well enough to recite it with confidence in front of so many strangers. The first slippery feelings of being a disappointment crept into my consciousness. He must have felt it. He was protective and proud of me, when it came to outsiders; he sensed some of his own maverick nature in me.

One of the earliest conversations I can recall with him is about his frustration about something I had done and how it would have been all right, had I been born a boy. That's been both of our deepest disappointment, my mismanagement of my gender in an irrevocable twist of genetic cruelty.

"There's no reason to feel ashamed," he said gently, "It could have happened to anyone. It was your nerves."

His words of comfort didn't fill the shreds of my battered pride and he could see that.

"The most powerful man in the world can make a mistake and get things wrong sometimes. Do you know who that is?"

I had no idea but I liked this side of my dad, the kinder, sober side.

"It's the President of the United States. He is the most powerful man alive. He walks around with a suitcase and he can press a button and start a war."

Somehow, this was meant to comfort me.

"So if he can make mistakes, how can I expect you not to?"

The burden of being perfect was lifted. I no longer had to be as brilliant and dutiful as those expectations, which although unspoken, always emanated from him. I wish he had swallowed his words then so he might remember them.

December; the year was drawing to a close. Christmas holidays loomed and the winter's greedy chill gobbled up most of the hours that should have been daylight. It was HH's birthday.

Our celebrations had to be restrained in the new *axis mundi,* we couldn't indulge in great feasts and killing goats to commemorate another year in the life of our living god, we had to settle for renting a large school on a Saturday night, big enough to accommodate entertainment for the children and the adults.

There were the traditional stick slamming dances which originate from Gujarat and gave away our Northern Indian tribal heritage. Women wore long skirts that flared like red carnations from their waists, to reveal slim ankles decorated with chains and bells that glittered and sang as they moved.

There was *rasra,* the clapping dance formations in circles, which our ancestors had performed to express their gratitude for good harvests and plentiful rains. For the kids there was a disco, complete with flashing red and green strobe lights, for these were the colours of My Flag.

Rishma's mother collected me as she was chaperoning my friend, her sister and another young girl, part of our gang. Rishma's dad was dark and exciting. His mop of jet-black hair and hooded eyes only added to the dark rumours about him being an arms dealer and involved in money laundering. They lived in an even bigger house than ours, still further north along the reaches of the sprawling Metropolitan line. He drove a dark gold Rolls Royce, with a personalized number plate and an imported Kenyan slave slept on a rolled up mattress in their kitchen.

I had been looking forward to the event, it was an excuse to mix with the Ismaili boys and see how they danced (badly), and (how) they were dressed (geekily) and to see who would get off with whom. I had begged my mum to let me wear her new, navy blue chiffon blouse and skirt suit with white polka dots on it. It covered the shape of the woman I was becoming, something my parents studiously ignored. I was still in an uncomfortable training bra. I walked with my shoulders permanently hunched forward and down in an effort to look smaller breasted than I was. The blouse, which hung down to my knees, had patch pockets in strategic places which suited my purpose for camouflage perfectly.

Something about those sweaty school hall dances spikes up the sex hormone in adolescent kids. I was a little over twelve, no longer a girl but not quite a woman. My periods had started and Yasmin had made strange biological drawings, which I pretended to understand, in her attempt to tell me about the birds and the bees.

I had been ashamed when I saw my green school knickers stained a deep purple colour but sex was something dirty, never to be discussed, and avoided, even in thought, at all cost. I'd lived through multiple short crushes on different sloe-eyed Asian boys with chiseled features I had seen in the mosque; they had caught my eye, in passing, like trinkets in a shop window.

My face has always looked older than I was. But at the age of twelve, after I had furtively applied burgundy eyeliner and smudged on some Strawberry Soufflé lip-gloss, I was unprepared for what was to happen to me that night.

We, the girls had separated ourselves from the boys in that respectful and time honoured way which is required of Muslim women. Ismaili culture latches on where it is convenient to old Mohammedan dogmas. We watched the traditional dances, lured in by the bantering brutality of the hand clapping and the wooden sticks crashing together.

There was a part of me that craved more of this, I wanted to know where it was we came from and what it was we were running away from. These vibrant, twisting Hindu dances that had wended their way into our colourless, idol hungry Muslim culture were calling me. I was that Indian princess again, the one from my childhood, who had watched the birthday processions.

She still lived in my mind and I loved watching the dancers make shapes with their long, lithe bodies. Brown velvet curtains of hair snapped against brown arms and licked bare midriffs, like tongues of silk strands whilst their eyes flashed heat. Kilos of gold glinted under school hall lights. We stood there, transfixed.

This was as far as I could get from the laboratory sterility of St Helen's, with its dank, moss green uniform which we bought with boring regularity every year at John Lewis, the department store that knowingly resold recycled air. The heavy scent of *masala chai* spiced the atmosphere, cardamom, nutmeg and syrup teased its way from across the room where a large metal dispenser was set up.

I felt him standing a little too close to me and instinctively, I stepped away. I didn't know him well; we'd seen him around when all the congregations gathered for large events at Alexandra Palace or the Commonwealth Institute. He was swarthy and seventeen, and he wore a polyester suit and tie, like most other good Asian boys that night. Immediately he entered our orbit, I could feel Rishma start to bristle. He asked me if I wanted a Coke. I replied by flashing the can I had in my hand. I wasn't ready to let go of this reverie binding me to the laughter and the colour, the mania of movement which had seized the young men and women still twirling in the middle of the room.

"Let's go and see what the disco is like," said Rishma, in an effort to rally her troops for a show of solidarity against the intruder. They say there is safety in numbers.

"I want to watch this for a little while," I said, doing my best to ignore her meaningful glares. The Mughal fantasy hadn't finished. I was daring myself, silently, to hold this older boy's attention for just a few minutes longer. He bled danger.

"I'll find you in a few minutes," I assured her.

I'm sure she didn't want to leave me there alone; she was like a sensible older sister. When we re-met, twenty years later in Nairobi, in another life after Imran was born and I was doing my Karen Blixen trip, she and I were immediately close again but the unspoken trauma of that night lingered over our friendship.

I didn't really want to go outside with him, when he suggested we go out and get some air. But the dancers were so close, swirling in the sounds and lights, and they would still be within earshot. I was woven into the spell they were spinning, I felt safe. My heart was beating a little faster as we stepped outside. We crisscrossed the playground, avoiding the climbing frames and jungle gyms that glowered like ominous fortresses in the cool frown of a high moon.

"Let's go in here," He had taken my hand now, a little too tightly and there was no one else around. I was conscious of being on my own with him. A shadow crossed my thoughts, was it fear or excitement? I had never been alone, or this close to a boy to whom I wasn't related for this long.

36

"I want to go back inside and watch the dance." I tried to pull away from him; fear had overtaken the desire to taste something unknown.

"Are you scared?" He was teasing me. No, I wasn't scared. Why should I be? What could he do to me? My youth overestimated its own fortitude. I felt my strength slipping through me like sand in an hourglass.

"Do you want a drink?"

"I told you I have one." I pointed again at the can of Coke I had put on the ledge behind me.

He had led me inside a covered rain shelter, in the far corner of the playground, as far as it was possible to get from the memory of colour and the sounds of the dholl drums but I could still hear the distant beat and the far-off laughter, I must still be safe.

"Let's put some of this in it, it'll taste better."

He took a small colourless bottle out of his inside jacket pocket and unscrewed it. He poured a copious amount into my can of soft drink and I watched a bead of sweat collect on his furry upper lip. He hadn't yet started shaving and he wore the fuzzy down that covers the faces of adolescent boys, that itches like Velcro. I wanted to wipe the sweat off him, to laugh at his bravado and break the moment but I didn't move.

"I'm not allowed to drink that, my dad will kill me. And then you."

"Your dad's not here is he?" His eyes were doing a crazy dance in the half-light and I didn't know if he was jeering or laughing. There was a part of me that said I shouldn't walk off, I should have been born a boy then I would have hit him hard and turned on my flat heel. As a girl, somewhat restricted in motion by the suede court shoes I had snuck out of the house, that I had slipped on in Rishma's mum's car, I felt I should stay.

Here was an older boy, much older and obviously interested in talking to me. I was torn between the safety of my girlfriends and the dark promises of a stranger boy I didn't know. There I stood. I must have lingered a moment too long on the threshold of my question.

He had pulled it out, pulsing and engorged.

"What do you think? Look how hard you have made me." I could have, should have run, with my mother's skirt hiked up over my knees, as fast as those silly heels could take me but the vodka had numbed my sense, the dance in my head was going faster and the dancer's skirts swirled like Catherine Wheels. I closed my eyes.

What was it that Yasmin had meant when she talked about a man loving a woman? I didn't feel him insert it. I wasn't aware that he had pulled my knickers down. He had manoeuvred his way inside me, pulling me closer to him and crushing my back on the wall behind us. We were both still standing.

I felt my stomach retch and its contents curdle when he pushed his tongue deep into my throat, forcing it down as he went deeper inside me.

He satisfied himself and I closed my eyes tight shut. I thought if I closed them hard enough I'd wake up, this could only be a bad dream. I tried to see the sparks that flew from the dancers' feet, but no image came. I opened my eyes a few seconds later and I saw him recoiling, the light in his eyes had gone out and his mouth hung slack. He was pale in the yellowish light and sweaty.

"Shit. There's blood everywhere. Why didn't you tell me you had never done it before?"

My fear hit him hard across the face.

"What have you done to me?"

I wanted to cry out but the sound was stuck, it was constricting my throat. There was blood all over the hem of my mother's designer skirt, it had pooled, like a dirty secret, accusatory, on the little white dots which were stained fresh blood red. I could see in the yellow safety light that burned over our heads that there was blood all over my legs. All I could think was that I was surely dead meat, she had let me borrow it reluctantly and I had ruined it.

He went inside and left me shivering, with his jacket over my shoulders for consolation. I was in shock and it felt like a lifetime elapsed before he returned with Rishma. The hangman's cloak he had left for me didn't help, it smelled of him and the bile rose in my throat, first a trickle then it gushed out, all over me, my clothes, his jacket. I vomited till only yellow liquid made runny pools by my feet. I had thrown up everything in me. But the stickiness and the putrid scent of his seed still remained.

"What did he do to you?" Rishma was trying not to panic but then she saw me in a scrunched up heap in my own sick on the floor. She saw the blood and fell silent.

"Let me go and find my mum."

The next day was a Sunday. I spent the whole day in the giant bathtub which lead off my parents' bedroom, I was in it for hours. I hand washed my mother's suit which was meant to be dry-clean only but which survived the watery ordeal. I scrubbed myself with a loofah, scraping the top layers of my skin off till I was red and raw, bleeding in patches. I had to get the stench off me. If I could shed enough skin cells, perhaps the experience would rub off. I wanted to eliminate what he had left inside me and get back a part of me I hadn't said that he could take.

"You can't stay in there forever, ET," although he was trying to sound casual by calling me by my nick-name, which had come about because of an unfortunate, self-styled haircut, I could hear the concern slipping into dad's voice. I had been in the bath for five hours. I knew Parin Nanji had called my mother earlier that morning. I was shriveling like a prune but I wasn't ready to come out of the bath.

"Do you want to talk about something?"

"No, nothing, I'm fine." But I wasn't.

I couldn't put words to what had transpired, less than twelve hours earlier. I knew about sex, Yassi's crude diagrams had been accompanied with a perfunctory spiel, she'd started,

"When a man loves a woman, he puts his penis into her vagina," and that was how babies were made. I was repulsed at the thought of people, like my parents, engaging in such perverse acts. Now I had done it.

Had Amin Ali loved me? Did he want to make a baby with me? I gathered up the pain, I screwed up the questions and I buried all of it, the pain and the shame into a corner of myself where it festered. This was my first experience of love; I hated it. If this is what it was, I wanted no part of it. All I wanted was to forget his Golum-like stare and the crazy look of lust in his black eyes.

Rishma confirmed later that her mother had indeed called mine, to tell her what had happened and to find out if I was all right. But mine never said a word; she didn't ask me anything about it.

Later, I saw her surreptitiously look over the hem of her skirt carefully, before she hung it back up in the cupboard, with all the other beautiful clothes which she kept locked away. She chose to see no evidence to believe what she had been told, that her daughter had been raped. Her skirt wasn't bloody; surely it would have been if anything like that had transpired.

Probably another pre-adolescent fantasy, she thought to herself. Besides, it was easier to believe than reaching out to protect and make the child feel safe. She had never been able to do that. Her daughter was out of her grasp. She had abandoned me long before that, and she knew she would never regain me, what was the point in comforting me? Or even trying to understand what had happened? My mother has always lived devoid of emotion and compassion but that was when, in my world, she started to die.

Stairway to Heaven

The suburban enclave we lived in had been clawed out of the edges of the green belt. It was called the Copse Wood Estate. Although it wasn't gated or fenced in, a strict system of proprietary apartheid existed, not with security alarms and barbed wire but with the surety that affluence brings. It was the comfort of being amongst ones own tribe, we were preserved and pickled living in our big, sad house perched second to the end of a private road.

Love, whatever that was, wasn't something that I wanted to try again. That first horrid encounter and the earlier years with my cousin made me wary of men. I was conscious of what I elicited and I felt objectified by my adolescent body and attractiveness. I hid my feelings of curiosity and natural teenage crushes deep below my tough facade. I found that if I didn't act on them, these infatuations came and went, as sure as the new moon grows swollen and recedes again. It was just a matter of time and waiting.

I found that there was some truth in the fairytale of opposites attracting, we always want what we can never be. He was fair and tanned, a year or two older and he had the right quantities of bravado and tragedy to take on my feigned non-interest. His father was an alkie and in one of his drink-fuelled rages had come through on a threat to move them all to Sedona, in Arizona, land of red rocks and golden pink sunsets. Two months before they emigrated, Peter came crashing into my life, like the Little Prince in St. Exupéry's tale, who lands inadvertently on an asteroid, and is stuck there.

He was staying with us, on a sojourn back from America during which he was organising the packing and moving of the household and deciding which of the family's belongings were to be sold or stored. He was respectable, my parents had met his and besides, the Wells family had owned a grand house round the corner, they were one of us.

I felt the first flush of being noticed and it made me feel alive. It was a melting feeling, of sitting next to a boy I liked who expected nothing. It started as a crush but this one didn't pass. Peter wasn't trying to prove anything. He was gentle and soft-spoken and something about him, at fifteen, was melancholy. I collected broken souls, they resonated with the angry four-year-old that sometimes still rules me. I am the child who wants to fix her daddy and so searches out the damaged, in the vain hope that maybe she can fix another, or be fixed as a substitute.

He was transparent and quivering, he had the fragility other children of alcoholic parents live with. We saunter about our lives, with a devil-may-care attitude but we are the walking wounded. We are bleeding in our hearts for all the hurt that our eyes take in. We are unable to stem the mixture of helplessness and pain that burns us awake in the night.

It was his last evening and we wanted to go for a walk, into Copse Wood but I didn't think my over-protective mother would agree. Several glasses of gin and a music party at home had softened her resistance, she allowed us to go. My older cousin, one of the Kenyan boys was staying with us, at the end of the long holidays.

Peter took a boom box stereo system and I packed an old blanket to sit on, some cans of soft drink and some snacks. It was a shimmery, end-of-summer evening. The sun had exhausted all colour out of the landscape and it descended by degrees, leaving with a lingering French kiss, full on the lips of the earth. The memory of the day was spun-out in still-warm pools of grass.

We walked some way and we took an entrance into its shaded canopy. We found a clearing. I lay the blanket on the floor and he put a scratchy cassette into the tape deck. No one dreamed that CDs would ever catch on; they were mini flying saucers, back from the future. We nestled down and settled into each other. We found the places where we fit, this joining up which was comforting and asexual.

We were picnicking on the grave of what might have been between us, but neither wanted to acknowledge it, the words were bigger than we could articulate. If we didn't give it a name or a voice, perhaps we might steal a little time, and enjoy the limitation of what we had.

"Have you heard this before?"

He looked at me, with his pale, blue eyes as the first few forlorn notes of Led Zeppelin's *Stairway to Heaven* played on the tinny system.

"No," I replied, nonchalantly, "What is it?"

"Aw man," he mocked me with his fake, recently acquired American twang. "This is the coolest band ever."

And so we listened, as the trees left their voluptuousness behind and receded in the twilight.

They appeared to be sketched in charcoal. They were barely outlined in the gathering dusk. The evening shuddered a little closer around us and the first, bright blue, neon light of the night settled in.

Every leaf on every tree resonated with his music and after the twentieth replay, it still sounded new to me. He sang it to me, a lonely ballad of a woman who was set upon acquiring all the treasures money could buy her. She wanted to pile them high to reach heaven through what she owned. I started to feel the cold and shivered a little but neither of us wanted to go back.

No one had noticed us slip away so they hadn't been able to extract a curfew on how much time we had left together. Peter took off his sweater, which was worn and patched at the elbows, and handed it to me. It held his boy smell, patchouli and sweet sweat. I breathed him in and closed my eyes to remember the scent of him.

"Here put this on." Although he was pretending to be gruff, the affection in his voice touched me. I felt safe.

"But you'll be cold."

"No, I won't." He lay down, his head in my lap and pulled his army surplus woolen coat over us both.

We were locked away, in a space where nothing, not the encroaching darkness or the unfamiliar sounds could intrude. I stroked the place on his forehead where his soft skin gave way to tousled hair. There was nothing to be said, it would spoil the sweetness of knowing that this couldn't last. When morning cast her first watery rays of light, he would wake up and get ready to catch a plane for another life.

Love lasts longest where there is still longing. Nothing happened with Peter, other than some intense French kissing, I felt calmer and restored. He brought laughter and light, there was innocence in his perfect smile and golden halo. Although he never put it into words, for I had told him about that evening in Hatfield at the function with Amin, he made me a loose promise that all could be right with the world again.

Finally we untangled ourselves, we gathered up the empty cans and the cassettes. It was dark. Silently, we walked back, hand in hand through the woods to the place where our private world met another.

Our story ended then, it couldn't survive the perfect Home Counties lawns and the shiny sports cars parked up on gravel drives. Like a sapling exposed too early to the sunlight, it never grew. I never saw him again. I think he wrote to me and we spoke on the phone once or twice but the distance swallowed up the words.

Did his love catch me? Men have tried to love me since him but I can't let them in. He helped me to regain myself, to get back to that place in myself before what had happened with Amin, a few months earlier.

Romance has its place; Conrad wrote that we should seek to go "in search of romance, for that after all is our business in this world." I bought the fairytale in hardback but in return I gave up my own story and its truth. I lived for romance and lived out a life that might never have been.

The vain rose told the little Prince that one is always responsible for the things which one tames. She was an ordinary garden-variety rose, no exotic hybrid, but by loving her, he lent her specialness, she felt as if she were the only one of her kind in the world when he found her. Peter was my first prince. There was no expectation, no promise of a future, we knew that time was limited and that was what made it bittersweet and necessary. It ended as sweetly as it began.

Ex Africa

Africa is in me, pernicious like malaria. It's as if she consumed me and I belong, some essential part of me, in her. She is like having a mad, dark dance of a disease that recurs when I least expect her. Her long shadow sleeps on top of me, weightless, like a resting storm. Then she is evoked by the pungent scent of fresh tuberoses or the smell of the rain, hanging like a promise in the air before it falls. That ripe, greenness raises my senses makes me look up, and then, as sure as I can feel the first few drops on my hands, the skies start to weep.

We visited Kenya often, it was an easy place to take three young children, and it was a holiday that fit easily like slipping into a pair of weekend jeans. My mother's older sister lives there and we stepped into the pattern of the days easily. It was home. Something of us still belonged there.

We were the children of the original corner *dukka-wallah,* Alidina Visram. He survived the European partitioning of Africa and the demise of the colonies. When all vestiges of empire were torn down, his own bust was allowed to remain, although it was moved from Piggot Place to a less conspicuous spot in Treasury Park Gardens in Mombasa. He and his peers had been the great pioneers; they were merchant traders but they weren't afforded political opportunities. The British needed them, to arrange missionary and hunting expeditions and to provide food and tents for the necessary excursions inland. Aga Khan Sultan Mohammed Shah encouraged them to look to the ports for industry by bringing commodities in that others needed.

The Ismailis descend from the Khojas, a tribe steeped in Hindu culture from Northern India. The Imams were Persian and they tolerated influences from other religions to allow some cohesion and something of the old and familiar in the newly converted. There was also the small issue of Aurang Zeb who paid a price for every non-Muslim skull that was brought before him and who built mountains out of these, a loud message from the unspeaking dead Hindus.

Alidina Visram set out for Africa in a dhow. Parts of my mother's family had settled Nairobi and street names bore silent witness to the long years of their lives they gave over to the infant city. The Alidina Visram School which was built as a memorial for him by his son is still a credible educational institution in Mombasa. His house has been turned into an art gallery.

44

His uncomplicated generosity was legendary. Once when he had nothing to give someone who came to the house begging, he gave away his wife's ornaments. He died poor and on his deathbed he whispered that he wanted to be buried in India but there was no money to pay for his passage. His son took the gold wedding ring off his father's finger and said he would sell it so his last wish could be observed.

Stories of his wealth and ruthlessness compile a complicated portrait of a man who is seen as the first merchant trader amongst the Asians in Uganda, although through his shops and his plantations he was able to give thousands paid employment.

Another summer. I was uncomfortable in a body that was budding in places I didn't want it to. The first embarrassing patches of soft, down-like hair were visible. I was flushed with the spotty embarrassment of girlhood around anyone of the opposite sex. I was getting used to living in the tension of being a teenager, that contrary feeling of being pulled in different directions. The markers were laid out, pointing the way for me to become a young adult but I didn't want to go, I hadn't been a child for long enough. Even then, I felt the loss of my childhood.

We were in Malindi, instead of Mombassa. It was a friendlier resort and not quite so commercialised. There were less loud European tourists who were determined to share their *Out of Africa* experience with anyone within earshot. We stayed in Serena hotels; they were owned by the Aga Khan and combined five-star luxury with a child-friendly atmosphere. It was another way of putting money into the coffers of the Aga Khan.

We spent lazy days by the pool, swimming and laughing. We were segregated from the real Dark Continent which lay crouching like a sleeping lion, just beyond the gated compound. Speckled with crumbling, white sand, the beach lay splayed like a flat, upturned palm, towards the sea. Where the two met was a space for a silent prayer on which two disparate worlds balanced.

This summer had been different; I felt something incongruent in the packing of the suitcases. When my mother told me to pack sweaters, it made no sense. It was hot summer in the southern hemisphere, why would I need them? My father didn't intend to join us; he usually did, half way through. This time, he was too busy.

But there had been something final and determined about the way in which my mother closed the front door and shoved her weight against it with her shoulder to make sure that it was locked properly. It was as if she was making a final exit, walking off a stage. As she approached the car, she flung the bunch of keys into her bag and reversed the car down the slope of a drive. She didn't look back at the house.

45

On another continent, twenty-four hours later, it was dusk; the inky blue sky had donned her shimmering sari, with stars for diamond drops that glittered to cast a spotlight on the evening's entertainment as we walked along the beach. The open skies gave way to the song of the night, the cicadas and the rustle of palm fronds. My mother and her sister walked a little way ahead and the other children were still further along the beach. I felt safe, on this silver sliver of coastline, lit up with the borrowed light from falling stars. The oceanfront was heavily guarded where it gave way to expensive hotels and beach bungalows. Blue-uniformed *askaris* stood sentry, every so often along the beach.

They were the gatekeepers of our cloistered world. They held ebony *pangas*, sticks made of shiny wood, in their hands but they would never use them. Nothing was likely to go off, they expected no trouble.

This was our beach-blanket paradise. This was the soft-sell Africa of banana trees and *Jungle Book* beach huts. Every so often we passed a group of German or Italian tourists, who were sitting in a circle, singing songs only they understood. Their burnt bronze faces were flickering and animated by the firelight. This was as far as they could get from their own culture and identity which were all the things that we craved.

I was tangled in the strands of my own thoughts. The memories of an African childhood, which had become faded and forgotten by longing and memory, were being stoked by the soft whispers of the wind. The moon above was a crescent, a carved out capital C but still the sky blazed. It was laden with its sparkling booty.

The warm, white sand curled between my toes while the warm evening breeze tossed strands of loose hair around my face. I was aware of how the elements were working together with all my five senses to delineate the edges of myself, to me. Together they conspired to create an unreal moment but I felt sure of myself, I couldn't see my feet yet I was sure-footed in the dark.

Africa opened up and I stepped in. For once, I felt whole, as if I was part of something bigger. She yielded herself to me, and our entwined legacy of blood-spattered earth and not belonging melded and came into focus.

The sea was flat; it was a still dish of mercury. It was lighting up silver where the moonlight caught it, giving off instant strobes that slipped back into darkness as fast as they had appeared. The water stroked the edges of the beach with long, sensual lashes. The scented wind still whispered somewhere over my head. This frozen platinum print of a moonlit world slotted into place. I was part of it. It soaked up my anxieties, Atlas shrugged and at once, everything ugly receded and solidity unified to give my world a coherent pattern.

Nothing was lacking. I stopped; I was still being pulled by the allure of the moon. The others had wandered off a little further but my mother and my aunt hung back a bit. She was beautiful then, my mum. The photos from that holiday are now corner scrolled with age but she looks out of huge Jackie 0 framed sunglasses from the deck of a boat and her mahogany coloured, shoulder-length hair is curled from the sun and the salt water.

She was clever, she'd been a Math and Physics professor at Makrere College in Kampala but in the holiday pictures she looks caved in. Her broad brow is furrowed, she's frowning, and the expression, behind the dark glasses is sadness, faintly visible though her tinted, plastic shield.

Her soft, sibilant voice edges close enough to me on the sleeve of the wind and though she speaks quietly, only for her sister's ears, I can hear her fighting back tears. She is on a precipice. It was the voice of longing, a young girl's wish from long ago for a different future.

"I could have married anyone you know. There was Akbar, he became a doctor. Do you remember him? He loved me…" Her voice faltered as her thoughts crossed over to the other side of what might have been. The unwritten chapters and distant worlds of possibility started to unfurl in her mind.

"What are you going to do? You can't leave him; you have three small children…"

My aunt's concern for our welfare was touching but her husband was devoted, faithful. She was also a fan of my father.

"We could all have married someone else, Zari, we chose the paths we were meant to," this was vintage Gulshan, down to the last drop. She is a firm believer in god and destiny, "Look at everything you have, your children are bright and healthy, you have everything you could want…"

I could see in my mind's eye, Gulshan's hazel eyes clouding over, her perky face losing its smile. Something in my mother couldn't stand it any longer; her voice had a jagged rasp to it.

She'd chosen adventure instead of love with my dashing dad. He whisked her away in his convertible sports cars and slicked down hairdo. She'd given up predictability and sacrificed Adoring Akbar to the dark glamour of my dad. She must have had some inkling, even then, that he was no saint, and there was always volatility in him. He could change suddenly, without warning. Something in him churned, he was as restless as the sea, which was his birth sign.

"What are you going to do? You have three children to think about," Gulshan's voice was almost pleading, gently coaxing back the practical, sane and long-suffering sister with whom she had started the walk on the beach only half an hour ago. Her sibling had stepped into the abyss.

"I thought we might come and live in Kenya…"

Her voice trailed off as she was struck with the impracticality of her own proposition. How would she pack up a house and three children and move them to another hemisphere, to a life opposite to the one we knew? To top it all we were three achingly aspiring-to-be-British children. Kenya was fine for holidays.

"The fights are becoming bad. I never know when he is coming home anymore."

Gulshan tried to soothe her, "But all men are like that, you have to make your own life."

"But my life could be so much better," she sighed and the sea sipped her breath, "I used to dream. And what will I do when the children are grown up?" My mother was already anticipating a life without us, when we were all long gone.

As the vastness of the sky and the depth of the ocean fused together, I knew that if her life had been different, if it had been the way she was imagining it now, it would have been one without me. Just one more step into the sea and I would be free. I strained my ears to catch the lullaby which had soothed me, seconds before and I closed my eyes to emblazon the patterns of the stars in the firmament, inside my eyelids, so they'd always be there, they were something to fill me up, because I felt hollow.

The tide was coming in faster, and my ankles were caught tight in the colourless clutch of the sea and the rivulets of swirling sand, tracing runes over my skin. The sea was daring, black but dancing, and I wanted to keep walking, a little further. It was up to my waist, then still a little deeper so her cool fingers began to caress my neck and my shoulders.

I heard my name, they were calling me and then my mother's voice was closer. Her sound reached me; she was suddenly so close I thought I could feel her breath in my ear.

"I'm here, behind you." The sea released me.

They turned and started to walk towards me. I was kneeling in the water as it came in, the backs of my legs were wet and my clothes had freed themselves from the shape of my body and gravity and were streaking towards the ocean. The sound of my mother's laughter brought me back,

"Why are you sitting in the sea?" She smiled and reached out her hand.

"You silly thing!" My aunt chimed in, she prodded me and took on a contrived Indian accent, "You are going to get all wet, like the monsoon. Come on *lurki*, let's walk,"

Gulshan's Hinglish impersonation always made me laugh. I stood up but she felt years away, my mother. The wet clothes clung but I didn't mind, their clamminess defined the edge of me, where they left my skin indicated where I ended. The outline was where something else began, they were proof that I existed. I took my place between the sisters and they each took an arm, and so we walked away, we three, a little lop-sided.

My mother has a favourite Doris Day song, she sang it when I was tiny, the one about the little girl who would ask her mother what life would bring, when she was older. It's the anthem of impatient youth. We so long to reach that day when we know we are adults, when things are firm and secure.

We walked back to the hotel, singing out loud. The wind raised the sound of her whisper to a soft moan and the long scaly trunks of the palm trees hunched a little closer. The sea puckered up where the moon descended into her and the stars grew dim. The bonfires on the beach glimmered and faded.

Somewhere under a moonless sky, where the Indian Ocean nestles into the coastline of Africa, the irresistible song of two sisters and something of an adolescent girl caught the tails of the scurrying, colourless clouds. They sang in clear voices, of those who had made choices, whose lives had taken the paths they were meant to. The girl cocooned herself in the cadence, the words could have been written for her.

Memories of the magical city of my birth were thrown alive. A fistful of stardust flickered making light where darkness had hidden my memory for years. I could imagine the valley below. The half-remembered dreams took my thoughts by the hand and led me back to the vista high on the hilltop. Kampala's city lights burned way below us. Me and my mother in the car, her favourite song on the radio which she was singing to me.

That evening when the song and the sand had ended, I understood more about my mother's disillusionment.

I learned the sacrifices she had made and the loyalty that was ingrained in her that distended her soul, made her live out a life she shouldn't have had to; my heart broke a little for her. Maybe this explained why she could never hug me or show affection. Her sadness began to drizzle through me. Her anger at my father let itself loose in me.

Years later, back in England I was going through my mother's jewellery, fantasizing about a time in the distant future when it would all be mine. There was a light blue vanity case, the kind that actresses use to store their potions and creams, and in it, besides the heavy gold chains and collection of mounted sovereigns that she had had made into necklaces, were a handful of faded blue Aerogrammes. They were addressed to my mother but they bore Gulshan's address in Nairobi, in my dad's squat scrawl. His handwriting formed letters that were cursive, ballistic, written fast. The letters dated back to that summer, I learned as I read them that she had left him and taken us. She had not intended to go back.

The walk on the beach, when the sea had held me close had been a turning point in her own life, for whatever reasons she justified to herself, she had decided to stay. The letters were full of doubts, he had met someone else and he loved her but he didn't want to leave us.

He's been a consummate adulterer, my father, but in his own way, he was feeding his own neurosis to be loved enough. He once loved me; I know how hard it is to let go of him. My mother, who was stronger than I, couldn't let him go. But his love is too much. We are like jihadi moths to a flame or the stars on the beach that night; we, who loved him once, are extinguished, one by one.

Travels with my Aunt

Yasmin is my father's youngest sister. Our relationship has always been complicated. When I was younger I worshipped her. She was the big sister who had to navigate the same stormy seas, years before I did. She was a safe harbour along the way; the more I advanced into my adolescence, the pricklier my father became. As I grew more awkward, he grew more unreasonable. The comments in passing, from years before, when I was still a knee-bumping, shin-grazing six-year-old, and I had fallen out of a tree, when he told me it would all be fine all this tomboy-foolery, if I had been a boy, that throwaway remark had grown legs and a personality and come home to roost. The only thing he wanted of me was the only thing I could never be.

Yasmin worshipped my father; he brought her up with his silver tongue and the back of his slipper. Love in my family comes with heavy chains and a no-refund policy; it's strictly cash, *caveat emptor*. The padlocks that lock you down have no key to let you out and the love is draining and bound by conditions.

Its definition changes, constantly, you are never quite right or quite enough. I tried unsuccessfully, to shape-shift to fit the latest decree, but as soon as I made myself fit by pleasing my parents, or at least one of them, by displeasing the other one, the boundaries shifted again. I became resilient to the constant motion; it was like being seasick on a small boat. I learned to fix my stare on some far-distant point, not to move around too much and hold on for all my life was worth.

I didn't realize that I shouldn't expect affection, in order to survive. I soon grasped the concept that negative attention for being bad was better than no attention at all. The day they gave out the book on parenting my parents had been absent.

Though he was always ambiguous with me, I thought he had a lot of dignity and I admired what I thought was his integrity, as a small child. He sees everything in black and white, with no room for greyness. He's made fortunes and although he loves his fast cars and his cavernous, impeccably furnished houses, they don't define him. He's quite comfortable squatting with the

51

gardener to discuss what plants can be uprooted so his beloved grandchildren can plant sunflower seedlings.

This is different from my experience of him; he was always too busy for me. He's a difficult person to grasp; there are so many shades of him. He's the super-cool buzz-cut, sports car driving man-about-town, with his aquiline nose and Bollywood hero looks. There's the uber-dad, holding his baby Farah close. There I am, in pale, colour photographs, looking sulky, a bundle of frills.

There are relaxed pictures of him playing with me on a bed with an inflatable Esso tiger towering beside me. It looks scary and emphasizes the awkwardness of that space between us.

Growing up was tough on Yasmin. There are more than ten years between them, which was enough of a gap for him to step into their father's empty shoes, for he was another one who was never there, even when he was. My dad went nuclear on her; he banned miniskirts, lipsticks and heels over two inches high. He kept her tightly screwed under his thumb. That wasn't unusual for the time; it was Kampala in the mid-60s. While they embraced western culture for their own generation, my father's peers were terrified that it might corrupt their young. My father pretended that the Beatles were the anti-Christ and although he listened to rock and roll on his car radio, it was banned in the house.

Yasmin was seventeen when I was born and I was the first acknowledged grandchild as Allegra, Julie's child, had been illegitimate. As she and her mother lived in England, the family avoided controversy by pretending she didn't exist. When my grandpa chose my regal name, Yasmin was at that uncomfortable age when teenagers spin out of the comfort zone of their family's orbit. She instantly disliked my mother who was then a beauty: she had an hour-glass figure and wore her hair in a beehive with a heavy fringe over her pretty face, which gave her an almost Egyptian look, like Elizabeth Taylor as Cleopatra. She wore close-fitting clothes to set off her curves and spiky toed high-heeled court shoes; the same ones that Yassi coveted and was denied. My mother represented womanliness and Yasmin was gawky, and angular in a geeky way.

Yasmin lived in her head, where it was safest. She wrote and read a lot, plays mostly as they offered a gateway from the torment she thought she was suffering. She caused a scandal when she kissed the black Romeo, as Juliet in the school's play. I don't believe the invective she describes in her largely fictionalised autobiography. My family is too uptight for public outcries. Our rage is expressed behind closed doors, where it has the potential to be more deadly.

She wore square framed Elvis Costello glasses. She had to sneak makeup out of the house if she wanted to wear it. I learned that trick early on. I'd put my burgundy eyeliner and plum mascara into my gym bag with the shoes I wanted to wear but I'd leave the house looking how he wanted me to look. She had been frightened of him but I learned, early on that anger is a great weapon. Mine was more potent than his, and scarier, coming out of a teenage girl. I dealt with him differently. As a child I was aware of the power my temper had over my parents so we played a cat and mouse game of tolerance and when I had had enough of him, I would take the long tube ride to Ealing Common where Yasmin lived and still does, in a sprawling, damp-smelling flat on Gunnersbury Avenue, which faces the park.

It was bought with a loan she never repaid from my father who paid the deposit. When Yassi and Sky moved into the flat in Ealing Common she asked Jena to move in with them to help with the new baby. I liked being around them, they presented a united couple, the front my parents had given up. But that was nuked into meltdown, thanks to my father's own brand of protean destruction.

Sky was athletic and handsome, he was a lecturer of Zoology at London University and she taught English to foreign students at an expensive college, in a salubrious street off Holland Park. I watched her, then, in the embryonic stages of becoming the great media controversialist she is no longer. She fitted well into the automatic authority that words and teaching lent to her as she imparted phonetic wisdom to her students. She used to be petite and pretty, but she had become podgy. Middle-age spread her out too early and at some point in my mid-teens, her jealousy crept in.

She was looking at me and remarked nonchalantly how lucky I was to be high-breasted as this was the fashion; it meant my legs looked longer than they really were. It was a bit of a backhander but I didn't understand that then. Sky called her Chubby, the layer of puppy fat that leaves most women in their twenties, had clung to her and she was conscious of her weight and how she looked. The smell of damp had permeated her, it was in her clothes and she tried to disguise it by dousing herself in scent, like the fake Moroccan, tawdry, smell of Opium.

Sky started to take courses, which meant he was away a lot of weekends, and Yassi was left in splendid isolation. She couldn't drive, she didn't learn till much later. It was part of the lifelong dependence on men, which she pretends to rail against because that is her game. She went from my father's house to her husband's and shed one skin for another, overnight. From being defined as younger sister she became the young bride. She didn't like her father, my Kassam. The most awful things I have heard about him have come from her. She never forgave me for taking the focus off her. That was when she fell under the radar of my father's attention. She became and has been, since my early childhood a non-entity in my family.

She encouraged me to come and stay with them, not that I needed much encouragement, life at home was like living on the San Andreas Fault. It didn't take much for me to throw some clothes and a toothbrush into a carrier bag and head their way. She encouraged me to talk to her about school, boys and in between huge bouts of self-consciousness I'd tell her bits and pieces. Maybe she thought I had it easier than she did, maybe she thought my father loved me more. When I left her house, I felt stained by her gnawing envy. I had my own battles to fight with him but I didn't realise how she was manipulating me because of her jealousy towards my parents.

When I became a pawn in their struggle, I'm still unsure. She started telling me about my mother, adding to the mistrust I felt after the confessions on the beach years ago and she stoked the antagonistic feelings till they became toxic. I disliked my mother as a person and I didn't see why I should like her as a parent, I certainly didn't choose her, whatever the Buddhist Lama says. Yassi cruelly exploited the rift, piercing voodoo pins into the remaining effigy of the illusion that we could be a happy family again. As if we ever were. My siblings were loved, they were close and they fit in. Sometimes I felt as if they could well have been a happy foursome if I hadn't been there. I wanted to disappear. In spite of the mutual dislike (my mother couldn't stand her sister-in-law but was too clever to show it), we continued the charade of extended happy Anglo-Asian families around the table over our Sunday lunch. She, Sky and Ari and sometimes one or other of my aunts from my mother's side would come to eat with us.

My father would play king of the castle. He became the personification of patriarchal supremacy as he carved the sacrificial lamb from a silver platter with an assassin's knife. We ate off china plates, they were Royal Doulton and they bore sprigs of country roses, yellow and burgundy. To all appearances, we looked affluent, happy, immersed in the new culture.

Sky tolerated us; he came from a large loving family who had emigrated from London to Canada after the East African exodus. They were the real deal, not the fantasy we created which was then reflected back at us in prose and programming. People bang on endlessly and erroneously about the loyalty of the extended family in the Indian Diaspora. It's our displaced genetic hankering that looks back at days when we basked in sub-continental security. But those days never existed. We had no stories, our reference points had vanished. I clenched the wholesome lie of big family love in my fists and it disintegrated like confetti and rose petals in the heat of my hands and the need I generated. It was never there.

Sky was sneering, arrogant. He was Herculean, compared to most of his tubby Asian contemporaries. He was a good head and shoulders taller than them and so he literally looked down on nearly everyone. But they seemed happy as a couple. I had reservations about him as a child; I'd refused to call him by his name, referring to him in some ego-denying way as "that man with the moustache." I grew to accept him and I was fond of him.

It was another tortuous Sunday lunch, in that brooding house in Northwood. We were all seated around a large oak dining table, some mock Tudor travesty

54

my father had bought from somewhere far-flung. It was more English than the English would have brought into their homes, but that was the trick, we had to be whiter than white. We were forced to sit upright by the straight-back dining chairs with wooden posts that served no ergonomic function. Lunch seldom passed without some gastronomical upset; my brother would flatly refuse to eat what was put on his plate or my sister, who couldn't manage her cutlery properly, would ignite the wrath of my father, by being clumsy and dropping her knife. Today there was a different tension, rare but discernible which mingled with the smell of *masala* roast beef and Yorkshire Pudding.

My dad had spotted Sky at Baker Street tube station. His office was now on Euston Road, so he had to change at Baker Street to make the connection back to Northwood. Sky had been kissing a woman, much younger and very passionately on the platform. They hadn't seen him. Dad still saw himself as the defender of the honour of his younger sister. Or maybe it was his mission to set about her destruction.

It's practically impossible to step out of the shade that my father's protection throws around your life; it's hard to wrench yourself from the influence. It binds us to him, even when we are thousands of miles away and separated by continents. Sometimes I think I'll only really be free when he dies. I have killed him off in my head hundreds of times, not in any graphic or explicit way, but just by ceasing to speak to him, sometimes for years at a time. I have imagined them both dead and felt the freedom of being an orphan. In my visualizations there are no crocodile tears, only relief.

Yassi was teary and they left soon after that. I remember angry shouting; she thought my father was shaking the tree in which their carefully constructed domestic nest balanced. She had spent her life so far building it but it was still fragile, held together only by her will, not by any mutual sense of commitment. If he shook it hard enough, there was a danger that it might all come tumbling down. Sky promised it was all a lie but then he stopped lying and promised he would stop. The dream of the life they had shared shattered that afternoon. My father was smug.

Years later she came to stay with me in New York, when I was an art dealer. She'd lost too much weight and the flesh had fallen off her bones except where it gathered under her eyes from too much grief, to form circles of mourning. Ari, her son, was still a great, buoyant child. We were watching him play in the kids' playground near NYU and I tried to listen while she unburdened her pain. She still blamed my dad, she was convinced that he had been committed to ruining what they had had because he could never have it with my mother. I couldn't explain that my parents, for all their dysfunction and the unhappiness that encircled them, were content. They had made compromises and settled themselves to accepting them. They were perfect at it and they didn't know anything else.

It transpired later that Sky's weekends away were an elaborate cover-up for another life which he had created with one of his young Zoology students, Zoë. They had set up a home. Zoë had his child. Yasmin was inconsolable for years; the life was gone from her. She couldn't understand how he could sacrifice what they had, what she thought was real love, for someone else.

Coming from where we came from, it was only natural that we should fall into bear pits of tragedy and messy relationships. How could we possibly extend love and nurturing when we had never known it? That was when I fell out of love with the aunt I had loved so much.

She was wrecked, like a picnic ruined by an unexpected summer shower. She became too human and tragic. She knew I had fallen out of her magic circle of power and later she did things to hurt me, because if she can't have the thing she loves, or if she feels love has betrayed her, she has to kill it.

That's how we handle pain, to lash it outwards at others, particularly those we once cared about the most. When we know we have killed the opponent, they are no longer able to hurt us, like the satiated lion that licks the blood off his lips after the kill, we can saunter off and never look back at the mess and destruction we leave behind.

Amazing Grace

She entered the black-painted room, wrapped and bound in an Azzedine Alaia bondage-style cat suit and a sexy hangman's hood. She electrified everything around her. She picked a corner and posed her way over, her movement was defined by angles and refracted light. It was like watching shapes as they delineate motion but in freeze frame. This was L'Equipe Anglaise and she could pick out her own spot. Her violet eyes and white teeth flashed, she was feral like a human panther.

Grace Jones hemorrhaged sophistication; she was a black diamond. It wasn't unusual to see her there, Shariffi's members' only club was the forerunner to the gulag of private clubs that came later. Then it was filled with the finest Eurotrash, those who swanked around London with credentials but no cash in the early 80s.

But Grace was different. She was feisty and languid; she didn't walk, she undulated like a string of pearls being laid down on a table. She was an enigma in our midst and a contra-flow of cultures crashing. Ideas exploded in her orbit. She had resurrected the sounds of Mistinguet and Piaff at La Gouloue with her espresso and Gitanes rendition of Piaff's song, *La Vie en Rose*. She looked like a weapon from Modesty Blaise's arsenal, something dangerous and surreal with the vertiginous spikes of her heels and the red, arching fingernails which were always poised, ready to claw.

I was bored with St. Helen's, as I had learned anything that it could teach me. I was no longer the only non-white, by 1983, there were enough brown girls to form the chorus line of a Bollywood film. Some of these, like me, were the daughters of immigrants who were desperately seeking some or other identity. We had one common factor, we wanted to belong and our clever parents thought money could buy that.

Other students came from India. They boarded, but we carefully skirted each other's paths. We didn't want to appear to be getting too friendly with those who knew our secret, for they were of us and they knew where we came from, and what we were about. An inverted snobbery took hold of the existing social order: the young Indians shone, they were confident of their culture, school was something they did to fill the time between vacations, when they went "back home." They laughed amongst themselves at us, the Anglo-Afro-Asians, and at our wholesale allegiance to the west's cardboard, cut-out culture.

They knew themselves and were sure of their sense of self so they were fluid like light. Their identities were as negotiable as coinage and like notes of an international currency and they gained access unhindered. Their inherent sense of self-worth opened doors to other worlds in which they didn't have to leave themselves at the gatepost. They commanded adoration with the lightest flutter of their extended eyelashes and a flash of pink, buffed fingernails. These were the new maharanis, in our midst.

They jazzed up the boring bottle green uniform with spangled glass bangles that tinkled as they walked. During the weekends, when they were allowed to dress mufti they wore exotic silk, jewel colours and they glimmered like the semi-precious stones embedded in the old Taj Mahal. They smelled delicious and warm, of spices and rose-petals. We, the Asian contingent, were yellowed, atrophied distant relatives. We were unsure of who we were, or how we fit in. We would never be white enough to fit into the west's idea of how Western Oriental Gentlemen, or their daughters, should behave. We were meant to be quiet and reserved, still clutching on at some faint hope of "belonging" with the barely recognized status of tax-paying guests from the colonies.

I longed to know more about these glittering girls who traveled from places with names from Jena's stories, Mumbai, Rajasthan, Jaipur. They had maids and horses. But I didn't dare ask.

I enrolled myself at the Lycée Francais Charles de Gaulle in South Kensington with another girl from St Helen's, Kate Fox. I wanted to get away from the stultifying atmosphere of the Independent Girls' School. The Lycée, in spite of its reputation for being liberal and cosmopolitan, had more rules than St Helen's. At least it was mixed. With red-blooded boys amongst us there was a handy supply of prospects for teenage crushes and hormones flowed, as did contraband alcohol in dark corners, at boozy parties. Napoleon was onto a clever idea when he set up the Lycée system, in which every school, everywhere in the French Empire taught exactly the same syllabus.

It was summer, 1984. London was a global melting pot. Live Aid had spread its powerful message across the world, that Africa was not a self-contained problem. With my distracting boy friends, Indian and Turkish hybrids or thoroughbred Lebanese, my schoolwork started to slip. I had to buckle down. The Sixth Form was fast approaching and the consequences of my lack of effort could be life defining. A-Level results determined which university would accept me, and the rest of my life.

I took English, French and Politics, with a view to becoming a journalist or writer but my father had other ideas. He'd only agreed to let me go to the Lycée when it was clear that my decision to withdraw myself from St Helen's was irrevocable. They were only too happy to give my place to someone who wanted to attend their prestigious Sixth Form. It wasn't that I was inherently naughty or a troublemaker, but because they could see I was chaffing at the bit. I felt bound by all the rules and pettiness. They could no longer control me and before the situation became disruptive, they let me go. It was like a friendly divorce.

My father is a frustrated advocate. That was what he had wanted to be when he was younger, when his mind was clean and sharp. He thought the law would be a good way to discipline my unruliness. Reluctantly I applied to study law at University College London. I was invited for an interview, in order to see if I was good enough. I crammed ferociously beforehand, and I read the newspapers from cover to cover for a week before the appointment.

Mr. Cobrin, our politics teacher had written me a glowing reference. I was his café-au-lait Lolita, a star-turn pupil. An element of attraction existed; he was the champagne socialist who wore yellow ties and pastel coloured shirts. London had ground to a halt in the midst of Red Ken's standoff with the Iron Lady as she legislated with the might of a steamroller to get rid of the GLC.

We had a couple of one-to-one tutorial sessions when his bald head had leaned in a little too close to mine, when his stumpy, nail-bitten fingers had rested a moment too long on the back of my hand. His eyes behind their glasses were misting up but there was nothing more to it than that, a schoolgirl and an attractive teacher who taught her favourite subject. He was confident I would get into whichever college I chose. Appropriately, Sting was on the radio, singing about teachers, frustration and schoolgirl fantasies.

After the initial agonies of adolescence, I was a little more secure. Whilst I still reveled in my rebelliousness, like the nymph Danae, I had finally found the light which made others see me. I was clever. I had shaken off my hunched shoulders and bad posture and I started to glitter with the self-assurance, which comes with being sixteen. We all shone, we were full of expectations, demands, and we had a list we wanted life to deliver to our doorsteps, longer than the ones kids compile for Santa at Christmas. We were barely able to contain all the carefully lain plans we had concocted. Even as we slept we counted down the hours to adulthood.

I told myself I wasn't nervous until I strode across the lawns of the campus. Law had sounded fine, I had gone along with it to please my father although I hadn't thought this one through; I had envisaged the courtroom victories but not at the end of long years studying. Finally I decided that if I had to do this, I wanted to practice criminal law.

I was shown to a seat and I waited nervously outside his office. The full weight of academia and the burden of the next three years leaned in on me. A cupola above me let in the light through glass panes, which were cut in the ceiling's stonework skin. I waited, barely breathing. I felt afraid to take in their oxygen in case I couldn't repay it later. Those felt like a long few minutes.

He seemed pleasant enough; he smiled warmly as he stood up to greet me and indicated one of the leather seats next to him. He didn't sit in the stiff upholstered leather chair behind the heavy wooden desk. He sat on the enemy side of the desk, next to me. His leather upholstered number facing me stared empty.

I tried not to look at the piles of papers and books that were spread everywhere. They appeared to grow organically, radiating like fairy circles from his desk. There must be some order to all this, I thought.

His office was exactly how I imagined it might be, lined with bookshelves. I hadn't expected the disorder over every surface. The law requires an ordered mind, I told myself. Whilst I was no neat freak, this sort of chaos left me clammy. This started to feel like a bad mistake. When he started to speak, he asked me polite, non-invasive questions about the Lycée. He told me my references had been very good and that I should have no problem in attaining the grades I would need to attend his college. He was Oxbridge personified, from his owlish glasses to his button-down stripy shirt and he had the way that men of that ilk, of being both superior and self-deprecating, so you never know where you stand with them. He reminded me of Tash Gulam, a friend of Karim who was at Cambridge then. He gave me copies of Machiavelli's *The Prince* and the Chinese classic, *The Art of War*. He'd lifted the worn copies from his own bookshelf.

The patina of the much-used books, the burnished leather chairs and the confluence of history and justice that resided in his study seduced me. Then he asked me why I wanted to be a lawyer, what could I bring to the study and its practice, what else interested me. He asked me about politics and current events and he nodded enthusiastically while he scratched a few notes, periodically on the pad with his old fashioned fountain pen. I felt at ease, maybe three years of law with the handsome professor wouldn't be so awful.

The longer we spoke and the more he explained, with reverence about the subject, the prospect of this ordered, sensible life started becoming palatable in my mind's eye. This was it, what I had been looking for all along.

He sat back in his chair and pushed his glasses up to his forehead. He tossed the notepad on the desk and screwed on the lid of his pen. We were coming to a close and there was a general sense of loose ends being gathered. He had placed his fountain pen carefully, so it made a perfect right angle with the edge of the pad, and now he was squaring it so it was perfectly central. It made me think about the Golden Ratio. I thought about what a clever thought that was to be having just then.

"Do you drive?" He asked me quietly.

"I'm learning," I answered. I asked myself silently what this had to do with my application to study law. I wondered if it was a trick question, I was seventeen and legally allowed to take driving lessons.

"Right, then my final question should prove particularly easy. How do you describe something that is done carelessly, without much thought?"

I had no idea and I looked desperately at his broad forehead, hoping that neon lights would appear from nowhere and flash the right answer at me. He noticed my scrambling but he didn't say anything else.

I felt as though the rest of my life, the one I had planned out as a female Rumpole of the Bailey for the last hour, depended on my finding this one, darned word. I asked for telepathy, silently willing the word to reveal itself, in a way he wouldn't notice.

"Well, let's try my driving analogy, shall we? If someone were driving in that manner, in a shoddy, careless manner how might you describe it?" Still nothing, all the golden light that had filled the room a moment ago, drained away, I must be stupid, I told myself but no word came that fit. I wouldn't get in if I didn't know, that much was clear. My future depended on one, vacillating word.

"Would it help if I told you that it began with an R?"

"An R?" I repeated, I rifled through the Roget's in my head but none of the dusty recesses gave up anything useful. No R words surfaced.

"Well maybe it was rather difficult, you know out of the blue, like that." He smiled and stood up, extending his arm to shake my hand.

I stood up to go. I was halfway across the room but his question was still hanging around, like the naughty child who refuses to go to bed.

"Reckless, the word I was looking for was reckless." That was strange, I had thought of reckless but in my head it had started with a w, just when I needed it the most, my superlative command of the mother tongue had done a Houdini on me. So much for law school then.

A few weeks later, the offer came in the post. It was a low offer, I should be able to achieve the grades required. But my being unable to think of the word reckless, on the spot had undermined my confidence. I wasn't going to be a lawyer. I had bigger plans. The world was unfolding in front of me, like a treasure map, and counties coalesced into countries which formed continents. New York chose me. I rushed through the last two terms of my A-Levels at the obligatory crammer, with a flying kiss and a prayer.

I left the day Live Aid was broadcast, with vague promises about coming back to England in a year to retake one exam for a better grade and then take up the deferred place at UCL. As I was saying them, the words remained unfinished in the air and they dissolved. Even as I was promising something else, I had no intention of coming back to the life I was shedding.

Interlude

America was inevitable. I sleepwalked through my teenage years, through the Lycée and through Collinghams the crammer, with all the expectations and ennui a young girl can muster. It all seemed possible, within reach. We spent nights at Shariffi's disco-dungeon and indulged in under-age partying at Pucci's, the Pizza Potentate of King's Road. I counted down the hours to my emancipation. Other nights were wasted at Annabel's or Tramp's. They ended with me quietly sneaking back to Tori's, her father was the Brigadier of the Duke of York's and they lived in a smart flat in the barracks.

A shy Princess Diana cast the shadow of her long legs over a generation of women's aspirations, she was Diana the huntress and the innocent nymph. The iconic photograph was released that shows her smiling coyly, wide-eyed beneath her heavy fringe, with the sun streaming through the midi-cotton flowery skirt she is wearing. She was the embodiment of Sloane Ranger. Love in that "whatever that means" way, spawned in the loins of Hooray Henrys all over SW London postcodes. We were the debutantes with dresses like cream puffs, who attended eighteenth birthday parties at the Dorchester or the Duke of York's Barracks, when it was still a working barracks for Territorial Army.

Life at home had become harsher, the fights between my parents more often, more violent. I was often the target for their frustrated anger at each other and it came out in regular beatings. My brother endured a lot of it too. It fossilized the love I used to have for them and turned the remnants of it to pure loathing.

I was often in the middle of their arguments and more than once my father snatched me and some clothes, threw them into an overnight bag and we'd storm off raging down the A40 to a house he owned in Shepherd's Bush. We were just pawns in the game of their marriage. He never kept his Airmail promises, they were as flimsy as the paper they were written on and faded as fast as his handwritten desperation. There were many other women but he kept them away, out of our domestic compass.

The final straw was when he started to pose impossible curfews on me, we lived far out of London and at eighteen I didn't want to be home by midnight.

My father sat up and waited, by then they had separate bedrooms at opposite ends of the house. I would creep in, my forbidden shoes in my hands, praying he wouldn't notice me but he'd always be there, at the top of the flight of wooden staircases with his shirt tales freed over loose boxer shorts. With the stale smell of a brewery oozing off his skin, he would launch in on a tirade, which I would try to ignore as I shoved past him to my room.

One night he started this regular routine of berating me for being an hour late and I stopped him dead, mid-sentence.

"Don't you dare tell me how to behave when you are the one who has carried on with God knows how many women and not come home at all. Don't you say anything to me." I flung the door closed in his shocked face.

He never said anything about my being late home again. He barely spoke to me after that, I had broken the spell. But the secret was out, I had put the unspoken into words. He knew he was no longer my adored daddy or the sun in my solar system and I was no longer his shining little girl. I had shown that I had lost respect and he couldn't buy it back.

Filthy Fantastic City

New York Squared

Landing a life in New York City is like stepping into the lead role in the Hollywood motion picture of your life. To be a New Yorker, I had to sign a contract with the city of More. But she is an addiction, from the first New York minute my soul hit Manhattan's grubby sidewalks, I felt as if I was home. It was the closest I have ever felt to belonging. The city is a shelter for the dispossessed, we who find comfort in each other's longing.

When empty eyes meet in the abyss of a passing stranger's gaze you know this is all that we all are. This is it, right here and right now. A persistent fizz permeates Manhattan nights. It's a barely discernable buzz that emanates from the streetlights, the subway tracks, the boiler rooms and the machinery that combine, many pieces of the same engine, to make it all function. This visceral vice soups up its residents, there's a constant loop of energy, passing between inanimate technology and the sleeping.

We need our fix of this to survive, but there's never enough, and we wake exhausted. The city, like a succubus drained us of everything we accumulated in our waking, during the night. Then she took some more. I was nineteen and pretending to attend NYU, studying French and Art History. It was an easy cop-out, this pseudo arts degree but I was fooling no one. My parents had realized that I wasn't coming "home" to take up the promised place and they sent me money for rent and bills and paid my NYU fees. A few days were spent attending some lectures if I felt like it; more often I was at the gym.

The Saint and Limelight took off, the latter in an abandoned church in the forgotten wasteland of eastern Chelsea. A bouncer in a Barneys' suit with an earpiece obeyed commands that only he could hear. He was the centurion at the gate of the altar where I worshipped. He stood there with the fierce look of a modern-day Hermes. They were the new oracles of Chelsea with immeasurable power. They predicted who was in, who was not. Life was lived behind the velvet rope.

The first time I sniffed cocaine was in a car, zooming into the entrance of the Midtown Tunnel that delves deep below street-level, under what was the Helmsley Palace Hotel. It was twilight and Maya Angelou's smoking carnivores scuttled like ants out of office buildings. It was a surreal time, when the limestone-fronted buildings of midtown seemed to sag a little, stooping into the central reservation that separated the traffic.

It wasn't a life changing moment.

I can tell you with all the fervour of an addict, I swear, I wasn't addicted from the first hit. I didn't feel anything straight away. Then, about halfway through the pale orange-lit tunnel, the lights started to sizzle, they were brighter.

My friend (who cares who he was, one of half a dozen interchangeable yuppies) was more handsome and his eyes shone, highlighted by the reflecting chrome from the dashboard of his sports car. Immediately, it felt as though a blueprint for a real life had been overlaid and there was wholeness where previously there had been incongruence. I could feel the freshness of an early autumn evening more palpably on my flushed cheeks.

Cocaine in small quantities feels like coming home. It's surrendering back to the embrace of an old lover and that same seductive comfort of someone familiar in whose bed you've been before. It takes less than a minute to come through the tunnel but by the time we reached the other side, the sky was velvety, cobalt blue. Manhattan sparkled as we raced up her Grand Avenue. We thought we could handle it all and have it all. We were untouchable.

Those early New York years are a blur. I was out every night, at every gallery and nightclub opening. Nello had recently opened his chic Madison Avenue trattoria and the Ciao Bella boys were rapidly expanding their posh pasta chain as they colonized great swathes of the Upper East Side with lengths of coloured spaghetti and pockets of perfect pumpkin ravioli.

Those were my roaring twenties, but it was love in the time of cholera. AIDS had not been clearly identified as a disease that could affect heterosexuals but it was sad to watch the beautiful gay boys who contracted it. It seemed life, which they loved with such vengeance, was cheating them. In our unbelieving eyes, it was tragic that they were felled in their prime, like adolescent angel-boys.

The excesses and purging with the potential to kill, left stains on all of our lives. I stopped eating. It wasn't through any conscious decision-making process, but cocaine was stealing my appetite. My antidote was to drink fruit smoothies so I could maintain the pretence of a healthy life.

New York is all image. It starts with perceived separation with the heavy, damask curtains that hide concealed and coveted booths at Nell's or Au Bar. They might as well have been the Berlin wall. They were the veils that separated the nightclubbing elite to those who were made to wait behind the velvet rope. It is a city that lives by extremes and it spits people out, when they are tired, the way the tide washes up pieces of driftwood.

New York is impervious. Even while Hurricane Gloria thrashed the streets and whipped up bus shelters, like matchsticks, nothing could bring the mean city to her knees. The sky was thick. Thor licked the slick grey cement pavements, with lashings of his switchback tongue but people still walked resolutely to work, took their children to school and they went about their lives.

Nothing can stop New York. I tried not to drink, I had enough experience from being on the receiving end of its unpredictability, to know what alcohol could do, but this was a permeable border.

On my twenty-first birthday, I wanted to see what would happen if I drank a whole bottle of gin. I felt sick for days; I couldn't get out of bed and lay in my bed with the curtains drawn and a pillow over my head. But those were my "happy days." In the limited scales of my emotions, I lived recklessly and I mistook that for freedom. Sex became something to do by rote, with handsome strangers I didn't necessarily want to see again.

It was an anonymous co-mingling of fluids, not for reproduction but for recreation. It was a pointless flailing of limbs, with passion but no purpose. I wanted the lurid, transitory delight of conquest, brown skin on white. If sex was a means to stave off my mortality; I fucked frenetically for a place in the fornicators' Hall of Fame.

Michael should have been a nice Jewish boy. He lived in a prestigious building on Sutton Place, the Our Crowd, Old Guard sanctuary of wealthy Jews who had crossed the Brooklyn Bridge. We met at Au Bar, Howard Stein's club on East 58th Street.

Howard was born of the mean streets, he was the son of a loan shark, Ruby Stein who was killed by the Westies and whose headless body was found floating in Jamaica Bay. Howard was the poster child for the 80s bad boy brigade. Rumours circled around him, after all, he had served prison time for tax fraud. He wore his deviation like a badge of honour. Instead of making him someone to avoid, it made him sexier, more enigmatic. Nightclubs were the religious centres and social clubs of the 80s. Howard had the best places locked down, Xenon was in a building owned by the playwright Henry Miller and Miller's upstairs offices were reserved as an extra VIP area by night. Peppo Vanini, the "manager" was legendary for what he could manage. He arranged a meeting, on a few hours notice with the Pope for Princess Caroline and Phillippe Junot who wanted a private audience. They contacted Peppo at the nightclub, if anyone could fix it, he could. Peppo's guys contacted a regular of one of the disco nights who was also in the Papal retinue and in awe of Caroline of Monaco, Grace Kelly's daughter.

Princess Caroline wore the same outfit to meet the Pope that day, as she did that night at Xenon, a black leather blazer, white blouse with a black velvet tie, black skirt and black heels. At night the black velvet tie was removed and the blouse a little more décolleté.

At Xenon, they famously refused to serve water at the bar, punters were told, "there's a fountain at the back, to the left." It was a place you could piss next to Christopher Reeves and watch Mick Jagger smoke from the balcony. The Royalton had opened recently, another Ian Schrager bijou boutique hotel in a part of midtown still to undergo gentrification. Its lobby was a clever engagement of all the senses, it was like diving into an empty swimming pool in a dream.

Philippe Starck, another transatlantic transplant had created a mini-mosaic tiled pleasure palace, like a diorama inside a Helmut Newton photograph with glass horn-shaped light fixtures and shiny railings. It was a festival of lacquered African mahogany book-matched wood paneling and a dominatrix' dream of leather and fetish-like chrome fixtures. Here was cruel beauty, like a sculpted Manolo stiletto.

New York had come of age and it wreaked sophistication, from the hypodermic profile of the Chrysler Building that pierced the early morning clouds right down to the excess of massive Soho lofts.

Michael was a drug dealer, that much was common knowledge. He owned a limousine and escort service as well as other legitimate businesses. He cultivated a couldn't-give-a-fuck swagger and he dressed scruffily with an overgrown Jew-fro, which framed his fat face. He wasn't ostentatious, he was shy. He told me that he liked my accent, which was still pukkah and British, cut-glass. He sold cocaine by the gramme to his escort agency clients and his girls became unwitting mules, who took the tricks their "cigarettes" which was the codeword I had to use when I started working his phones.

Working for Michael afforded me a grand lifestyle. I was ostensibly an NYU student getting $1 000 a month for rent and to help with bills from my parents. Michael paid me weekly in cash, I was given a percentage of every call I booked and a cut of the takings. I easily made a couple of thousand dollars a week, which I blew at the three Bs, Bergdorf's, Barneys and Bloomingdale's. I was a client of the super-stylist hairdresser, Oribe and at Chanel they took my cheques. They would call me to tell me they had a delivery of the new collection if there were some clothes I might like. I liked it all.

The money was easy but there was also increased access to cocaine. Michael never questioned the quantities I packaged up for him from the soft, white bundles that were delivered by his driver, twice weekly. It was tightly wrapped in cellophane, this flaky powder that looked like crushed mother-of-pearl. I dispensed it into tiny brown glass bottles, each held a gramme. I enjoyed the ritual. He got it fresh from Columbia, it felt slightly slippery between your fingers and it was almost pure, not having made its way very far down the supply chain.

Olga was a Russian immigrant who putatively held the position I had. She had met and fallen in love with Jose, a client but she still came by once in a while. She had a little black book of private clients who didn't mind that she had passed her peak, she was over thirty. Like dancers, call girls have a limited sell-by date. Yet they paid $300 an hour to see her. Olga taught me how to cut the cocaine from Michael with unscented talc, baby formula powder, even makeup and we must have done it well, no one ever complained about the quality of the product, we made sure not to cut it too much, so that it never lost its pinkish glow.

In this way, I ensured I had my own stash. I was never a big cokehead, a gramme would last a week or ten days. It wasn't about the quantity I consumed, it was more the psychological dependency, of knowing that it was there.

I could summon up the notorious combination of imperviousness and exhilaration at will. It was all I needed to take the edge off, to dim the ache of sunlight by day.

The girls who worked for Bel Air came from all backgrounds. The arrangement was simple enough; I agreed to answer the phones for $200 a shift plus a percentage of every hour I booked a girl out. He began to trust me more and I took over some of the manager's duties. I interviewed girls from ads we placed in the *Village Voice,* the downtown artsy paper that came out every Wednesday.

I was solicitous of my girls' welfare. They kept sixty per cent of the fee, the house kept the rest but I asked the clients to slip them an extra $20 bill for cab fare, even if one of Michael's limos was going to pick them up at the end of the call.

I could no longer reconcile my fake college life with being a stand-in madam, and there wasn't much of a question as to which path I should take. I felt a depraved sense of power when I heard my clients on the other end of the phone. They were media moguls, tycoons, bankers and politicians; these were the robber barons of the end of the century. They called on our "regulars" line, which had an unlisted number. First they exchanged pleasantries, and then they asked who was available. It was commerce in its purest form, reduced to its barest essence. This is what we had to sell and they wanted it.

Michael had a lap dancing club, Ray's Bar on the edges of the meatpacking district. About once every month he would ask me instead of someone else to pick up a parcel from there, containing the club's takings and paperwork that he needed to go through. He had given me an early mobile phone, a weighty Motorola brick, which meant I was always reachable. Strangely, this made me feel important rather than exploited. Michael was a master manipulator.

Tonight meant another trip to Ray's. I had quickly learned to dress the part, Maud Frizon crocodile spikes and Chanel suits. Various combinations of blue, white and black boucle became my uniform. The chain straps on the status handbags the brand is well known for gave me something to hold onto. Maybe they held me down; they were links to my reality.

At my age, twenty-two, I was a lot younger than most of the women who worked at Bel Air but the clothes lent me some gravitas. They teased me about how I looked more like a banker than a whoremonger. Looking good covered up feeling bad. I was in turmoil inside which I was perpetually trying to numb out of my consciousness; I was living on the edge, but I was deep into this dangerous world, which started when clubs and restaurants emptied out. Michael was well connected. I had the numbers of the Police lieutenants of Midtown North and South and the 19th Precinct on speed dial stored on my phone. The Upper Eastside and midtown where most of the expensive hotels are located were prime whoremaster territory. Paid for sex was an easy at-home game, like take-away food, for bored husbands, when their wives were safely ensconced in a beach cottage in the Hamptons or a Connecticut farmhouse.

I used to wonder about the women behind these megalomaniac men. Our clients were stud-horses of men, the iconoclasts that controlled every aspect of our lives, from the financial markets to global politics. They were the men who decided foreign policy and the height of a hemline. They influenced what we saw, how we bought and what we thought. Did these little women know? If they did then they looked the other way. Was theirs where the real power was then, to be in this situation and still stay?

Hearing these grown men, grinding their teeth from cocaine dry-mouth, desperate for company, changed my conceptions of sex and relationships altogether. Sex was stripped down, raw. I was highly paid to enable a service that wasn't hurting anyone. Michael's enterprise rescued Venus from the boulevard and ensconced her in the boudoir style décor of the Bel Air townhouse, where she could wait for the phone to ring.

Reason, right and wrong, blurred my preconception of what was normal between a man and a woman. It seemed straightforward enough; the girls protested they would only do it for a short time, that it was a means to an end. The men considered it less dangerous than picking up someone on the street or in a bar. It was less expensive than supporting a full-blown affair with a high maintenance mistress. In the middle of this transaction was I, the conjurer of fantasies. I could invoke demi-goddesses out of darkness over the phone. I had the power to grant their sexual wishes.

Bel Air was spread over two floors of a townhouse in Kips Bay. The office had its own entrance. Ostensibly it had been set up to resemble a simply furnished home. The overhead fittings had been removed throughout, and desk and table lamps scattered pools of watery light. There was never enough ambient light to be able to see clearly but Michael liked the semi-darkness. Some of the girls came into the office to work, to get away from the inquisitions posed by their families. Others wandered the city, with their pager worn on their waistband.

My world occupied the corner of the living room that was an amalgamation of Michael's old furniture through the years. There was an old wooden office desk with an antiquated cream plastic box switchboard that had nine lines attached to it. With one earpiece I could switch between lines. We had a private number that was unlisted and was used only by Michael or regular clients. One of the buttons would light up red to indicate which line was ringing, but they didn't ring, they purred, like an electronic mog.

It was like a Tardis, this cavernous half-house. Night after midnight, when classy Cinderellas had fled the ball and Prince Charming was left musing Portnoy's complaint, the phones would start to ring frantically. Our ads came on cable TV at the same time. With only MTV for company, I felt locked in my own media-manifested world: television, phone and me, communication without any.

All over the stealthy city, the girls were being dispatched by drivers, once I had verified the callers existed and that they were where they said they were. Checking with directory enquiries whether such a person existed at the number I had been given was tricky. If it was an unlisted number, I could access a reverse directory through a police-friend, but I rarely bothered. I'd listen for the blanket denial of the operator's pre-recorded voice;

"We're sorry, the number you require is not listed and does not exist in our records." This automated denial proved that they were somewhere.

Nothing had ever happened to anyone on any of my shifts. I was judicious about time keeping and if I left to go home and we still had girls out, I forwarded the phones to my cell phone or my home number. I'd set my alarm to wake me so I could check in and see if they were staying or leaving. It was, I kept telling myself, simply providing a service, I was just a facilitator. There didn't have to be anything inherently sleazy about it and it felt more honest than some of the transactional relationships that existed around me. My mother for instance, why had she stayed in that loveless relationship but for the safe comfort of money, homes and the facsimile security of luxe?

A trend was emerging of second wives. The good and the great had recently started to acquire svelte, younger women with slightly dubious backgrounds. But that didn't stop their dizzying ascent: their pedigree was rewritten by a savvy press person overnight. Some money to a favourite cause or fashionable charity from their benevolent and bedazzled older husbands helped others to forget.

A young Jewish working-girl became the second Mrs. Someone Important, although her new identity was as fully rounded and well-structured as the designs which emanated from her atelier. Her husband-patron had set this up for over $20 million.

Michael liked the art of Patrick Nagel, who designed the cover for Duran Duran's *Rio* album. Limited editions of his works on paper hung like ancestral portraits in our office. Nagel's depictions of women were slick, idealized and flat. They were idealized geometrical planes of gouache. Their mouths were always perfectly lined and lip-sticked. They were painted in impossible angular poses. Such perfection could only exist in two dimensions. Because Michael collected Nagels, I started to buy them as well.

The nights were so long, the hours between three and six in the morning dragged and I was fully saturated with the smell of smoke that permeated the house. I felt as if I was being watched by the staring Nagels. I didn't smoke myself. The stench rose up from the beige carpet and had seeped into the walls and the permanently drawn curtains. Even the plants that managed to survive our toxic environment exhaled carbon dioxide and tobacco fumes. No amount of air freshener or carpet talc wiped out the odours.

I witnessed the darkest side of glamour that is the unreconstructed carnal lust just a notch above the base instinct for survival. I lived within the boundaries of its spectral shadow, a mix of mortality and desire. It was impossible to maintain the separation between sitting behind my desk with the illusion of sexual power and my personal life. I no longer saw men as equals or as capable of having or participating in loving relationships; it was all about the hunt and the game.

The women who worked were from all sorts of backgrounds, some from good middle-class stock with a college education, who went in with their eyes wide open. They were whoring themselves as a means to an end. They all had big dreams, perhaps to open a shop somewhere or to pursue a degree later. The common denominator was that they all craved money. Soon, those dreams were ground like glass on the three concrete steps that lead to the front door, which opened up to their secret life inside the innocuous looking town house.

Men sought women who looked pretty and smelt nice, like the inside of an apothecary or a perfume counter. They wanted women they could unwrap, like bow-tied and candy-wrapped parcels. Their faces lit up with delight, and as each silk covered button was unfastened it served to sharpen their anticipation and their need. Bel Air girls didn't look like prostitutes, they spent money on expensive clothes and impractical lingerie, and they had regular manicures and pedicures and were waxed, massaged and polished to a feminine ideal. They read the papers, listened to the news and had some idea of what was happening in the wider world. These men wanted women who would immediately reflect their glory and their success, someone who wouldn't ask too many questions; certainly not someone who was going to make any demands. Paying for someone else's time is a wicked, lonely concept.

All that was required was an ear to listen, without judgment or expectation. The women saw the men as a means to a better life, some of them were generous and tipped handsomely, all of which the escort could keep, but they were under strict instructions not to give out their personal numbers. Bel Air was the Chinese wall which kept both parties in the transaction safe from one another.

Michael's reputation was enough to keep most people in line and like the little man who pretends to be the Wizard of Oz but is only the projectionist, there was enough scary monster myth thrown out about him to keep people at bay.

Some did exchange numbers and they embarked on promising romantic adventures with ex-clients. Once a man has paid a woman for sex, he has bought her and all sense of that woman's integrity is drowned in his shame; she is just a commodity. I'd watch from a safe distance, they would confide in me, knowing I wasn't about to tell Michael but inevitably expectations were set up along the way and couldn't be met.

Sex is a powerful tool though and for the women who went into the romance with the practicality of a business venture, these extra-curricular romps could prove to be a lucrative sideline. More often, they were heart-crushing affairs that were doomed from the start.

It was hard to know any of them. They all used working names they'd invented and whole back-stories of such depth and detail; I wondered if they actually believed them. They seldom saved their money; it seemed to wound them, like stigmata. The lure of designer clothes and long exotic holidays was too much. Many of them had little to show for working on their backs except a closet full of desirable handbags and the fading tan-lines from a recent South Beach holiday. It was hard to get off the game.

These women became hollow, the Chinese say that when a man sleeps with a woman younger than thirty, he takes her *chi*, her life force. They had the life fucked out of them. There was no blatant drug abuse but tiny blue 10mg Valium and their less soporific yellow cousins were discreetly consumed with champagne and cocaine, to ease the step into the zone where numbness descends and the harsh edges fade. I needed the twilight zone too, the chemical cocktail gave the lights a warmer glow, I could feel alive enough to function and dead enough not to feel.

Sidney Biddle Barrows was on the verge of being busted. The Mayflower Madam thought she was untouchable because of the names in her little black book. The blue-blooded could never fall into Giuliani's zero tolerance policy, they thought that they were above the laws made for the masses. Thousands of miles away, on another coast, Heidi Fleiss served up sex in sunny Californian Beach houses. It was a tough world out there, there was stiff competition but the Bel Air bubble, this make-believe universe, somehow thrived above the noise of the dirty city, because in the end, the sex game is a man's world.

Ray's Bar was no different than any other private lap-dancing club. I let my driver go and told him I would page him when I needed him. He had been with me all day, running errands and shopping, filling up the daylight hours whilst living for the night. I told him to give himself an hour, to go and eat something. I was bored, and bored was dangerous.

The limo slinked up Tenth Avenue and a gaggle of street hookers came into view as its headlights doused them in tungsten light. Bare legs and high heels flashed and the streetlights caught their hair so it looked like golden candyfloss. Standing there, trapped and frozen they could have been dressed up for carnival, in Venice or Rio. They were unreal, their glossed-up lips popped like pink flashbulbs, and their dead eyes glimmered for a second, like fish catching the light at the bottom of a pond. Here was the prospect of some business.

Their faces hovered disconnected from their bodies; their heads were unanchored like floating balloons. They saw the woman descend from the car and teased me,

"Hey girl, you want some woman loving tonight?" I stuffed a feeling, is this what my life had come to? It looked glamorous and shiny. I had beautiful things but if I scratched the surface ever so slightly with the lightest touch of a manicured thumbnail, I could feel the Farah-shaped void. I stepped into the dark gloom of Ray's and my eyes adjusted to the chequer-board marble floor. Bluish pinpricks of light spilled in pools on the café-style tables. I thought of the streetlights outside. Different prey, same hunt.

There were groups of cookie cutter Yuppies in Brooks Brothers' 365 suits and cloned haircuts. Some stood, propping themselves up against the wooden bar. Some sat at tables in clusters. The place stank of easy-sleazy money. On a raised platform in the far corner a white spotlight flooded the dancer. It made her appear ghost-like, unearthly, as it blanched the colour off her skin. Her emerald green eyes pierced the darkness. I stood in the doorway; I dropped my Chanel tote by my feet. I realized I was the only other woman in the room and suddenly I was self-conscious, I could feel many pairs of eyes looking at me.

She was voluptuous, immaculate. Her skin was milky white and she glowed, like alabaster. Thick coils of auburn hair curved over her full breasts and slipped easily, like dripping honey, into the hollow of her back. She danced as if in ecstasy like a dervish in slow motion, a smile barely grazed the corners of her lips. She looked at her audience full of desire but she didn't engage her gaze. That song, which followed me wherever I went in New York, started to play. It was Lou Reed's anthem for misfits and cranks, *Walk on the Wild Side*. I crossed the room, I wanted to get a table where I could sit alone. I wanted to watch her. She was mesmerizing, like a mermaid, the sequins on her panties shimmered like a fishtail mirror.

I hadn't looked at a woman like this before. Naked women were to me what hole punchers and staple guns might be to a secretary. I was perfunctory but polite in the way I dealt with the nudity of the women because I had to see them stripped down to make sure they weren't hiding track marks or ugly tattoos. I learned early on that men have different definitions of sexy and that their ideal includes zaftig curves and bouncing breasts. Shiny, healthy hair is important too. It's those mummy memories they look for, as they reach for wholesomeness in a whore.

Women I thought were shriveled up and past it had men calling for them regularly, spending thousands of dollars to spend time, something they could have found for nothing. But they were reluctant to invest the time in dinner and theatre with a non-working girl. Paid for sex has its own allure. There was no guessing about the prize at the end of the evening, it was theirs for the taking.

I held unannounced lingerie inspections; men crave infantilizing, impractical scraps of lace. All Bel Air girls wore stockings and garter belts. I insisted on monthly Dr's notes from our bent gynecologist, Terry Andrews, to ensure a clean bill of health. If something was detected then it could be treated early on. Dr. Andrews' letters did little but salve my conscience; he would hand out clean bills of health and anything else for the $100 payable after the appointment.

High heels, the highest they could walk in, were essential. If they couldn't walk in them, they wore flats to the building they were attending but had to put on their show-time shoes before they entered the lobby. Manolo's fetishist fantasies embodied the legend of elegantly packaged sex with grosgrain silk ribbon to tie into bows.

Ray, the front man of Ray's had spotted me and came out to greet me from behind his seat at the bar. He was an ex-Ivy League English Professor. He couldn't have been more than thirty-five but he ran the establishment with the precision of a clockwork general. There had been no incidents or violence since he had taken over. His strong hug engulfed me. He overcame the vampire pallor that was a hazard of his job, by working on his tone and his tan during the empty daylight hours.

"Hiya doll. How are you?" Ray was too elegant, too New England for this vernacular greeting to come from him. I let myself be held by him, and he kissed both cheeks. I felt myself shrink back a little, involuntarily. Intimacy, extended for a second by someone I liked put a chink in my armor. I couldn't afford such a weakness. He pulled away and was scanning me in a brotherly, asexual way. I knew what was coming and braced myself.

"Jeez Louise, you've lost more weight. You not eating enough?" I lived on takeouts from the Carnegie Deli, which delivered to my office and my flat. They remained largely uneaten in their foil containers. His concern was real, I didn't doubt him but we were skating away from the usual banter.

We shared pleasantries. That was safe, it kept us well within the confines of what we had in common, which was this Vesica Pisces space where our lives had intersected because of Michael.

"Been eating, just been working a lot," I tried to smile. I didn't want to meet his gaze. It's hard to con a con. He picked my bag up off the floor and crooked his arm into mine. He led me over to a table in the VIP section, which was close to the stage. He had set up a booth, which he had transformed into his personal domain. From there, he could entertain punters who were big spenders. They liked to come and sit at the big man's table.

"You sit here, I'll go get the books M wanted, it's all ready to go, just needs to be put into a folder. Can I get you a drink?"

I didn't usually stay at Ray's for any length of time, I'd ask the driver to circle the block so that he would be outside waiting, by the time I stepped out again. Tonight, I wanted to linger a little. I was safely tucked away from a hundred pairs of inquisitive male eyes at this table.

"Sure, I'll have a Diet Coke, no ice please." I had anaesthetized myself to the point I was no longer curious about what was in the envelopes and files handed to me. I would put the lot in an LV holdall, put a padlock on the zipper and drop it off with Michael's doorman. I didn't have a key. It could have been drugs or guns. I carried danger, I was used to it. Maybe it aroused me.

I was drowning in my denial by not consuming alcohol. I could therefore tell myself that I was not an addict because addicts drank while drugging. I couldn't be an addict because my latent fear of needles prevented me from crossing over into the final taboo of injecting. I never did cocaine during the day and seldom on my own. These were the parameters that fenced in my addiction. They allowed me to function though I fooled only myself. These were the thoughts that were going through my head, as I sat in the darkness, letting it take me in.

I looked at the girl serving me, the waitresses didn't dance, they were one notch further up the pecking order, one step further away from being for sale. Ray didn't demean his waitresses by making them dress like tarts. They wore black short, short skirts and white tank tops, the lace edges of their bra cups played peek-a-boo over scooped necklines. Michael had sussed, a long time ago that sex and class sold, he had mastered its commercial viability and he ran his operations with the flair of members' only clubs. From cars to cunts, his ventures were branded and exclusive.

All Ray's girls raked in the cash. Cavorting with Wall Street boys keen to wear the magnetic strips off their Platinum Amex cards, it was easy to part a fool and his money, with a flash of inner thigh or a hint of taut midriff. Sex is an easy sell. I thanked her and handed her a $5 bill from my wallet.

"Oh no, it's on the house." She seemed to blush.

I don't know what they made of me, who I thought I was but they treated me with a cocktail of respect and careful indifference. I'd been here a few times with Michael and I'd been part of the main table as King Rat and his cronies partied. They fawned on Michael, he carried cash and cocaine, and he was their meal ticket out of there.

"That's for you." She was surprised but she smiled and she walked away.

I had had a long day. Michael wanted to expand Bel Air so that our girls (I had started to feel proprietary towards them recently) could do calls in Los Angeles or London, over a long weekend or even longer. *The International Herald Tribune* was a rich hunting ground, it brought in clients from a tiny one-column ad, from all over the world.

All day I had been researching where I could place wanted adverts for women in other cities. Now I wanted to get the grime off me, leave it behind for a while. Ray came across and cut into the thoughts that were spiraling my mood deeper downwards. He cut an odd figure; it was hard to reconcile his old life, the comfort of tenure, with what he was doing now. How could this be the same person? Living in this neon-lit, twilight zone had made me both blank and immune to experiences, yet I craved them. The less I could feel, the more I sought them out. Something in me wanted to push hard against the boundaries of the known and the safe, even if it meant walking headlong into a typhoon, I craved physical sensation, extremes of any kind. It confirmed to me, this combination of pain, fear and danger, that I was still alive.

"That's all you are having?"

I could see he was buzzing; his eyes were filled with euphoria. Freebasing, or smoking coke had just become fashionable. It was the rich man's version of crack. There's so much paraphernalia, cooked cocaine rocks, filters, heaters. I had tried it once with Michael and the immediate chemical hit which slammed me left me feeling as if I had been punched in the chest. I didn't like it, it was a hit I could see others chasing endlessly as they went through piles of coke and thousands of dollars in a night. I wondered if Ray had started to freebase. "Yes, I'm fine."

"Are you in a hurry to go?" He was curious, usually I didn't sit down, and I'd wait by the doorway, impatiently tapping my snakeskin-clad toe as he brought the bag to me. I was always raring to leave. He sensed something different in me, tonight.

Ray and I had had sex. It was just one of those things that we did, in the circle we inhabited; it was a short cut, a substitute for intimacy, this coming together and a rite of passage. It was fine, he was athletic but in my mind it was filed away as another event, committed for no particular purpose, not for mating or pleasure, just something to do so we could get on with the business of friendship.

"No, I thought I might hang out a while. I need to unwind a bit. Is that all right?" I asked the rhetorical question out of politeness.

"I got something great in today…You want?"

This shorthand way in which we spoke was another identifier, it was a code only another druggie would appreciate. Fucking had removed the need for the fineries of grammar or punctuation.

"Bolivian P. Five grand an ounce, some dealer wants to supply us…he sent in a sample with one of the ladies."

We sniggered, Michael had all his joints sewn up, and there was no way another dealer was going to get a look in. He had no say in the matter. Neither did I.

"Go on then, let's see what you're about."

Bolivian Pearl was the beluga of cocaine; it was oily so it didn't tear the septum apart. It came, almost pure, and so the thick tongued, cottonmouth and teeth grinding that come with a cocaine high, which are brought about by the mixers and fillers and bring on the hangover concocted in the inner circle of hell, could be avoided. He came back out of his office a few minutes later and returned with a little silver platter piled high with a mound of shimmering pinkish white powder. It was a generous fistful.

He handed me a silver straw and walked away. Ray's was protected in the same way that Bel Air was. M had officers on the payroll and some of the most important city cops were our clients. There was no threat of impending drug or vice-squad raids to worry about. I lifted the engraved business card he had left on the tray that bore his initials in a raised Tiffany font.

It's the rituals of taking cocaine that make it so compelling, the trammeling out of a line, the upside down reflection of my face as I lower my nose closer to the straw, then the moment I have to close my eyes. I anticipate the sharp sting in my nose passages into my sinuses as I raise a finger to close off one nostril by pressing the wall of my nose to the septum. There's always the heartbeat of hesitation but still I crave the rush of that first ever line. Every single line of cocaine I took after the first one in the Midtown Tunnel was an empty lie; I was chasing something I never really had. But that didn't stop me trying, another thousand times.

I blinked and tears stung my eyes. It was good stuff, I could feel the pressure lifting off my shoulders and the invisible permanent head brace that gave me tension pain was fading. It was like breathing out after holding in my breath for too long.

When I looked over, she was still dancing. Her movements flowed like well articulated sentences. She was dancing a story. Her eyes seemed fixed in my direction, in my dark corner where I thought I was invisible, and she smiled confidently when she was sure she had my attention. I was locked into the cross hairs of her stare.

I noticed that she was curvy with full hips that quivered as she gyrated. Her large, round breasts lifted as she arched her back and raised her toned arms over her head. She manipulated her hair so it fell like a veil, sometimes it covered her face, sometimes she would scoop it all up and twist it up to reveal the curve at the nape of her neck. She couldn't have been more than eighteen.

The men in the room were transfixed, Ray's was a repository for yuppies who wanted a place after work where they could wind down, where they could drink and drug unfettered and where the sensitivities of female colleagues did not have to be taken into account. This was boys' toy town. Tonight however, they fell silent. She was supine, spread out like butter, her breasts rolling out to the sides of her ribcage, inviting, like dough waiting to be kneaded. The song ended but no one wanted to break the spell so she stood up and took deep bows as she toured the perimeter of the stage.

The men in suits clapped and let out yelps and catcalls, they broke into a collective movement as they reached for their wallets. Then they stuffed money into the shard of cloth that covered her cunt. I watched as she left the stage. Yet still she lingered, ghostly atoms, something of her appeared to remain and was held aloft by the shards of sex that winked off her, and then that too was gone.

She was bound to come out and find me.

"Hi, I'm Shona. Do you mind if I sit here?"

Her hair was pulled up into a loose French knot and her skin was damp from the recent exertion of the dance. She was wearing a black silk kimono with oriental poppies scattered on it. It covered her completely, but not at all, as it wrapped around every curve and indent, like an obscene satin shroud.

I looked up at her, "Sure."

She sat in the chair facing me and a waitress stepped up to take her order.

"Hi, angel, I'll just have a fizzy water with ice and a twist of lemon. Can I get you another..." Her voice trailed off.

"Diet Coke. Yes please, no ice."

The game had begun, but I wasn't sure what I was playing. I had never been with a woman, I had never thought about it. She surprised me with her flat, midwestern accent. Her eyes dazzled green, in the dark night of the club and I could see a few stray freckles that crossed the bridge of her snub nose. Her neck was long, where it showed proudly, beneath her up-do and on the planes of her cheeks she had sprinkled glitter powder so they scintillated as she spoke.

She looked like a child playing dress up. The voluminous kimono added to the little-girl lost look.

"I'm Farah."

"Oh yeah, I knew who you were when you came in." She was confident. Now it was hard to put an age to her. She could have been anywhere between eighteen and forty.

"Really?" I wondered what she had heard about me but I didn't want to ask her, I wanted to leave that version of me behind for an hour or two.

"Yeah, I met Michael and he said you came in here sometimes."

"Oh, I see." I was the gatekeeper. I looked out at the sea of tables of men. I realized that seeking anonymity in Michael's world probably wasn't such a great idea after all. I would always be defined by him, within the borders of his empire.

She noted my silence and she continued, "He said really great things about you and that you dress nice."

Her drawl hadn't been tainted yet with the rifle-like percussion of a New York accent. I was relieved, she was intrigued by the same stardust they all were, the allure of his money and the lifestyle were what attracted her. Not me.

"Oh. I just work for him." I forced a smile. I saw she was trying hard not to look at the pile of cocaine.

"Try some. I won't say anything."

"Oh no, I can't I'm working." But she did, she bent her head forward so the front of her gown fell open to reveal the orbs of her breasts. I watched the back of her head where her hairline met her neck. I wanted to reach out and trace that shape with my forefinger so I could commit that shape to my memory of her.

When she lifted her head, she let out a sharp breath, "God that was good."

Any residual discomfort fell away. There was room to breathe again.

"He said you ran Bel Air. Is it true that the escorts make so much money just by hanging out with rich guys?"

I searched her face for some irony but there was none.

"Is that what he told you? Yes, something like that." I smiled to myself, M was incorrigible, always recruiting, and while we did have the odd request for a genuine dinner date, these were few and far between. But why did every conversation, every person I met have, to drag me back to the darkened living room where I was chained to this other life by a telephone wire?

"Is it safe?" She ventured, she was coming close again by letting go, like the whispered words of the Irish poet. Maybe she wanted to work, to go out on these elusive dinner dates he had promised her.

"It's safe enough," I had never yet had an incident of violence on my watch. I explained to her how I called in every hour to make sure the girls were still all right and to ask whether they were staying or leaving. I usually had someone close by, a driver, waiting in the car downstairs and I would make sure the girl called him from the client's room so he knew someone was waiting for her.

A lot depended on the way a woman handled herself. I hoped that told her what she wanted to know. Looking at her as a commodity for me to sell, she was a blank cheque for Michael's business, a 100 carat rough diamond, mine, waiting to be cut. She leaned in a little and let the edge of her palm touch mine,

"Do you think I would make a good escort? Could I be a call girl?"

There's something in the psyche of a woman that knows instinctively that we can't have the same zipless sex in which men can indulge and delight. But we can pretend. By reducing sex to money, there's an illusion of power. Power is sexy, however you can get it. Her eyes conspired to draw me closer.

"Stand up." She did and shrugged her gown off her shoulders, so it sank to a pool by her feet, she might have been Aphrodite, stepping out of her shell. She arched her back and the triangular sliver of rhinestones between her legs which crossed her lower belly, winked.

"Well, you have a great body. You hold yourself well, you are certainly sexy. Are you thinking about it?"

"Maybe. I just wanted to know what you thought," she lifted her chin so I was covered by her shadow. The only light in my vision were the pinpoints of brightness given off by her spangled crotch.

"I think you'd do well. You look young and wholesome and guys like that."

I was flipping through the mental Rolodex in my head, thinking of punters who would love to spend time and money on Shona. It was all about chat in the end. The girls that made the most money were the ones who could talk, make their clients feel desirable, listened to and important.

I'd wonder when a girl came crawling in with the first light what she had done for fourteen hours. The most virile of men would find it hard to have sex more than a couple of times with the drugs and alcohol that had inevitably lubricated the encounter. More often than not, the escort, a few thousand dollars richer but tired and aching for her own bed would say,

"You know, we talked."

The shrewd ones kept their minds and bodies flexible. An intelligent women is sexier than just a pretty face when the lights are out, although a pretty face can take you a long way with men who throw gold coins at the water's edge, as they to try and buy the wind.

These men who acquired sex in the same way that they might acquire a painting or a new car wanted someone who presented the opposite of what they had at home. They wanted someone who wouldn't nag or pour blame and who could accept them for who they were, with no expectations. Money merely oiled the transaction, greased its wheels and it removed the guilt and any lingering sense of obligation.

There was a chubby woman who didn't look like the models I had on my books, but when she dressed in her silk and lace La Perla underwear she became every man's fantasy, whether he was an Indian Princeling or a Greek shipping tycoon. They could, under any circumstances have had their pick of glossy Park Avenue models or socialites, anyone they chose. But a call-girl stays just beyond reach, they can buy her time but they can never possess her in the same way.

"What else do you do, Shona?" I flicked a quick look at the room as she stooped to pick up her gown. All eyes were on her.

"I'm at NYU. Didn't you go there too? It's my first year."

"That's really great. Don't stop doing that."

I had been right about her age, about nineteen, three years younger than I was.

"What are you doing this for?" I had looked, discreetly for abscesses or bruises where she might have injected herself but I hadn't seen any, there were no track marks, no collapsed veins although when a junkie wants to use and go unnoticed, she'll inject in her groin or between her toes. The fatty tissue in the abdomen is also a good place to hide needle marks and scars.

"I'm saving money to pay for my tuition. I've enough to pay for college and living expenses for three years, almost. What happened to you at NYU? Michael said you quit." I wondered how much more about me she knew.

"It just wasn't for me; I'd like to go back one day…" I trailed off and laughed, "Don't be like me. Lots of girls do it and save, just hang onto the reason you started doing it in the first place."

And lots more girls didn't, the lure of pretty things was too irresistible when money was made by lying on your back. I tried not to think about what had happened to my plans for my future. I was aware of how much I had lost and the high price I was paying for having glittery trinkets in my life. Money seemed to have wings.

"Anyway," I reached down into the bag by my feet and pulled out a silver business card holder, "Here's my card, it's got my cell number on it so if you decide you want to try working as an escort you can call me." Someone had sent a bottle of champagne to our table. I couldn't face this aspect of my sexuality, these neo-nascent Sapphic urges without chemical balance, so I poured some into each flute and raised my glass.

"I thought you didn't drink?" She looked a little worried, as if she might be responsible for this slip in my sobriety.

"Sometimes I find it hard to stay sober." I drained my glass and watched the champagne bubble along the line of her lips as they reached the rim of the glass, the same way they were dancing in my head. I was resuming the chemistry in my body at which I could function without feeling. The internal operating system recognized the code and started, life was better if it was lived out between bottles of Bollinger.

Shona slid round so she was sitting next to me on the banquette. I could feel her bare leg against mine, she was relaxed. She was at ease, not predatory and the next move seemed natural. She was very close to me now, her face not an inch away and I could smell her sweet breath. This woman was going to seduce me. She had been down this path, many times. "Have you been with a woman before?"

I didn't answer and her voice slipped over me the way water covers sand on a beach.

"Do you want to be with me tonight?" I didn't have a chance to answer her. A woman's kiss is soft on the tongue, it's made of air and wetness, and it is gentle and questioning, By the time I realized she was kissing me, sometimes in my mouth, I was kissing her back.

The room took flight. I was giddy, giggling. Her glittery porcelain face covered my view, she was all I wanted to see. She slipped her hand under my skirt and stroked my thigh with the lightest touch. Then she retracted her hand. She teased me and licked her finger, with the tip of her tongue. She closed her lips around it for a moment and she looked up at me, for just long enough. As if it was the most natural thing in the world she took my hand, easily.

"Let's go home," she suggested and so we left.

The End of the Game

Life was a game I played. I made up or changed the rules as I went along. If it had been a poker game, I played as if I was holding only aces. A part of me thought I would drift along this way for the rest of my life but to relieve some of the boredom, I stepped out of the shadows and committed the cardinal sin of carnal commerce. I put faces to some of the names on the other end of the phone. Not for sex or money but out of loneliness, for we shared the solitude of sordid secrets.

There was a surfeit of sex in my life. It wasn't driven by a particular desire or hunger for a man but there were many affairs which began with intercourse and climaxed with nothing. I stayed in this pattern of non-starter relationships until I was twenty-seven. Older men came with a set of prescribed habits and I liked that; it meant that one of us could be a full-time grown up. I went through these affairs playing the part they needed me to enact, chameleon-like, I could fit into the shape that they made for me in their lives. I wasn't naïve, so they couldn't have wanted to be in a relationship with me for some sense of innocence that they had lost. I didn't bring that with me. I needed them for a sense of stability. They appeared rooted in the shifting sands of New York to which they were attached by family or profession. I wanted to devour their experiences, to make them the legend of my own life.

Michael became more elusive. He disappeared like the white rabbit into the black hole of cocaine psychosis. Freebasing simply fast-forwarded to the end of the movie. He had started with the latest chemical weapon in the arsenal of the addict, the speedball, which was a hit of heroin, injected or smoked, followed by a puff of freebase. He started to unravel at the edges and was so short tempered, it was almost as if his frayed nerve edges were being exposed to the light, which he avoided as much as he could.

There's a night that stands out. We started at some club; it could have been La Goulue on Madison on the Upper East Side or the Milk Bar, which was hidden behind an unmarked door in the Lower East Side. It could have been anywhere else in-between.

I started the evening with Charlie, who, by day was a steely, respectable, arbitrageur. At night he became a charismatic cokehead. He was one of our best clients. He was nearly fifty but hypnotic. He had the body of a man twenty years younger and the nickname Silver Fox. Charlie lived both in high society and on the edges of New York's seamy underbelly. He lived by extremes, with a weekend house on the estate of Henry Kravis and Caroline Roehm in Connecticut and suspicious connections with the city's leading mafia families. He was from the Deep South he had kept his accent and smoky drawl. Charlie was my guardian angel. But he couldn't put the genie back into the bottle.

There was no question that he still functioned, after a full night of partying, he would put his head down for an hour, get up, shower, shave and shit, as he'd say, and slick back his silvery hair. He'd put on a dress shirt and a tie, and look as if he'd had his full eight hours and sufficient REM. A driver was waiting and ready to take him to his office in midtown. Each step of his hand-stitched leather soled brogues shook off a little more of the debris of the night before as it touched the sidewalk.

His unspeaking, unseeing maid was already busy in the flat clearing the empty double malt bottles, the used condoms and the cocaine residue off his coffee table. In a couple of hours all the evidence of the previous night would have been removed.

The evening started with him, so we might have been at JG Melon a bar and burger joint he frequented or 21, the steak house. Or maybe it was someone like him. I had been drinking bellinis at Harry's bar on the corner of 59th and Fifth Avenue, I liked the sugary buzz they left more, with every peach, fuzzy mouthful that I swallowed. Life was a twenty-four seven party.

People who couldn't hack the pace fizzled out and moved to South Beach, Miami, like Peter Ehrlich, but others popped up to replace them. Everyday was Mardi Gras; a parade of stoned and smiling faces that floated by like indistinguishable figures riding fairground horses on a carousel. All the pretty, clever, glittery people were here, bobbing up and down while the ride lasted and the music played. We were like apples in a barrel, sometimes visible, sometimes drowned.

Light is cruel in Manhattan; it's not just the angle at which the flat, North American sun hits the dirt. It makes rough shadows on the most buffed and botoxed of faces. In the East 60s, between five storey townhouses that are occupied by single families, restaurants like Lutèce and Le Cirque light the faces of the ladies-who-lunch crowd with bulbs manipulated to let off light similar to that given off by candles. At these *grandes dames* restaurants, tiny lampshades lined in the palest pink silk pongee illuminate with a colour corrected glow which enhances the impression of prosperity and health.

The city lives and dies by its image, and its residents are parties to that deceit. As long as you looked good, you could get away with anything.

It is night, the red-soaked sunset of October skies have finished their painful bleeding, every corner is neon lit and buzzing. The red-for-stop and green-for-go man break dances, as if he is on amphetamines. He flashes that it is not or it is safe to cross the road. We go anyway. The taxis blaze by like giant goldfish, their numbers lit up. There were lucky numbers to look for, numbers like runes that held the mystery of the secret city. They meant something only to me.

It was just another evening, one spent between places, in cabs. Somewhere at one of these joints, I met someone I knew; I must have known him because I left with him.

I noticed how tall the red the arrangement of roses in the hotel lobby was, as we crossed toward the elevator to go up to his room. I was holding his hand; I caught a flash of a reflection, in a flat-brass panel of an elevator door. He was a distinguished looking city gent. I saw me, lost but pretty. Normal people doing normal things, like having dinner or returning from the theatre, surrounded us. I remember the brass sweep of the heavy doors of the elevator entombing us as we ascended. Then I remember nothing.

The next morning, I stumbled out bewildered in the early light of another day, straight into the rush-hour traffic on Park Avenue. My stockings and panties were stuffed into my handbag. I felt bruised and sore between my legs. There were marks around my wrists that I couldn't explain. I had been drugged with a pill.

The scary phantom of that night dwells in me. It's a blank page, and a blank in my history that I'll never be able to fill. The realization that I could put myself in such danger crept into me, slowly, like shock. I retched and felt sick to the pit of my stomach but nothing came out. There was nothing left in me.

Something in me snapped into place that morning; I knew it was as simple as change or die. I stood on the street, wishing for rain to wash the dirt in me away but none came. Instead, in a cruel and dazzling grimace, the morning sun shone, lighting up all the ugliness in me for the passing world to take in.

I had been trying to move out of Michael's world, I skirted a little further away from him. Larry Gertz was the accountant Michael used to clean money from his various ventures. I used him to help me keep my bills paid and he could sign on my bank account, to ensure that money went out monthly so my life ran smoothly.

He had cerebral palsy and he dealt with it by imbibing copious amount of cocaine. His offices were in midtown, in the West 40s. Larry was responsible for laundering hundreds of thousand of dollars of dirty money, not just Michael's. He put it through offshore holding companies and dummy corporations. He had a stunning girlfriend, Monique, who was an accomplished dominatrix.

A few days after the hotel incident, I was detoxing and getting clean, because I was too frightened to do drugs anymore and I was more coherent. I realized that Larry had been stealing from me. In my detoxification rage, I screamed in front of a room full of people that I would kill him. I forgot what I said as soon as the words left my mouth. But walls have ears and eyes and there's always someone around you with a bigger secret they don't want exposed. Chances are they'll sell you out.

Christ Church sits on Park Avenue between East 60th and 61st Street. AA meetings were held in its basement and out of necessity, as I couldn't do this solo, I started to attend. I was also trying to extricate myself from a relationship with Jim Harmon. He was from Connecticut and he'd retired when he was thirty-five. He had managed to save a couple of million dollars in the bank and he had bought an architecturally interesting house off Route 27, on Flying Point Road in Southampton that had been designed by Stanford White and was once owned by the American Impressionist painter, William Merritt Chase.

He had the obligatory yuppy apartment in the East 80s. We fell into each other's mess. He had been a big client, not just of Bel Air but also of the other agencies. I should have known better, a man who buys sex can't respect any woman, we are all whores in their eyes, everyone has a price and it's just a matter of negotiating the deal. But I was intrigued by this superman look-alike. He was a lot older than I was, he was thirty-eight and I was twenty-four.

I was aware that I had reached a nadir, I was scraping along at the lowest point of my life but I had to take myself there to understand the sickness in me, with Jim. It was like seeing who could do the most degrading dance to their grave faster. He was good to me when he wasn't drinking or high, he was generous, there were pretty things: a diamond Tiffany tennis bracelet, a bespoke platinum and diamond engagement ring, holidays in Florida and weekends at his beach house.

I denied that there was anything unhealthy about the relationship. His self-abuse and addiction made mine look as dangerous as naptime in kindergarten, and this helped to reinforce my lies to myself about how bad things were becoming, in my own life. When he tried to get sober, I would go on massive drinking and drug sprees. When I wanted to try and clean up my act, he would get deliberately off his head.

I was spending a lot of my time sitting in church basements, trying to get my head around the mess I had made of my life. We were in another ropey patch of our relationship which had been going on and off for about eight months. I was hanging on by the frayed edges of my nerves, not wanting to let go completely because I didn't want to be alone. His drunken rages were better than sitting with myself. I had been out and come home later than I had told him I would. I hadn't bothered to call, all the niceties and concern that make the day-to-day of a relationship bearable had long since been abandoned. I turned the key in the lock to his apartment and the first thing I saw was the bunch of lilies on the table, already placed in a vase.

The lights were off and there were candles dotted around the room, which were reflected in the full-length mirrored wall. I was pleased, a little relieved, I had expected a fight, screaming and ranting when I got home. I didn't anticipate that the scent of my favourite flowers would greet me.

I closed the door behind me and when I turned, as my eyes were still adjusting to the dim light, there he was. He was standing in front of me, almost on top of me, completely naked. I looked in his face, and in a second and I could see he was wired. His skin flared up when he took cocaine and there were red blotches on his face. He was grinding his jaw and his eyes were wild. His cock hung slack and shriveled between his legs. He was rudely unaroused. His pupils were dilated, they were tiny ink spots in fields of blank parchment. All the life in him had been blotted out.

He snatched my bunch of keys out of my hand and he locked the door behind me. He slammed the keys in my bag and threw it on the floor of the coat cupboard. It groaned from the force with which he had forced it shut.

"What's going on?"

I was frightened but if I didn't let on then he might back off. He thrived on fear. He had never hit me but the crazy energy bouncing off him and the dull fixed look in his eyes was scaring me. I instinctively flinched and tried to back away to the perimeter of the room, I was hugging the wall behind me. I thought if I retreated to the sofa, I would be safe.

"Where have you been?" His voice was low, if he had screamed, lost his temper I would know how to react. This was different. I stood still.

"Out with Sam, I told you."

"Out with Sam…" He tried to mock my accent but his eyes were bulging with rage. He looked vulnerable and much younger without his horn-rimmed Armani glasses. He said it again, in a childish sing-song way, "Out with Sam."

Then he grabbed my wrist.

"Jim you're hurting me." I tried to shake his grasp free but he held on, harder and it started to burn.

I have mistakenly thought I have fallen in love so many times in my life and I thought I loved Jim. He was tender and he didn't judge people, I liked the unconventional strain in him. When he had enough, he kicked it all in, he

90

dumped his waspish wife and lived the life he wanted. That was how it looked to me from the outside.

"Come and watch this. I got bored waiting for you." He snatched a handful of my hair and pulled me into the bedroom. The pain made me wince but it made me angry enough to start shouting at him.

"What the hell do you think you are doing?"

"You are going to watch me fuck this hooker, because that's what you have been doing isn't it? You whore."

I hadn't. Sam was a girlfriend who was trying to help me to get out of the bad situation with Jim. We had dinner once a week, it was a regular girls' night out.

"You are going to watch while she sucks me off and you are going to enjoy it when I go down on her." He laughed.

The romantic setting, my favourite lilies and the scented candles, they were all chicanery to court someone else's affection, which he had already secured by paying for it. In our bed, the one we slept and made love in there was a girl not much older than I was. She had short brown hair and her eyes were empty. They had been at it for hours, the debris of paid-for sex was spread out over the floor, used condom wrappers lay strewn next to empty brown cocaine gram bottles.

In the half-light, I could see the damage to Jim's body was beginning to show, his once firm muscles had started to lose tone and he used to get terrible nosebleeds, when pieces of his septum would literally come loose from the chemical abuse. There was a pile of blood stained tissues on the floor. He had no colour; he was a ghostly shade of white. The veins on his forehead were straining, he looked as if his face might explode.

I didn't know the girl splayed on my bed. Jim liked light bondage; I went along with it if I was stoned enough. He kept an array of women's silk scarves in a drawer and there she was, tied loosely to the four-poster bed with silky knots at her wrists and her ankles. She wasn't straining at all, she was lying there. She might have been a dead animal on the butcher's block. She was waiting to be desecrated.

Just then, I remembered he had kept his ex-wife's passport, he claimed she had forgotten it when she left him. I began to doubt his version of events. He started to kiss my neck and to undress me. His paws were grabbing at my dress but I felt sleazy, if he had poured a barrel of crude oil over me, I might have felt sexier.

"Get her out of here and get off me!" My voice was thin and shaking.

He pulled my dress and I heard the thick, muffled sound as it ripped. At another time and place, this might have been arousing but now I was furious. I pulled away, clinging onto what I could of the dress around my shoulders; I saw he had torn my bra too.

Then he hit me. He didn't hit me hard; it was more the shock of the smack than the pain it delivered. He did it again, four or five more times, enough for me to sit dumbstruck, half-naked in a heap on the floor. I didn't know what I should do. He had a look of contempt on his face and where he had hit me I couldn't feel any pain. My scalp still stung where he had pulled me by the hair. I put my hand up, to rub the sore spot and strands of my hair that he had yanked fell out.

He had turned his attentions on the prostitute; she was now lying on my side of the bed, making soft low moaning noises as he put his head between her legs and went down on her. That was an intimacy we had shared. I understood her pretence, this act was more for his benefit than from any real pleasure she might be deriving but still it felt like total betrayal.

A pro, in my bed, with the man I was living with. His mouth on her. My long hair that I had put up in a loose knot, only a few hours earlier had fallen all over my face and strands of it were mixed with my tears and hurt pride. I had not been paid for sex, not in this directly transactional way; I had never sold myself for money but I had sold myself out, nonetheless.

In spite of all the elegant clothes and my mid-Atlantic accent, I might as well have been a professional. That was how low I felt. I collected what was left of my dress around me and quietly, so he wouldn't notice I stood up. The dress was in shreds, the edges of it dropped out of my clasp. I slipped out of the bedroom and found his keys in his coat pocket. I let myself out into the hallway. As I eased myself through the living room, I caught a glimpse of the morning rising.

Outside, fifteen stories below, life went on as normal in the city. The first grey light of dawn scraped the edge of the night and the sky was crackled like dirty foil from the discarded apparatus of a heroin hit. I banged on the door of a neighbour I had never met. It was five in the morning and he had been asleep but he let me in and gave me his dressing gown.

Later the police came and took Jim away in handcuffs. I didn't ask myself, for another fifteen years why I was picking men as damaged and destructive as he had been. I did understand, in some sick, sad part of me, that I had picked men as angry and addicted as I was. These relationships fuelled the furies in me. They came out through these mad and dangerous encounters.

Something in me wanted to destroy them, to hurt them before they could hurt me and in the end, each just eviscerated the other. But they kept coming back.

I was nobody's friend, I was the demolition woman. I don't know who chose whom, but I had to start asking the questions.

New York is the epicentre of therapy. Whatever ails you, the cure is to be found there and it is dispensed by gurus. They give you words and weeds. One of the shamans that lead me a little way down the road to try and gain some insight into my increasingly erratic lifestyle told me in no uncertain terms it was the demon of my father that was manifesting itself in these sick relationships.

I would have to kill the king to marry the prince; it was a game to the death, for one of us.

Daddy Dearest

It was a smoky New York evening; autumn was conspiring, long spells of winter and heaps of leaves appeared from nowhere to gather at the feet of street lamps. I tried to commit to AA, to do the ninety meetings in ninety days ideal and I did more than that. I lived in dull, smoke-filled basements. I was in shock from the end of the affair, I knew that it was over but still we kept stopping and starting in fits. He called me, his voice as thin as a reed in the middle of the night, he asked to see me and he sounded so hollow and fragile, I'd agree to meet. He said we could get through this, that he, we, could change but we were two overloaded dumpsters backing into each other. Every time it was a crash of emotions and raw pain, every time failure and disappointment.

That church on Park Avenue had solid beginner's meetings, where old AA lags said you'd meet "a better class of drunk." AA felt welcoming and safe and there was a hint of a brighter future, one in which sobriety was a cornerstone, a day at a time. I could see it becoming a part of the rest of my life, but at twenty-four, the rest of my life was a long time.

My father's drinking had cast long shadows in my life; it was why I had left home. I hated the person he became when he was drunk. The echoes of my mother's voice still rattled around in my head, and it took me straight back to being a confused and crying child, thwarted by her own power. She would tell me that it was all my fault that he drank, that if I would behave better, if I studied harder, if I stopped fighting my siblings, he'd stop. Now, I drank to stop feeling that guilt. If I didn't want to own anyone's pain but I certainly didn't want to confront my own.

My drinking started once we were safely separated by an ocean, and a few years when his drunks could no longer affect me. I drank for oblivion, not to feel. I swallowed whole bottles of gin, as I had done on the night before my 21st birthday. Nothing changed. I still felt sick. Drinking induced the same anesthetic state that men and shopping did. I felt as if I didn't exist and when I was drunk, that the pain was rubbed out.

These intakes of excess further blurred the frayed edges of me. I tried so hard to fit into my reflected self, like Narcissus, but my mirror was dirty and cracked. The ends of my nerves stopped transmitting any sensation. I could have been living between giant sheets of blotting paper. The hangovers were awe-inspiring, I felt as if an acetylene torch was burning holes in the frontal lobes of my brain. It hurt when I tried to think and I couldn't make the simplest connections.

I could feel the physical deterioration. I was tired. I acquired an AA sponsor who was an enthusiastic friend. She listened without laughing as I detoxed and the muck filtered out of my brain and my body.

AA precluded having any outside life. It felt a little cultish. I quickstepped through its program of Twelve Steps, which marshaled every aspect of my life: past, present and future.

I tried to conform but it meant surrendering to a power greater than me and I wasn't ready to accept that anything could be greater than my imagined omnipotence. I preferred to hang onto the craggy precipice than to let go, for fear of what I might fall into.

It was Wagnerian, my addiction, like a ring story, I always came back to the familiar threshold. I wasn't ready to quit and I easily surrendered to more ugly adventures. Fluorescent lights in old church basements do little for the chiseled features of the actors, celebrities and journalists that eventually find their way into the rooms. I drank strong filtered coffee in styrofoam cups, laden with heaped teaspoons of sugar, as it softens the effects of withdrawal that accompany not drinking.

Hearing other people's stories of drugs, dependency and degradation made me feel less like a sorry failure. I settled into this world of aggregate freakishness and my story fell somewhere in the middle of the catalogue of horrors that we alcoholics compiled. AA inductees, when they have reached the ninety days milestone have a freshly exfoliated look. We venture forth, detoxed and replenished, with our shiny (plastic) ninety days medals, which we carry like St. Christopher's coins, to guide us through the Mephistophelean maze which is life without substances.

It was taking longer than a little while to clear the fog in my own head. I was oblivious to the posse of undercover detectives who had been following me around, who probably wouldn't have permeated the permanent state of short-sightedness my vanity inflicts on me, in any event. I had ascended from the pit back into the choking car fumes and boisterous noises of my city's Grand Avenue. I stood by the curb and watched the swarm of taxis, they were lit up, like locusts as they glided on a swarming carpet in a choreographed formation up the wide avenue.

I always looked for the taxi number 9E16, which was my street address. There were two behind me, climbing the old, narrow cement staircase gingerly and two more greeted me as I reached the top of the stairs.

"Farah Damji?" My mind was still elsewhere, as it tried to weave together the incongruent strands of my separate lives, to form a new shape into which I could fit.

"Yes?" I thought they were AA folk but something pricked in the back of my mind when I realized they were using both my names. That's a big AA no-no, you are only known by your first name and the first initial of your last name. Anonymity is the cornerstone on which AA is founded.

"Farah Damji, I am arresting you on suspicion of the murder of Larry Gertz."

More detectives came from out of the shadows and I was soon surrounded by eight or ten of them. They handcuffed me and read me my Miranda Rights.

Larry's murder had been front page news on New York's daily toilet paper, *The New York Post*. The unspoken conclusion was that it had been an ordered mafia hit. Larry was mixed up with the wrong crowd and had embezzled from people he shouldn't have. The smart money said he got what he deserved. I hadn't stopped to ponder on it since my outburst that day. The devil deals the cards in that world, murder was part of the pact if you were caught lying, stealing or cheating from one of the Grand Masters of the game.

The ride to Central Booking underneath One Police Plaza was long and quiet. They must have been expecting a gangster's moll, judging from their excessive number. A detective sat either side of me. They were relieved I had volunteered to go with them demurely, but there was no rush. They were on overtime, it was a Tuesday evening, they could have sprung on me anytime prior to that.

One Police Plaza is an ugly grey municipal building, which was having a bad Bauhaus day. We passed in a procession, through the regulation wooden paneling in the lobby; we went into an elevator up to the floor where the DA and his assistants lived. I was shown into a boardroom and the handcuffs were taken off me. They didn't fear an arachnid escape from the eighteenth floor. They left me on my own. This felt insane.

I was barely twenty-five and though I had done a lot of impulsive things in my short life, murder, even the thought of it, hadn't been one of them. Larry had been another person at the periphery of my gang. He hadn't been more than a casual acquaintance. The amount he had stolen from me was paltry compared to what he had taken from others.

I'd asked Charlie what had happened to Larry and I had been summoned to a "meet" in the middle of the night at his flat. I had started to receive strange phone calls, consisting of vague threats and unspecific demands. I put them down to M's paranoia. People said he had learned that Olga and I had tampered with his precious cargo and this was him, trying to reign me in. Michael did things in metaphors; he couldn't confront me directly so he'd mind-fuck me with the paranoia that he projected from his own fear. I'd seen him do it to other people.

His skin was so dry it was flaking off and he hardly left his darkened flat on Sutton Place. He had aged fifteen years in six short months. The purple blotches had spread and where he picked at them, ugly scabs formed on his face. He looked crusty.

The door opened and a young man with a springy step bounced into the room. He introduced himself as Dan M Rather Jr., Assistant District Attorney. He looked like a young Kennedy; he had the same rich, suntanned look of the privileged scions of America's first families. Dan M Rather Jr., less than thirty, was going through a rough patch. He didn't have the same assured good looks his father did, he was a little fish-eyed and rumpled.

His father, CBS's long-standing news anchorman had recently had an episode in which muggers had attacked him and kept asking, "What's the frequency Kenneth?"

He was walking up Park Avenue on his way home and although his doorman had corroborated the story, there was a lot of New York snickety-snickering about the incident. Some versions of the story claimed he thought he had been privy to alien cross talk on the airwaves. Others were less kind.

I tried not to smirk as I said: "Oh, like the news reader?"

"That's my father." He wasn't smiling; we all have our paternal crosses to bear. He could think of better places to be than here, during prime drinking time on a weekday evening in the Irish pubs a few stories below. Tonight was his father's birthday, maybe he would rather have been there than intimidating me. He rummaged his hand through his thick blond hair.

"Look at these." He slammed an A4 manila envelope down in front of me so it landed millimetres from my hand, which was resting on the cherry conference table. It looked innocuous; I tipped its contents out on the table.

Immediately, I recoiled.

The glossy 10 x 12 inch colour photographs depicted the crime scene at Larry's death and there they were, Weegee style, spread out in front of me. There were close ups of his neck which had been slit from ear to ear, it was known as a Mars bar, in gang slang. He lay slumped on his desk, with his head lolling too far forward. I retched loudly and Dan Rather moved his precious photos away before I could throw up all over them. I didn't, I tried to remain stoic. He could see that I was shaken but he didn't stop, he picked up the half dozen pictures in his hand and fanned them out, like a tarot card reading, in front of me.

"What do you know about this? Did you have Larry Gertz killed?" Had this not been happening to me, it might have been funny,

"What are you talking about?" Indignation rose in me and I could feel the fear which I had managed to keep suppressed, quickening in my veins. My hands started to shake and I couldn't stop them. This wasn't happening.

"We just found a cashier's check for Connie le May for $1 000 in your purse. How do you explain that?"

Connie was a professional dominatrix we sometimes employed when the need arose. She was a one-stop bondage shop and charged upwards of $500 an hour. I couldn't explain that. The client she had been with was a leading fashion designer. His silk swathes enveloped starlets and socialites from Metropolitan Museum of Art charity balls to the Oscars. He paid by credit card, which would go through one of Michael's companies, and we'd pay her by cashier's cheque.

She had spent two hours with this hard-core sex freak. Cold and hard as cash, only she could bear to dish out the level of degradation the oily Levantine immigrant wanted to have inflicted on him. She made thousands of dollars a week on the administration of pain, she had made it into an art form but how was I going to explain this to Dan M Rather Jr.?

I stayed silent and as I did I wondered how he would interpret that. Silence can be seen as a way of holding onto truth, or in the words of Thomas Moore, it can be seen as an admission of guilt, a tacit collusion to the facts presented. He scraped the chair he was sitting in noisily away from the table, and slammed the door as he went out of the room.

For the first time in my life, I got on my knees and I prayed. I hung onto the leg of the table for a little physical stability during my devotion, I felt as if I might melt away. I was put through the system, in the subterranean sewers of the building. My fingerprints had to be taken twice as the first detective hadn't taken them accurately, "accidentally."

It took another twenty-four hours for my prints to come back as clean from Albany and I began the endless circuit on the fairground Ferris wheel which is America's court system.

That night I had a dream which seemed to prophesise what would become of me, down the line. My bones were ground to a fine powder as I was crushed between stones. But I still believed that I could get myself through this. I was arraigned the next morning and went home, back to bed to try and forget. I woke up flailing in the sheets. The sky was a shroud the colour and grain of a pumice stone dawn while the horizon was being bruised with brutal punches of purple.

I called the number, which hadn't changed in all the years we had lived in that house in Nicholas Way. I can never forget that first phone number; it's been digitised into my memory. I held my breath and whispered a prayer as the phone rang, thousands of miles away. I could imagine its sound scoring through the silence of the early morning, resounding off the parquet flooring and climbing the stairs.

"Mum?" She had been fast asleep.

"Hmm?" I heard the sheets rustle as she sat up in her bed, in my mind's eye, I could see her pink silk nightie sloping off her shoulders.

"Farah? Is everything all right?"

My phone calls home were sporadic at best. Sometimes, when I was feeling nostalgic, over the holiday season I would phone, pretending to look for a recipe for Yorkshire Puddings or to ask her how to cook a turkey. Whatever time it was, my mother would gather her wits about her and explain over the phone. She must have known it wasn't the recipe I wanted. I sought the reassurance of knowing where I came from, of hearing her voice, but the link had been broken long ago.

These cold midnight calls couldn't defrost the tundra that lay between us. I'd asked to speak to my father; he was still the distribution system through which everything had to go. I told him briefly what had happened, without embellishment and I felt so small when he comforted me and told me he would be on the first plane the next morning.

"I'll call Lou Rivlin, he'll know what to do." Lou was the DC based ex-Judge who had invested in my father's business. Lou had become a larger-than-life Father Christmas figure in our lives, he brought toys for us, and wisdom for my father whenever he came to visit, about twice a year.

I had telephoned him when I first arrived in New York, to lay out the markers for a friendship away from home and he'd call me sometimes when he was in town and once, we had dinner together. He was a wily, world-weary character, going on seventy but he didn't look a day over fifty. He had recently married a much younger woman who had made him a father again. He was always slightly grumpy, he had forgotten that young babies cry a lot and wake up in the night. His first brood was all grown up and had left home decades ago.

Lou didn't let us down. The next morning I was at the offices of the attorneys he had recommended. My dad came straight to the sky scraping office in midtown Manhattan from the airport. The large wall-to-wall window sucked in the panoramic view. The sky was stooping weary and low, heavy with the burden of proof and the weight of low grey clouds.

This is the image of my father that has frozen in my mind. He was in his mid-forties; he wore a camel-coloured cashmere coat and an immaculate fine wool suit underneath it. His hair was thinning but it was slicked back and wavy and he wore a beard. He looked like a rainmaker, a high-flying executive, one of those men who occupied the executive floor in the stratosphere of power, in any metropolis. But now he looked small with the big city crowding behind him. He must have been tired. He had taken an early flight and although he had traveled extensively, by First Class, for as long as I could remember (I had the doll collection of National Costumes from far-flung places to show for it) he was worn out and grey.

His voice faltered as he tried to greet me when he entered the room. It was a lot to take in, much more than the extravagant breadth of the window, in the expensively appointed partner's office in a midtown building. Robert Kasanof was our man. Lou Rivlin had known him from his old judicial days, he was part of the Washington circuit, Kasanof had been a prosecutor. Armed with his loaded Rolodex, he had siphoned off a young bloodthirsty ADA from the Manhattan DA's office, Mary Shannon.

They had thoughtfully left us together in Robert's vast partner's office so we could come to terms with the seriousness of what lay ahead of me. He held his arms out and I stumbled into them. The daddy-scent of Benson and Hedges and Simple soap filled my senses. I was taken back to a less complicated place in my life, when I was younger and he could still fix everything.

His warm overcoat felt as soft as a blanket and I thought if I buried myself in it for long enough, I might wake up out of this nightmare.

"Are you all right?" He sounded gruffer than I had expected and when I pulled away I saw tears rolling down his cheeks. I didn't answer, my mouth refused to form coherent words and my mind had stalled. I looked down at the antique Persian rug, sprinkled with colours that looked like crushed spices.

There they were. All the answers that never came to the stillborn questions of my youth, they hung onto us, like shackles. The distance grabbed both of our elbows and it rooted us to where we were standing. We could no longer reach each other. That moment had passed.

"We should have – I should have explained it to you when you were much younger, then you wouldn't get into these messes." I winced a little, whatever childhood scrapes I had manage to entangle myself in, they didn't come close to being up on a murder charge. My back stiffened.

"Told me what?" I needed advice, not moral lectures.

I retreated a step. He half-turned away from me, as if he wanted to step out into the forest of buildings behind him. Now was not the time for confessions but the words had already slipped away from him and they'd formed boulders between us, it was too late to put the secret back into the drawer. He let out a sigh and slumped into the sofa. His body collapsed, in one swift movement. He looked small in the chrome and leather bucket seat. He sat completely still and only his mouth moved.

In flat tones he told me a story I already knew, about being kidnapped when I was three, about how we had left Kampala, complete lives and our dreams behind.

"Oh that. I know all that." What it had to do with now was beside me. I wondered if this was going to turn into an analogy, like the President and his suitcase bomb.

"But it was an important... if you had dealt with it when you were younger... we should have..." His voice broke off because he didn't know what he should have done.

He dealt with it in the best way he knew. It was too late for recriminations. This navel-gazing rumination, so unlike my father, left me cold. How odd, I thought, as I tried to take the first faltering footsteps into adulthood, that I should fall and there were no hands to catch me. I felt uprooted and my centre couldn't find a place to balance. All I could see was fear in the eyes of my father.

Mary knocked on the door and the light tapping brought us back. She entered and was followed by Robert and Lou, who had flown down from DC for the day. They asked for a $50 000 retainer to take the case. Salvation came in the form of a torn leaf from my chequebook; I paid half, and my dad paid the other half.

Through Mary's erstwhile connections she gleaned that the DA's office had hit a brick wall with the investigation into Gertz's murder. They knew that he'd been involved in cleaning money, they knew about his underworld connections and the affair with Connie.

They had been deliberately drip-feeding misinformation to the media, who sucked it up. They recast Larry as just another innocent New Yorker who got caught in the mad, bad mafia wars that peppered pockets of the city. He had been sliced and diced to create fear in the hearts of New York's denizens; it was all part of a larger plot to destabilize the city.

The reality was that it was part of a political agenda that had stagnated and was meeting some difficulty in the city's administration. They played on and exaggerated his cerebral palsy, how he had overcome his affliction to become a successful accountant. He was recast to become a local super-hero in their aggrandizing urban legend. No mention was made of his cocaine addiction or that he was stealing money from his clients. The murder took place in broad daylight, in midtown Manhattan. The police had found a carving knife at the scene but it had been wiped clean. There were no traces of DNA or fingerprints. This was a professional, ordered, contract hit.

Rudolph Giuliani had recently taken the helm at the Mayors office. New York had dumped Ed Koch, the old, flamboyant homosexual. Ruddy was the new chairman of the city, with about as much charm as a cold pizza. He had declared outright war with his corrupt compatriots, the Italian mafia. He was going to give the mean streets that had long been divided up between the ruling families, back to the people who lived in them. He started the neo-con dogma of "Three Strikes and You're Out," and with it, he succeeded in warehousing vast sections of undesirable New York stock, the white politician's favourite folk demon, the gun-toting, gang-banging, young black male.

We learned that they had decided to lean on me, as I was the youngest in the crowd and given my newly found sobriety, they were aware of how fragile I was feeling.

I had been fascinated by the clutch of power, which held the writhing city. I'd been seduced a long time ago by Charlie's mobster friends. They would sit around in his apartment for hours, "shootin' the shit," he called it; these streetwise, outwardly normal people whose beliefs were reinforced with the clang of gunmetal and the flash of knife blades. They had New York sewn up, in an all-encompassing protection racket. Business people knew they had to pay, in the same way they paid their rates, to have someone watch over them. If they didn't, they lived in fear of what might happen.

I had met John Gotti, when he was *il capo di tutti cappi*. He was charming. I was introduced by Tony, a man I was seeing for a short while who was also connected. Tony used to take me along to some of his meetings. The photograph the DA's office produced of me taking Gotti's extended hand as he plants a kiss on my cheek could have meant anything. It looked like a familiar embrace, between two old friends, but it was the first and only time I had met him. He was of that old European ilk that welcomes you warmly, with a double Italian kiss-on-each-cheek greeting. I wasn't being singled out for particular affection.

Those were the grainy pixels with which the DA's office could link me to the mafia hit on Larry's life. Gotti spent an hour telling us about his plans to go to Florida for the winter and all about his family. When he spoke about his children, his sun-tanned face crinkled, around his eyes and a smile opened like a leather billfold. In the mind of Mad Dog Dan Rather, if I had nothing to do with it, I must surely know someone who did and he was determined to lean on me hard enough so that I would break.

I wondered, as I looked at the incriminating evidence, what a bored Grand Jury had made of it. What would they think when they saw the evidence of a self-destructive woman stupid enough to put herself in the hands of men like Tony, who were criminal and dangerous. Charlie, as much as I loved him was crazy, unpredictable. I was a neophyte in a new city, running with a motley crew, I didn't know well.

It was Shiva, the God of destruction that wreaked havoc in my days, in the way a child draws patterns in the sand and waits for the sea to come and wash them away. Everyday there was a clean slate and everyday I manifested more drama and destruction. I stepped closer to the brink of my capacity for danger and then Nataraj, snake-hipped and sibilant, drew me in even further. He tempted me to come a little closer to the edge. He was leading me into the ultimate dance, towards self-annihilation.

Already, Kali was waiting, she beat a rhythm on the ground beside my grave. It was already dug and open, waiting for me to simply step in.

Undue Process

Whoever said the law is an ass, underestimated the inherent sagacity of a donkey. It's like being inside a rat's ass, and any involvement in the criminal justice process with the chief rat-catcher, Rat-bag Giuliani was guaranteed to be no fun. The case dragged on and on, I frequently spotted detectives tailing me when they thought they were undercover.

The shock of Larry's death had started to sink in. I maintained my sobriety and was hit by the new found insight that this wasn't normal, to know people who became murder victims. Worse still, I was suspected of being a murderer myself. Mary, the solicitor who had assisted in our defence of this case, had sent me to a hypnotherapist, to see if he could unearth any deeply buried trauma or memories, about that event. She told me she had seen him and that he had helped her identify "her issues" but the experience was surreal.

More out of body than in my head, for $400 an hour, Dr Robert Reich ascertained that I was not susceptible to being hypnotized. He said, as a rider, before he began, that a certain small percentage of the population can't be put under, and then he tried a crude transference. He told me to project whatever I could see, as he spoke, into an imaginary silver screen, on the wall in front of me. I did but I remained self-conscious throughout the process which he was recording for Kasanof and Shannon's files. The screen shimmered with crystalline pixels, but nothing came. I was truly and deeply blocked.

On that chilly morning in those expensive offices, change presented itself, again, as the only option available to me. I applied to enroll in a one-year course at the School of Interior Design on East 58th Street; all pretence of going to NYU was ditched. I enjoyed the simplicity of matching colours, of learning about antiques and different designers and their signature styles and I was good at it. Life started to assume normal dimensions, I was tired at the end of the day and I usually had homework or an exhibition or a gallery to visit.

Slowly, almost unnoticeably, Michael and his world slipped away, it was the change of scenery between acts at the theatre. Him and his seedy world had no place in it. He had heard about the investigation and knew about Larry's death so the best place for him, and his shady business empire was well away from me.

There were only a few people I trusted with whom I dared to stay in touch. The permanent police presence helped keep a check on the company I kept.

The DA's office was no closer to finding out the truth and finally, almost nineteen months later, the charges against me were dropped. No one was finally brought to book for Larry's murder, I suspect it's another of those New York stories that turns into an urban legend, whose memories seep into the buildings and pavements and are forgotten over time.

After I was arrested, and been allowed to go home pending my case appearing before the court again, Charlie was the second call I made. He asked me to go over to his flat after the meeting with the lawyers and my father. Charlie knew the Rathers, the newsreader, and the Junior District Attorney and he smiled cryptically when I told him everything that had happened.

His blue eyes danced and he said simply,

"Baby-doll, you tell them everything you know."

"But I don't know anything."

"Exactly." He smacked his thigh with a resounding clap and his whole body rattled with laughter.

"So what do you mean tell them everything?"

"You don't know anything my darlin', so you surely can't tell them anything." This seemed to make sense in some inverted and convoluted way. I was trying to play logic with Charlie who was coked out of his head but still sane. It felt as if he wasn't really taking any of this seriously.

Maybe the money we handed over did it, or maybe it didn't make the slightest bit of difference. I couldn't see how the illustrious Mary Shannon spent it. They convinced me I needed a bodyguard with me at all times in case the DA's office pulled another arresting stunt. This ate away at a lot of the initial retainer. They certainly weren't worth it, Kasanof was not around much. But if the fee was meant to grease the wheels of justice, then perhaps it did. I suspect somewhere in a gym in the recesses of a gentleman's club in New York City, a deal was made. Two silver-haired waspy men, one of whom was rather fond of me, shook hands as they steamed. I was delivered from the eye of the maelstrom.

When I gathered up the courage to ask Charlie, years later, he looked at me blankly.

"I fixed it. It's gone. Forever. Now if you stay clean and sober and stay out of trouble, no one will ever bother you again. All right, darlin'?" And that was as much as I got out of him.

He became a sort of lover in my early sobriety, maybe he was that bit of the disease that I wasn't ready to let go of, just then. By day, he moved money in great quantities around the globe, as an arbitrageur he speculated millions of dollars in global markets. There were nights we went out and came home late, he crashed as soon as his head hit the pillow.

When the phone rang, in the middle of the night with an urgent inquiry from a trading desk in Hong Kong or London, from the depths of his sleep, he reached over me to get the phone. I'd listen, half asleep as he made sense while his eyes were still shut. He grunted some directions down the phone and cursed as he left the receiver on the pillow for me to put back in its cradle. Then he closed his eyes and curled up against me and started snoring, picking up the thread of his dream exactly where he left it.

I didn't kid myself, Charlie had lots of girlfriends, and I was one of three he was seeing then. I just happened to be the favourite for that moment. I looked for safety in him and I found it. He was kind to me when I needed him; after yet another failed affair, and an unwanted pregnancy, for which he planned the abortion for me.

The following weekend he took me to his cabin in upstate New York. We walked and talked and played happy couples as we crunched the leaves underfoot. He looked after me. We both wore his oversized, hand-knitted cashmere sweaters.

We went into the local village and he had to buy me flat shoes, as I didn't own any. I left the wellies at his house, for another time or maybe another woman. The secret with a man like him was to have no expectation.

That Saturday evening, with my insides still sore from their recent scraping, he made love to me passionately in front of the fireplace and the feeling of having him inside me, as painful as it was, eased the emotional pain that I was going through. I didn't mind any amount of physical pain, I could handle that.

Office Space

I landed a job. Not just any old job. A great job.

I was a very junior decorating assistant at Parish-Hadley, New York's waspiest decorating firm. Sister Parish was old and dotty by the time I arrived, but she still had an office, all chintz and gimp-edged, oversized, overstuffed sofas strewn with cushions like confetti. She looked a bit lost on the days her liveried, black driver brought her into the building on East 63rd Street. She was like a relic from another age. She sported chubby magenta dots where her cheeks should have been. She wore her hair big, in fixed pin curls that were white and coarse and unmoving and her mouth was marked out with a glossy red scar, like a wound.

Parish-Hadley spawned three generations of designers and decorators whose work fills America's swankiest homes. There are countless spin-offs from the trademark Parish-Hadley style but I was with the real McCoy. They had redone the private quarters of the White House for Jacqueline Kennedy, the first lady of American Style. They gave the magic of Camelot a fitting and elegant backdrop.

Albert Hadley's style is more minimal than Sister Parish. He likes chrome and glass and Le Corbusier, but he'll pick and mix Arts and Crafts with stylish French Empire furniture in his white-on-white interiors in a way that is his hallmark. Only he can make it work. He admires Jean-Michel Franck, and his own furniture designs often bear Franck's marque, the X in the cross of the legs of tables and stools. He is a short, tiny man with the innate authority of a schoolteacher, which is what he was for a long time. Albert's low-key style and tolerance were a natural incubator for the best design talent.

As the most junior decorating assistant I had the task of sorting out the sample library, a tiny square of a room which was lined with shelves. It was situated in the middle of the hall, so either end of the corridor could access it; one opening was just outside Mrs. Parish's office. I sent back the fabric and wallpaper swatches the designers no longer needed, to the D+D building at 979 Third Avenue, where most of the wholesalers had showrooms.

I was also tasked with meeting prospective vendors who lugged their heavy suitcases of sample books and paint treatments, to the office. They wanted to ply us their wares. I had set Fridays aside to meet them, and gradually I built up a broad array of material and stone samples from as faraway as Italy and Provence. We had pictures of reclaimed fittings and fixtures in photo albums that could be shipped over quickly and a collection of hundreds of coloured fabric samples all neatly folded and displayed.

David Kleinberg was one of the two senior designers, alongside Gary Hager. They couldn't have been more different both in decorating style and in personality.

I had been hired by Dianne Miller, Albert's tiresome, meddling secretary who had learned assertiveness and acquired her people skills through EST. Gary and David called it her cult, they laughed at her and said she practiced mind control and sorcery. She was tightly wound and they made it a point to display how much they disliked her, they refused to call her by her name, she was addressed as the dragon, or just "she."

She wasn't that bad, but sometimes, out of mischief, they took on caricatures of themselves, and they parodied other people and every situation. David was flamboyant, he loved colour and chintz. Gary was sober; his schemes were subtle and clever. He could juxtapose the grandest gold leaf Rococo Louis XIV armchair with an oak Settler table. His interiors were classic and sophisticated, they emphasized good materials and taste. David would frequently send me scurrying off to Scalamandré to find some exorbitant hand loomed $1 000 a yard silk, from their Gobelins factory in France.

They were different in the way they treated me too. David would find occasion to comment on my Chanel suits, to him they were a brand, I was acceptable because I looked the part and I happened to fit but Gary noticed details like the buttons on a vintage suit, or the way the company's emblem changed from season to season. Gary taught me how to look at colours and texture, he helped me define my own style and grow comfortably in it.

I had a bijou jewel box of a flat on East 65th Street between Madison and Park Avenues in an unrenovated townhouse that had been split up without much love. My flat had been the first floor drawing room and it boasted long walls and high ceilings. *House and Garden* photographed the fireplace for a feature they did. With treasure rescued from Parish-Hadley, such as the gold leaf sconces the socialite had rejected (but still paid for), and white silk tassel tiebacks (wrong shade of white for the ivory damask curtains they had been meant to restrain), I made it into something beautiful that I could call home. It had an unusable kitchen, in the hallway and a tiny bathroom opposite the main room. It was rent-controlled, more valuable than gold, in Manhattan realtor-speak. A broker in the AA rooms had helped me to find it.

Rob Yeoh lived two blocks away, in a similar studio on East 63rd Street. His position as Albert's sometime-assistant gave him access to Albert's genius design mind and his sitting room (the only room), was painted in broad black and white stripes. He owned beautiful gilded furniture and a wooden four-poster bed. It looked like a Cecil B de Mille set for a glamorous prison cell.

Rob and Gary had so much style and nothing to prove. They were both friends and allies at Parish-Hadley and without them I would not have been able to stomach the constant backbiting and bitchiness that pervaded the office's atmosphere.

The offices of Parish-Hadley had recently moved from a townhouse off Fifth Avenue to a purpose built design office block. John Saladino had the top floor and we occupied the floor below him.

The office was brightly lit; the designer's offices were decorated to their own styles and tastes. Gary's had an elegant rustic feeling; it might have been in the country palazzo of an Italian nobleman. There was an old farmhouse table that he and his team worked around.

David Kleinberg's was a gay man's fantasy of what a woman's boudoir might look like, tight buds and full sprays of magenta cabbage roses covered his sofas and window treatments and celadon silk lampshades cast a permanently cool morning light.

Each designer had a junior and a senior and then there was me; I was often called in to put together a sample board for a client presentation or to get bagfuls of samples from the D+D which they would then go through and select what they liked and what they would use.

Parish-Hadley has, at some time or another, decorated the homes of most of America's foremost families. Noteworthy names like Astor and Whitney on the spines of folders jostled with newer and trendy society families, Quasha, Novogrod, Ertegun.

Old and new images of spent money jangled in our design archives. We were in the business of selling the reflection of colours in the rainbow, as seen in the old Venetian mirrors hanging in Albert's office.

We sold style that couldn't be defined and was as untenable as stardust. We were selling an image. Having spent hundreds of thousands of dollars at PHA, a client might suddenly become bored with the look and rip out the hand-painted wallpaper and throw the overstuffed sofas out onto the sidewalk. Robert Star's hand-painted $1 000 square foot paint treatments would be scraped off. Then they would employ another firm, to start all over again. The perfect home ended up in a skip or a charity shop.

We were pimping a product, given credibility by the proprietary seal of approval, PHA, in red, engraved 14 point Times New Roman. It might as well have been an ancestral shield, this talisman-like logo of the three capital letters. We bought all the pieces of it, fabrics, furniture, trimmings, in bulk from massive design emporiums. These were like giant chests of drawers, spilling over.

We drooled over Christopher Hyland's tapestries of fabric, hand spun with gold thread, that he imported from Eurasia, which sparkled in his sun-filled showroom. There was such sophistry in this sale of substance, by the yard. There was the odd person who was passionate about what he did, who saw through the chimera but we were all cocooned by the fantasy, in voluptuous reams of silk and velvet.

We sought out the Gamatria in a piece of furniture, with the fervour of those who went in search of the Holy Grail. Proportion was the gospel. These purveyors were the people with style; we took it, moved it uptown a few blocks and repackaged it having marked it up. We could resell it to hungry, bulimic Park Avenue Princesses, who with their skinny necks craned, wanted some of what someone else was having, a piece of the emperor's new clothing.

Other than Rob, Gary and Albert Hadley it was hard to feel generous towards the other PHA employees of that time. Mrs. Parish was sweet but vacant. She'd drool when she fell asleep in her chair, after lunch and after a couple of clandestine gin and tonics, she was pretty much gone. She was wheeled in and out when the occasion arose to impress a potential client like an important painting or a piece of prized furniture.

She occupied a dusty corner of what she had been, but in moments of lucidity, was still as sharp as an acid-drop, the Queen bee of the decorator dowagers. She had brought her own style to America and spawned a thousand facsimiles.

Through Gary and Albert, I could see the value in paring down, taking away something when a scheme was finished to leave a space for the muse to settle in and for the occupier-client to leave his own mark so that he fit in.

The sublime ridiculousness of Parish-Hadley's place in the pantheon was made clear when Sarah Ferguson, still the Duchess of York, before her toe-sucking days, came formally to ask if Parish-Hadley would decorate Sunninghill. The staff were lined up at the front door to greet her, we'd been given a rudimentary lesson in how to curtsey (and how to bow in the case of the men, although some might have preferred to curtsey) and Sister Parish donned a new hat.

On her way out, Sarah Ferguson slipped on the overly polished parquet floor and she landed in a navy gabardine suited pile, all we could see and hear were her giggles and the silk dots on her blouse.

The Queen put the kibosh on any decorating plans that the young Yorks might have had. Sarah had to make do with someone boring, staid and British. The

American version of English Country house style, imported by Sister Parish half a century earlier was certainly not going to find its way back across the Atlantic into a royal household. The colonies would not dictate style to the Royals, who after all had invented shabby chic. Still, the delineations that marked out Empire and colony were subtly visible, like the fading lines of an architect's blueprint.

This was the early 90s and AIDS was coming into its own. Although no one ever spoke openly about Gary and Rob's condition, they often had to stay at home as they were too ill to come into work. Albert insisted that Rob should have the best anti-viral treatment available, and it was all paid for by the company's health insurance policy. No one said the word AIDS, even when the light scars of sarcoma started to tarnish Gary's jaw. Rob became so frail he had to use a walking stick.

They were both under forty when they died. At their memorial services, which followed their funerals, no one mentioned how they had died. In a manner befitting characters from *Bonfire of the Vanities*, no one acknowledged that they had been sacrificed to the awful, panic-creating disease, which was festering in our midst, whose name we couldn't speak, for fear it might catch us, too.

AIDS took them in their prime, in the same way that a proud gardener deadheads his favourite rosebush as soon as the blooms have blushed, fresh roses are allowed to come through. They were gone but some of the style they created lives on in dusty decorating journals from the time.

They had been ghosts while they were still amongst us. Maybe because they knew they were dying and they trod the earth more gently. They wavered between being alive and knowing that they were living on someone else's time. Maybe that's when we know we are really alive, when time is scarce and life becomes precious.

Brown and the New Black

The intersection of men who had been clients of Bel Air and who sat, bored and distracted in design briefings in the Parish-Hadley offices was more frequent than you might like to think. The same men who bought sexual pleasure also humoured their wives by doling out extravagant decorating budgets for second and third homes on Star Island or in the Hamptons. Powerful, ruthless men turned meek as mice when they were confronted by sneering designers and their cohorts. Customers were treated with barely disguised contempt. The men were buying peace, some harmony at a pretty price, and they were happy to let their trophy wives be accessories to the understated, overpriced interiors that they would all soon inhabit. These men were prowlers – they couldn't keep still. Perhaps changing houses and shifting landscapes and settings fed the same desire for change that sleeping with prostitutes did. To misquote Pliny, *Ex Homini semper aliquid novi.*

I was dismantling old design folders. Samples had to be returned or PHA would be billed. Clients had already paid, at some point, as the cost of the samples was incorporated into their invoices, but this was part of the old world frugality that lay behind the success of the firm. It was like looking through someone's diary and bank statements: I was privy to the intimate secrets of what name-check families, such as Whitney, the Paley and the Rockefeller, had paid for their curtains or a piece of furniture. Every item was documented.

The ultimate accolade was to have the new or improved home featured in the pages of one of the style bibles, on the East Coast it was Nancy Novogrod's recently revamped *House and Garden* and on the West Coast, the glossy pages of Paige Rense's cathedral of style, *Architectural Digest* would suffice. Anything else was considered less than enough.

Nancy and John Novogrod were clients of Gary Hager. She had an unwritten deal whereby she would acquire the specified fabrics and materials at well below the normal retail cost. As the editor-in-chief of *HG* she had clout. Nancy and John, the second partner in this A-list couple, her master-of-the-universe in training pants of a husband were part of the younger new, upwardly buoyant society that PHA needed to break into. She was young and stylish but in the presence of one of the two named partners of the firm, she slipped off her pedestal.

112

Senior designers treated their clients with great respect and decorum, while they were still in the room. The moment the doors closed behind them, the character assassination scissors would be drawn out alongside the proverbial tape measure to compare credentials and the real one, to measure a floor plan, and the bitchiness began.

Designers were only as good as their last gig. Their social status and design desirability was defined by their client list. The women were expected to maintain a presence in the gossip columns, just as the men had a place in the Fortune 500. The rolling out of the new design would be mentioned by one of the gossip sites in the *New York Post* by the arch-socialite septuagenarian, the kindly Cindy Adams, or her glamorous colleague, Liz Smith. Page Six was only for pop-stars or Eurotrash, Richard Johnson has never had the same gravitas in gossip as the two grand dames.

A well-placed item would appear in the *New York Observer* or the Home section of Thursday's *New York Times*, both were good incubators for leaking the grotesque budget of new clients we had acquired. By Monday, eager-to-impress editors' assistants called to see if they could have the first look-see of the property once it was completed and then it was a matter of clever negotiations, most prominent page placement, how many double-page spreads and which named photographer would take the pictures.

Every project was documented and professional photographs were placed with the tenderness that might be afforded to distant relatives, in red leather scrapbooks, embossed with the gold monogram of the company on the cover. Published articles were carefully cut out and stuck in the book too. By creating spaces and then enshrining these images of the created space, with the seal of the publisher's approval, the firm successfully ensured its own legacy and legend.

There was a big PR machine behind all this, endless press releases and photo opportunities but the appearance of spontaneity and madcap extravagance was carefully contrived. In New York truth is a secondary concept, it's the capital city of style and back-stories are created overnight to give credence to a newcomer's meteoric rise through the upper echelons of society. Money could buy power and prestige; iconic couples such as the Trumps, the Kravises, and the Perlmans raised slick monuments in the name of their wealth and laid serious coinage at the altars of excess and vanity. Trump Tower leapt off the sidewalk on Fifth Avenue like a golden Icarus, wet and gleaming, still full of fire.

Hungry property developers, who covered blasted out building sites with pretty, painted hoardings, ravaged whole corners of the Upper East Side. They promised a new urban paradise would soon sprout, to replace the rent-controlled squalor that had been allowed to exist until the Donald Dynasty. The names of these new buildings and their inhabitants were anglicized; they were made palatable, like crustless, quartered cucumber sandwiches where Subway foot-long specials should have been.

Jewish or Eastern European suffixes were dropped. Everything about Manhattan, my city, in that moment, was about smoke and mirrors and the reflection of you in it. We lived with the chicanery of air bucks or unreal money, paper or credit, which fuelled the commodity *du jour*, the junk bond. Greedy eyes grew wider than porcelain teacups as the fumes of hairspray from Ivana's up-do propelled the dream. The concept of air as a tradable commodity had taken hold.

I left Parish-Hadley to become a designer at Stephen Mallory Associates. He was camp (but straight) and had been a design luminary in the 70s and early 80s. He had done and redone sumptuous, slick interiors for a fistful of clients who adored him and returned to him, with their new yachts, their children's first flats and their beach condos.

Stephen had married an elegant Englishwoman, Jenny Mallory, an ex-model, who in spite of three decades of living in America, had retained her accent in the way many ex-pats do. I didn't. Mallory had forgotten his own humble roots and hitched his star to the scaffold which propped up the derelict townhouse he had recently bought on East 64th Street, between Park and Madison Avenues. He hadn't paid much for it, compared to the telephone number prices most houses in the vicinity commanded but still, it was substantially more than he could afford.

At the end of each month, there was a substantial shuffling of funds between the Mallorys' own bank account and the client account the firm established to hold client money in escrow. Every month, Jenny, who was honourable, would knot her bony hands and her transparent skin wrinkled more deeply as she tried to meet payments with money they didn't have and that didn't belong to them.

Stephen's biggest client was Herb Gallen, the founder and proprietor of Ellen Tracy, which was a middle-of-the-road but successful ladies clothes label. Then he found Linda Allard and installed her as his senior designer. Herb was married to a Jewish woman who had raised his children and looked after his homes in expensive parts of New Jersey and Florida. She was broken and wheelchair bound while Herb enjoyed a second flowering with Linda.

It was good for both of them, he could make Linda fit into what he needed, and she took to the mould perfectly. I worked on Linda's dream palazzo, in the middle of nowhere, Connecticut. Much to Stephen's disgust, her architect brother, who was also a professor in Ohio, was designing it. Money was no object, if Linda couldn't have Herb, she'd have the house. What Linda wanted, Linda got. She would roll her pretty dark eyes at Stephen's excesses and she might blanche theatrically when she was presented with an invoice but she was delighted to be the elegant cash cow he was milking. It was a clever con.

114

Stephen would present Linda with a few alternatives for an item; once it was dining chairs. He showed her pictures of authentic Savonarola chairs from Italy, the heirloom of a dissolute count's fire sale and some others that were respectable reproductions at a fraction of the price. Essentially, he could rely on the certainty that Linda who was still just a small-town girl, would defer to him.

The idea of spending $60 000 on eight dining chairs, naturally, didn't sit well with her.

"What do you think?" Her owlish glasses lent her seriousness but she still had some of the midwestern accent left in her voice and when she was unsure, it became more pronounced. She could be childlike, almost coquettish in front of him yet she was the wrong side of forty-five and controlled one of America's most financially successful fashion brands. She was the poster child for the American Dream, but when it came to making simple decisions about her own home, she floundered.

Stephen would take off the frameless glasses that perched on the end of his bulbous nose. He'd fold them meticulously and set them down in front of him on the table. He leaned in and touched Linda's arm, paternally, and then rubbed his eyes hard with his fists, as if he was trying to wake himself up from a bad dream. His fingers ran through his mane of white hair. He wore it a little long; he thought it made him look raffish. Finally, for he was a consummate actor and understood the value of a delayed reaction and the amount of doubt created in the space of a second, he would suck up his breath and with the particular patience of a father, addressing his favourite child, he said,

"Well, Linda, if you are sure that is what you want." And that was it. She might as well have handed him a blank cheque and her firstborn child. The dark, almond-shaped eyes would fidget with confusion and panic, she had picked the wrong answer.

How could she have been so stupid? She was still, and always would be, a hick of a girl from a small-town in Ohio, and here she was, making a fool of herself at the table of the great potentate of New York design. She couldn't possibly know that Stephen had passed his prime, as she was only following her mentor and lover's advice. The colour would rise to her immaculately powdered cheeks where two rosy spots of embarrassment settled. All her self-assurance, all her sparkling brilliance, and the street-edged determination that she'd had to steel herself with internally, to get to the position of power which she had acquired, it all drained away. In a quiet voice she'd barely manage to say,

"Oh well, I love these but if you think…"

Stephen seized his cue, like a lion hunter who has just clear-sighted his prey and he pounced. With the accuracy of a skilled marksman, he'd bagged her.

"Well if you love them, dear girl, you simply have to have them. That's all there is to it."

And his liver-spotted, gnarled hand covered hers completely. She was his. He could take her to lunch safe in the knowledge that his mortgage interest payment was going to be met that month.

"Now let's go and get some lunch and talk about shades of white." Like a dandy and his courtesan, he'd take her elbow and lead her out of the office to one of the local expensive eateries where he would pay for lunch and then double it and bill her expense account, for the next month.

Designers and decorators work on a fixed fee which is payable in stages. The amount is negotiated in advance and depends how much of a pain the designer thinks the client is going to be and how much he can get out of the job. Then there is the additional 20 per cent on top of the retail price of everything specified, although the designer gets a discount from the vendor because he will pay the trade price. It's called getting it from all sides.

Linda Allard undeniably had good taste, probably better than Stephen Mallory's but she lacked the cachet of confidence and possibly the time to go and source all the trinkets and treasures that made a house a home. Stephen called the service he offered, "let's make it look like nice people live here." We were to provide the texture that would give her Connecticut new-build some depth and some history.

Arthur Smith is an interior designer of the old guard. In true blue blood fashion, he kept his head down when his long-term partner, Andrew Crispo was found with a dead rent boy at the Rockland County family home of his assistant, Bernard LeGeros. He killed Eigil Dag Vesti, a Norwegian fashion student while Andrew was there. This was dubbed "the sex mask murder" by *The New York Post*.

Crispo had been an art dealer to the elite but went to prison for tax evasion. A week after he was released, his home in the Hamptons burnt down and he settled on an insurance deal worth $5 million. Arthur had given up designing interiors but his shop on East 61st Street was a statement of his considerable style. He never cluttered it up, the way some antiquarians did. He had important pieces he had sourced himself from all over the world.

I had found a dining table and two armchairs from Arthur Smith Antiques for Linda's house; I'd snapped Polariods (the weapon of choice for the daytime sortie) and Linda instantly loved them. I had phoned Arthur to place a reserve on them till Linda could go and see them herself in the shop. We would usually have the pieces picked up on loan for the day and sent to the client's house but in this case it was impossible, Linda's brother was meticulous in his draughtsmanship and plans were still being shuttled back and forth from her office to the university where he taught.

The foundations of the princess' palazzo hadn't yet been dug out. Stephen's silver mane was often left tousled after agonizing about what he described as "this suburban box, fit for an Ohio backwater." He would have much preferred that Stephen Mallory Associates oversaw the whole project, in-house. We had an in-house long-suffering designer-architect, Mark, who managed to maintain his serenity whilst deflecting Stephen's covert advances, while everything around him was going gradually into melt down. He worked well within the chaotic paternal way that Stephen Mallory ran his enterprise. It was all water off a duck's back.

A few days passed, Linda pulled up in her limousine outside Arthur Smith's. She liked them as much as she had their photographs and although they were expensive pieces, together they came to over $120 000, a cheque for half the amount was messengered from Herb Gallen's office later the same day. I left Arthur Smith delighted she had liked the items I had chosen and promised him that I would come back regularly; Linda had a whole house to fill. He was gracious and extended the normal fifteen per cent discount, which was not bad for a morning's work, considering Stephen hadn't had to leave his office.

It was hard to miss the glimmer of Stephen's greed, behind his bi-focal's when he opened the envelope which contained the cheque.

I liked Linda, she was pleasant to me and in spite of her success as a down market Donna Karan for the masses, I felt sorry for her. Herb was never going to leave Betty and Linda had squandered her pretty years and her youth waiting for him. Access to his wealth was her compensation, for being both mistress and muse.

Besides, she was a Goy, Herb was a prominent Jew and a significant and card-carrying member of his synagogue, he'd dispensed a smattering of millions to various Jewish causes on his way up and he wasn't going to leave the power and the prestige of the life he knew for a *schiksa*. He had feelings for her but he knew she would stick with him regardless of whether he left his wife or not. Linda had an apartment a few blocks away from our office, which Stephen Mallory had decorated. Herb spent most week nights there.

The Kips Bay Decorators Show house is a high point of the New York social calendar. An Upper Eastside townhouse, one that had recently been sold and was to be gutted was handed over to selected designers. Each was given a room to makeover. Vendors and suppliers would fall over themselves, once the announcement had been made, as to who was participating, to lend furniture and give materials to be incorporated into a favourite designer's scheme. In return, their generosities were mentioned on the designer's room page in the catalogue and a discreetly typed A4 paper panel on the wall.

That year, Stephen Mallory asked me to design and create the dining room in the dolls' house, which was auctioned off each year to raise money for the cause. It was seen as an honour to participate in any way in the event. The charity raised money by charging the public an admission fee and selling catalogues and advertising that listed the designers' firms and resources.

The list of the patrons of the Kips' Bay Boys Club read like the pages from the Social Register. Each year there was a gala opening, attendance was by invitation only. There were additional soirées, dinners and cocktail parties at the homes of society hostesses, and newly moneyed second wives, with husbands who boasted deep pockets.

My dolly dining room was pure Stephen Mallory with a twist. Grown women's faces lit up when they saw all the work that had gone into creating the house, all the different parts of it that had come together. A dressed dolls' house could bring in $1 million for the cause. Money and other people's taste, took wealthy onlookers back to the innocence of their youth. Stephen was pleased and took all the credit for discovering me, his young protégée.

A few weeks passed. Linda Allard sent me a card on her heavy signature stock to thank me for the work I was doing in her house. I started to receive calls from the accounts department at Arthur Smith who were concerned that they had not yet received payment for the pieces that we had reserved. I didn't think much of it to begin with, we were always slow paying bills but I passed the calls onto Liz in accounts. The calls and messages kept coming and when I directly asked Liz why they hadn't been paid she answered tight-lipped that I should ask Stephen Mallory.

I did and was repelled by the tirade that came at me. Linda was *his* client, the cheque had been sent to *his* office, I should learn not to tell vendors that a purchase had been approved, he could have gained a better discount. I realized what a precarious situation he had been in and that he had used Linda's money to prop up his own falling empire; he didn't care if we lost the chairs or not, in some half-upholstered fashion, he would make his apologies and an excuse to his best client.

The calls kept coming, other designers were eyeing the items. Arthur would have to remove our reserve. Stephen Mallory was inherently racist, he made horrible jokes about Jews and how tight-fisted they were. I couldn't help thinking at least they were tight with their own money. Linda was a hard taskmaster and not least was my worry that she was going to reject whatever substitutes we found for her. But Stephen would to find a way to pander to her perfectionism and still make a buck out of it.

118

Another coast was calling. New York's endless February winter, with its dragging sky and grimy slush piles gathered on street corners, went on and on. The colour and the life had been sucked out of this skinny bitch of a city. Her sharp knees and elbows, the needles of frozen wind and icy rain bore slits into my body, through layers of merino and cashmere.

The trees had lost their nerve and looked as if they had been scribbled in pencil on the dirty canvas of the sky. The children's boat pond in Central Park had frozen over and the rain, that endless grey drizzle like a runny nose, seemed interminable.

I had friends in LA and I needed to get away from my cruelest month and from Stephen Mallory whose financial shenanigans were making poor Jenny dash for the Diazepam with her Twinning's. But doubt filled Stephen's eyes. It matched the grey hooded skies. I asked him if I could go and he agreed, reluctantly, as long as I left on the Friday evening and was back in time for work on Monday. I knew when I booked the plane tickets that I wasn't going to be back for Monday, I made sure I had delivered up the work that was due from me. I needed time out. I felt fragile and the grip of the soulless design world had taken a hold in me.

There were more important things between heaven and earth than the length of a pair of curtains. This illusion of selling fantasies was precarious and I was falling into a pit. I called the office the Monday I was meant to be back at my desk and was told to come back as soon as possible, Stephen was angry with me, was the message. When I piled my bag and myself out of the taxi from La Guardia, back to my apartment I found an envelope, sticking out of my mailbox, which bore Stephen's flourish in brown ink. I had stayed a week. I dropped it in my bag; I didn't want it to break the memory of sunshine and surf. I wanted the holiday feeling to linger a little longer.

His note was brief. He accepted my resignation, although I hadn't offered it. His pre-empting me in this way canned any chances that yet another disgruntled employee could take him to a tribunal. He told me I was talented and I had star quality and that he wished me luck. I was free.

I set up on my own, operating out of my flat, working for friends and on recommendations. Through Jacqueline and Robert Norden, a brother-sister duo who had become close friends, I met Todd Black, another independent designer and we were soon the envied, young design partnership, with work in London and New York. Our clients were young, rich and stylish. Savvy magazines editors "spotted" us for their trends and up-and-coming pages.

The first Gulf War had ended and the boys were coming home. The celebrations were bittersweet. A ticker-tape parade had been hastily planned, as they came through Wall Street and people put on a merry face. But it was the first war in which journalists had been embedded with the soldiers. The images of scud missiles making their clumsy marks as rockets lit the night sky over Baghdad had been acid etched in our minds, in the way the shooting of President Kennedy had been in the minds of a generation earlier.

The live commentary that accompanied the visual feed was addictive, war had become a spectator sport. Collectively, our coalition generals should have known better after Dresden. I sat and watched, for two days and two nights, unable to move away from the television screen's jolting images.

Jacquie was a Daughter of the Revolution and the Republican Party had planned a homecoming ball at the Warldorf Astoria. We were asked to design the theme for the evening. We transformed the ballroom of the old hotel, as imperious as a dowager aunt, with swathes of white silk and hundreds of tiny votive candles. There were white linen tablecloths and the only colour was in the flower arrangements, which had some green, in their foliage.

Todd was talented and had heaps of style; he was as smooth as he was sophisticated. He was a svelte blonde and could have stepped off a Calvin Klein billboard. He was a good foil to my irascibility; he could be sociable when I didn't feel like it. He softened my own hard-headedness. I learned a lot about surviving in a particular set in those times, by learning how to play Truth or Dare and I saw the many faces and virtues of Madonna, he was her biggest fan. *SEX* lay on our coffee table in the office. The partnership didn't last and my sobriety slipped away, he drank jellied vodka shots. I like jelly.

New York is a perfect city for reinvention. In the memorable words of one of the best, The Donald, New Yorkers love a comeback kid. There's a sigh of relief, a sense of there-but-for-the-grace-of-god-go-I, when someone falls spectacularly off their pedestal in the sky. Social x-rays who graze on organic salad leaves (no dressing) for lunch whisper in hushed voices about the salacious details of the misfortunes of others. The encroaching sense of dread makes their gullets close up, so they can't swallow. It saves them shoving their fingers down their throat later. The city is both a vampire and a parasite; great wealth is amassed on nothing and everything's for sale, at a price. Fortune smiles like a great benefactress but sometimes, the curse, which settled on the original Dutch filchers of the land, reappears.

Karma travels at the speed of the information superhighway, on an endless energy loop. The actions that we play out, unknown, to anyone but ourselves, their consequences are played out on a stage in broad daylight. In a matter of days and weeks.

In Hindu mythology, Laxmi is the Goddess of Wealth and Sarasvati, the Goddess of Knowledge. They laugh as they lay elegant mantraps along the way so we clumsy creatures crawl about on all fours, looking for fools' gold in the concrete slabs of the sidewalk. It's all long gone.

Concrete desiccates the soul. We neglected knowledge and we chased wealth, only to find that wealth didn't want to be hoarded or flashed about in sickening statements of consumption. So the spurned Goddess shrugs and lives are smashed like broken toys. If we had sought Sarasvati, then would our success have had a firmer footing?

The skill of a good designer is to ascertain what the client likes. Decorating is about creating reflections; it's a bit like painting a portrait. The canvas is the empty space and the composition are the people, colours and textures in furniture and fabrics that inhabit it, they form the features. Colours and light create the client-shape he feels comfortable fitting into and all this has to be accomplished with breezy professionalism.

It's impossible not to want to put your own distinctive personality on it, but that would be too easy. It's easy to keep on recreating a mood or a nuance and adjust it slightly, so it retains something of the one who created it; it's harder but more rewarding if the client is involved in the process.

There are several stages of the client – decorator relationship, the initial euphoria, of getting to know and deciding if I like you, over lunches and drinks, followed by carefully observed window shopping, so that I can glean what attracts you. Then there's the stage where I have to draw you out, to take parts of your personality and make them into tangible objects that we can place around you so that they resonate in your own environment.

The last straw, the final one that put out any desire I had left to make nice homes for not very nice people was a mad Englishman. Robert Wylde lived in a brownstone on East 13th Street. He was festering at forty and his last girlfriend, a friend of mine, had been driven to distraction and had to move several states away to remove herself from him.

He had bought a house but he had no idea what he wanted in it. He had gutted it and was living there. It was impossible to pin him down and commit to a style he liked or one he thought he could live with. He was untenable, like a cup of water, which has been poured into the sea. There was no dialogue with Robert. He was impatient and flighty, he's made millions of pounds which he converted into cash on the copper futures market in London and then he decamped to New York where he wanted to reconstruct himself but he dived into drugs and drinking. It was as if he wanted to step into a life already set up for him and I wasn't able to provide the living space for it without his input.

My sobriety took a beating, hanging out with him. The situation with Robert Wylde worsened as his dependence deepened. He was the American caricature of the posh English gentleman, public school educated and rebellious with long hair and a desire to push himself beyond his own limitations, physically. He was a dapper, dusty scruff; he thought if he moved back into the half-derelict house, his builders might push on.

It's impossible not to make a career in interior design a twenty-four hour a day life choice; I often felt like a glorified, expensive babysitter. Linda was the long-term mistress of Robert Entenmann, the cookie and cake entrepreneur. He'd installed her in a non-descript block not far from the Museum of Modern Art, just on the wrong side of Fifth Avenue, but only just. Linda's fridge was crammed full of his confections, in white boxes with their blue logos, although in the months that I knew her, I never once saw her eating. There was always a still-warm cinnamon coffee cake on the glass dining table waiting when I came to see her in the morning and donuts for the workmen at teatime. I wondered if he sent cakes the way other men sent flowers.

Linda was outraged that Robert had declared he was not going to marry her. No man ever would. Linda was purely mistress material and high maintenance. She always had freshly applied lipstick, no matter what she was doing. The project started off quite small but like many others, it expanded as the recently renovated part of the home made the rest of it look shabby.

The baker was going to pay for his neglect, he was going to have to sell a lot of cakes for his oversight. But he couldn't have been that angry, my bills were paid promptly. Maybe money was easier than a confrontation. It became increasingly hard to deal with Linda's demands.

Her permanent Percoset smile and the helmet of sleek auburn hair that fell like a velvet waterfall, they never moved. She seemed frozen. She felt dead to me, and try as I might, to put some beauty and soul into the neo-seventies retro inspired apartment, I floundered.

Worse still, I felt as if she was sucking the energy out of me. She wanted a best friend, a confidant and a sister. The fact that I was her only decorator was incidental.

Charlie was a great client and one of the first. He asked me bluntly how much this nonsense was going to cost and cut me a cheque for the whole amount. He put the fear of god in me by telling me not to ask him for another red penny. We had calculated it together and it was a generous budget so he let me get on with it.

He had recently come back from a big game hunt in Africa. I was flattered he had asked me, he knew several society decorators who would have loved to do his flat for him. He chose me. I knew him well enough to know what he would like and we had fun recreating *Out of Africa* moments in his two bedroom flat, with a little help from Philippe Starck's recent obsessions with horns and phallic shapes.

Charlie settled well into his corner of Africa on East 68th Street. I went way over the initial budget and we had some memorable shouting matches about it, I think he forgave me in the end.

Mimi was about sixty; she had been a decorator a long time ago and had an elegant apartment she had tastefully decorated with some good pieces from her earlier married life.

She wanted fine gauze curtains, a shade of preordained peach she had imagined – but which didn't exist – to create a light wall and shield her from the southern sun that flooded the sitting room in the afternoon. It was on the hunt for this elusive paleness to block out the light, that I met Paul Stolper, a private art dealer.

The Business of Beauty

Paul was a younger version of Jay Jopling, his mini-me doppelganger, complete with rectangular fish-tank glasses. He was an independent dealer from London who represented the work of young, hip, contemporary artists including Jeremy Deller. Paul was the son of some friends of Mimi and was in New York trying to find a space to exhibit Jeremy's work, which was a series of oversized ciba-chrome prints that depicted fragments of a section of London life that I had known well. This was the next generation of excessomaniacs. The pictures intrigued me because these might have been the same people and parties from which I had stepped away. I had been eager to forget them yet they had found me again.

There's a picture I bought, of an elegant woman's neck; a diamond solitaire pendant sits in the concave of her collarbone. The heart shaped neckline of a black taffeta ball gown underscores the composition. Her face, her expression, none of it is visible yet the image captured the Sloaney confidence of Cool Britannia and the easy swagger of power and life under New Labour. From across the Atlantic it seemed quaint and exotic; like a mini Sampson girding its loins at the great American Goliath. My frozen-framed contemporaries had been anthropologically displaced in a cruel reversal of Orientalism.

Nothing had changed and I still didn't feel connected. New York is the epicentre of its universe, which spins on its own axis and rarely shifts to encompass anything beyond the boundary of Manhattan. It barely even acknowledges the three outer-lying boroughs which prostrate themselves towards her splendour, offering up long tunnels and bridges in supplication.

New Yorkers are hungry for news; but only about themselves. It's the only city that can sustain more than a couple of daily newspapers. There were the raging tabloids with their overheated headlines, which worked by the magic of smoke and mirrors and sturm and drang. There were the more serious newspapers, *The Wall Street Journal* and *The New York Times*. There was the broadsheet guide to social climbing, *The New York Observer* that peppered salacious articles about the good and the great, alongside party photographs and extended diary pages. But the news, in whatever publication, rarely extended the edges of the needle shaped island we inhabited; one of the unspoken rules was that nothing existed of importance beyond our world, across the waters. We were the children of a

Greater God. Yet Manhattan retains the mind set of a small community, a one-horse, two-pump town.

England's economy had imploded, thanks to the ham-fisted government of Mrs. Thatcher. People were losing their homes. Britannia's armor was decidedly tarnished and Mrs. T was going to leave a ruined legacy. Disturbances that came out of the Dark Ages, in the form of protests and strikes struck at the heart of the image of stiff-upper-lip Britain. But all this was an ocean away. It didn't touch us.

I occasionally saw people from the old life. A friend from St. Helen's, Deborah Colman had come over on a working holiday. Her father, a prominent barrister, had set her up in an arty job at the Lincoln Centre for Performing Arts. I reconnected with Aboudi Najia, a friend from my Lycée days while he was attending Georgetown University.

I envied how he and his brother Michael had maintained a firm hold on their staunch Lebanese identity. A full-size PLO flag took pride of place in their townhouse's living room. They were the heart of the tight knit Arab community, part of the rich foreign student contingent in Georgetown. America had changed his English accent, made it softer around the edges as he filled out a little, as well, but it hadn't changed him.

I had no sense of cultural identity. I reached for the familiarity of old friendships that had helped to define me in another life, at another time, but America had changed more of me than my talking. I couldn't find my voice, when I listened for it, when I tried to resurrect its timbre in updated stories of old dialogues, with people from the old life, there was nothing.

I could no longer feel the edges of myself. I felt floating and amorphous. I shrouded myself in the welcome anonymity of living in the moving city – nothing could stay still for long enough to stay the same. Impermanence was written in the city's DNA. In New York reinvention was part of the deal for those of us who had traded in our old selves for newer, shinier versions, in order to live there.

There's a wicked alchemy that rises up from the soil and the sidewalk. Whether it is by bridge or tunnel that you first enter into the confines of this city-island, she has you, on a hook. She plays the tune and you dance to it. I looked for self-affirmation in places I inhabited.

One of these was a loft on East 16th Street. I moved in as it was still being refurbished so I was able to pay to put in my own fittings and fixtures. It was a typical loft space with sweeping swathes of strip wood flooring and low voltage halogen track lighting. Behind a set of French doors and a heavy piece of gold and black brocade, I closed off a bedroom space. It was painted burnished bronze and it felt warm and safe. This was my space.

In the front of the building, which faced out onto East 16th Street, there were four large arched windows that framed the wall of the living space. They were original to its construction and had been stripped back to their iron structure.

There was an office off to one side, and in it was a Phillippe Starck sofa, like a red velvet lipstick kiss and Picasso posters, original lithographs I had found at a fair at the Armory on Park Avenue for next to nothing.

There were bits of me, memories of Africa in books and artifacts and piles of books on art and design. These were the visual clues to who I was. It was to try and plant some roots, rather than for anyone else's benefit.

There is no such thing as coincidence. People and events have fallen into my life with far too much intelligent design. The synchronicity of many situations has been too often and precise for me to believe that these were the workings of the hand of fate.

The exhibition after Deller's was a group of emerging downtown talent including Peter Ostrom whose perky collages full of childlike symbols and brave colours attracted an eclectic art crowd.

Bill O'Reilly was the leprechaun and rainmaker of the uptown art scene. He was one half of the Salander-O'Reilly Gallery and he came to see Walter Derby Bannard's and Tim Lefens' new paintings. These concoctions of acrylic paint that looked like the candy coated surface of the moon were by the heirs-apparent-in-paint of the art that Bill represented, which was the first generation of the New York Abstract Expressionists. Bill was encouraging and when I asked him what he thought of Peter's work, he smiled and snubbed it, cordially, as he murmured, "What's not to like?"

Clement Greenberg was the original exponent of the New York School. He rendered Jackson Pollock's dribbles of paint and Willem de Kooning's cruel cubist expressions of womanhood in words, making them easier to decipher. His book *Art and Culture* changed the way a generation of art-lovers viewed modern American painting. By transference, the greater art appreciating public began to buy, collect and participate in this emerging school of art.

Intuitive expressions of forms without structure were the symbols of the post-modern world. America had shrugged off the last vestiges of European restraint. The art of the time speaks volumes about America's steps towards her post-war, postcolonial identity. Clem was an art hero; his writings were the wheels, which allowed a moment of art history to get into gear.

The taxi pulled up to the apartment building in the Upper Westside where he lived. The mutual friend who set up the meeting, told me to take along a bottle of branded vodka. I had it in a brown paper bag in the tote bag I was carrying.

I had been nervous about what to wear, how to wear my hair and makeup so I'd settled on my uniform, an old blue and cream boucle Chanel suit. It set me up in my comfortable boundaries.

My relationship to art was still finding its sea legs on a journey I hadn't expected to undertake. It was visceral. I loved the curdled lavishness of paintings by Jules Olitsky, one of Bill's second-generation painters. The flat, coloured plains of Larry Poons' ordered canvases were cerebral. I was drawn to the rune-like mysticism of Ciao Fonseca's large canvases. They pulled me into his secret world, an old rich European heritage dotted with the spicy colours of Southern Italy and Moorish Spain. But what moved me the most were the windows into Mark Rothko's world of darkness and light. The ACA Gallery on East 57th Street held an exhibition of some Rothkos and that introduced me to his dark allure. I was seduced straight away. The paintings were crowded full of morbidity like fading spots of life, the paint seemed to slip into different shades.

There was a specially modified room at the Museum of Modern Art that held canvases the color of dried-blood on every wall, which had been designed for a chapel in Dallas. Limited natural light came in from a skylight in the ceiling and in there, looking at paintings became an act of worship. It was like learning to see colour for the first time.

Meeting Clem was the privilege of a front row seat, as the history of my life was being written. For once, I was participating and not being swept along, or being somewhere by default. I felt present.

He was a washed-out watercolour of the man he had been, he was almost eighty. A lifetime of hard drinking had left a spattering of liver spots and his eyes, which had been a deep, bright blue, had turned dark and hazel. They were watery, swimming.

Yet something of the younger man came out when he started to recount the stories of his trips to Montauk, where Lee Krasner and Jackson Pollock kept a makeshift summer studio. He seemed to shed forty years. He spoke about the power of art in that understated New York story apartment, with all the blinds drawn, so no light could come in. I wanted to see how he saw.

Clem belonged to another time, when the world was peopled with fearless men. Men who were giants in their art and artists who became like Gods and who broke the rules and smashed up the restricting boundaries of the old world. They made the art they wanted to feel and watching this old man tell it like it used to be, as he sat in his armchair in a camel-coloured cardigan with patches at the elbows, seeing him relive the passion that had burnt through his restrained writing placed me right in his narrative. He'd held the hand of history in his own and he had lead it down a path it might not have followed without him.

Clem continued to talk and drink. He asked me why I wanted to be an art dealer and the words slipped off my lips, although I hadn't known when I had arrived, a couple of hours ago.

"Because I think art can change us."

I must have said the right thing; he looked pleased and settled further into his armchair. He'd given me a couple of books to take away. On a scrap of foolscap he'd written, in his shaky pen, the titles of others he thought I should read. In the book by Ruskin, whole passages had been underlined in pencil, and were dotted with exclamation marks.

Dusk had fallen on the city outside, and it had blotted out the tiny horizontal hems of light that had formed on the window ledges. Clem had folded his hands in his lap and fallen asleep. I tried not to wake him, and to imprint this image of him in my mind, peaceful, resting, but the overflowing ashtray and the empty vodka bottle told a story of a real life. They defied my attempted imposition of an idealized, facsimile memory of him.

He had given me the tour of pictures, around the apartment, which he had received by artists who would later become both powerful and wealthy. They had been barters for a free lunch, or a thank you for a generous review. They had no money, but lived on fire.

I felt as if I'd witnessed the retelling of an important page of history, which changed not just the sleeping old man in front of me, with a silvery spool of drool falling from his chin, but everyone after him. And me. I stood, without a sound, I didn't want to break his dream and I put the sofa blanket gently over his chest and shoulders so he wouldn't feel cold. I left a low table lamp on, so its glow would greet him when he woke up. I had devoured and digested every word he had spoken, to hold it in my head.

Before he fell asleep he managed to extract a strict promise, that I would only show art I cared about and which I believed could change people. The secret of the outcome of every action, he told me, was in the intention. He promised to write a page long introduction of the Tim Lefens exhibition I had planned.

As I closed the door behind me, the paintings and sketches on the wall gathered closer and drew their protective shade over the sleeping giant who had incubated their creators and given them light.

There were only two times I broke my promise. Twice, I paid dearly. I never saw him again. He was too ill to come to the opening of Tim's exhibition and his greedy daughter put paid to any attempt to secure an introduction for the catalogue, we ended up using something he had written fifty years ago. The words still breathe life through dusty pages.

Truth Lies and In-between

Myles Pollin was a chameleon who changed his Zegna suits as often as his personality. He was Jewish, born to academic parents who were now both in their eighties. They had changed their name, in a swift act of social reconstruction from something offensively Polish. Myles had climbed the corporate ladder and was an associate attorney in the Mergers and Acquisitions department of a smart midtown law firm, Sidley and Austin.

We met through a vapid socialite who had dated him for a while and he crash-landed his way into my life with the force and strategy deployed to crush the Sepoy Mutiny some hundred years earlier. It was the full frontal attack: there were expensive dinners, vintage champagne and Oceania roses by the armful; they were my favourite, palest green singed with pink edges. He was a good ten tears older than I was and, unusually for a child of the New World, he had traveled beyond the shores of America. He played the piano beautifully on the baby grand in his apartment.

Myles had a cruel look about his mouth, his lips were too thin. They curled back, over his teeth when he smiled, in a reptilian way, so they almost disappeared. He was prematurely grey and prone to anxiety, people said he looked like a young Michael Douglas, I didn't see it. Kim had warned me he was well endowed, so it was more out of curiosity than attraction that the predictable first fuck happened at my loft. But he gained great pleasure from the pain his large member was causing. He enjoyed watching me flinch as he pounded me. He smiled in the half-light of my sexy bronze bedroom and said,

"Don't worry, you'll get used to it, they all do. You'll grow to like it." I didn't and no amount of lubricant eased the discomfort but I bore it. I thought I liked him.

He was different from the obviously beautiful boys around at the time. He didn't have the cool charm of Leigh Keno, the antique dealer, with his angular Brancusi face with fantasies of necrophilia. Leigh would get irritated if I moved while he performed but he liked to gnaw at the nape of my neck and I would burst out in a fit of giggles, unable to keep still.

But my discomfort didn't figure in Leigh's or Myles equation of pleasure. I was there to satisfy their perversion. With a lot of the men that preceded Myles, I made myself fit the shape in their hearts I thought that they wanted. Physically I fit their criteria, I was young and pretty. I was interesting and I had a creative and exciting job as an art dealer. People my own age seemed centuries behind me. An English school worth its fees instills a type of confidence and a sense of come-off-it-ness that can't be bought. Rob Stein describes it as a part of the British psyche. It's a sense of knowing and not believing, even when faced with irrefutable facts. It's about remaining skeptical and not taking anything too seriously. America, the New World was still fresh and impressionable.

Myles felt rootless, like I did, though he took great pains to hide it. He didn't quite cut the mustard. There's a caste of American families who inhabit a rarefied stratosphere in the hierarchy of the social order in Manhattan and thus, by default, the world. With old English names such as Whitney, Astor or Grace, they control, by being directly involved or by influence, the big banks, business, the judiciary and law firms. They are the Masters of the Universe.

The shifting sands of globalism tipped the playing field a little towards a truer meritocracy, but still but they had open access. They could buy the best education. If you weren't from that set, or you didn't go to the top Ivy League schools where you had formed the connections that would set you up for the rest of your life, if you didn't do the mandatory years with the Junior League with the same patriotic fervour with which an Israeli signs up for military service, you never entered the inner sanctum. You probably weren't aware that it existed. It wasn't even about entering they were just there.

There was an unspoken racial glass ceiling, which no one acknowledged but which left visible bruises on the widow's peaked Semitic foreheads of a lot cleverer Jews than Myles. The old guard, with scions who bore names like Thrush or Hayes or Scudder, was inherently classist and racist. They didn't bear the burden of shame, which was left by the aftermath of post-Empire, reconstruction gloom. The general liberal lie had taken on the patina of truth: America was this much-vaunted meritocracy.

The founding fathers had sworn never to give their allegiance to potentates or foreign princes, yet there was as much room for manoeuvre between the structures of class as there was space between the blue and white stripes of Old Glory. These old Americans revere tradition in the genetically disposed manner of all expatriates since Pliny, they brought along with them the rules and the strict social underpinnings of the society whose dust they thought they had shaken off their feet, when they left the place they no longer wanted to call home.

The Jewish community, "Our Crowd," had realized long ago that they couldn't be bona fide members of the waspy white world so they went about creating their own. They held benefits for synagogues, fundraising events to create new wings for existing hospitals or whole new institutions such as Beth Israel.

130

Museums like the MoMa or the Guggenheim, which had a long history of Jewish patronage and didn't care about the colour of their donors' money as long as it was green.

Indians were a rarer breed. There were posh, exotic women like Usha Singh and Bina Ramani who spoke with plummy English accents. Sonny Mehta was the reigning maharaja of Park Avenue and publishing and his pretty writing rani, Gita divided her time, as did most of them between India, England and America. These hybrid ambassadors of east and west who fluttered across landmasses were like colourful migrating birds with their retinues, oblivious to the dictates of seasons and cycles.

James Ivory and Ismail Merchant continued to churn out gorgeous sepia and rose-tinted versions of celluloid life from a bygone Britain, which perpetuated the belief that the little dotty island in the North Atlantic, that didn't have any relevance in a bigger world, was somehow still important.

It was easy to fall into place; on his way to becoming a partner at his hallowed law firm, I became the partner that Myles Pollin wanted. But it's impossible to live in the schizophrenic angst of the space in-between who I was and who I had to be with him. I used to steal money out of his wallet. He used to withdraw hundreds weekly from the cash machine, to feel safe. He didn't use it; he only went from work to home by subway or the firm's town car account. If we ate out, he charged it back to the firm, scavenging receipts, and found a way to make a corporate client pay for it. I never felt bad about stealing from him; it was payback in the transactional game of our relationship.

My relationship with Myles had deteriorated and he had made a complaint about me to the police, stating that I was intimidating him. I wasn't, I had moved out and I simply wanted my things out of his flat. I was arrested for harassing Myles. He turned out to be a lot more trouble than he was worth. By being deluded about himself, he held up an ever more unattainable illusion for me, to live up to.

Herb Minkel was the toothy bankruptcy-lawyer that bailed me out, when I was released by the police, on his recognizance. He'd been on the edges of our social circle but was a much more senior presence at his law firm; he had been a friend of Frank Battle, Myles' managing partner. We had met Herb at Shelby's a yuppy bar on the Eastside.

The loft gallery was successful. I kept art on consignment and sold artists I represented, some of who have gone on to become acclaimed talents internationally. Ironically Jeremy Deller's opening exhibition at the loft, which sold dismally, was my X-Factor moment. He went on to win the Turner Prize and is now part of the art cartel in London. He became a trustee of the Tate with the other art grandees. He confirms Art Buchwald's observation that if you attack the establishment long enough and hard enough, eventually they make you part of it.

131

It is expensive to keep a gallery going; most comparable galleries had big backers behind them, with the pretty girl as the front-person, and huge publicity firms behind the scenes to keep the machine churning. I was euphoric when Farah Damji Gallery had its first listing in the *New Yorker*, under galleries and exhibitions. In that tiny, uptight, paint-fume intoxicated world, with a three-line listing in six point type, scarcely legible, we had arrived.

The space on East 16th Street had been perfect for the kind of art I wanted to display but I was too mired in debt to try and salvage it. I thought a fresh start uptown would do the trick. I was too proud to disentangle myself from the financial spider's web by asking for help. The owner of the building had set his sights on my loft, which I had refurbished to a high standard to serve its purpose as a showcase and Maurice Leboz, a great swarthy lump of a man with faux French credentials and his smarmy sidekick, Robert Falcone, made my life hard.

I'd come home to find my locks had been super-glued shut, so I took to putting a hasp and a padlock over the lock plate, which was a pretty grim way to live, even by New York standards. It felt like coming home to a very grand prison. I had wound myself into quite a mess.

The county bailiffs at LeBoz's behest, impounded the property at the loft, including that of the artists who had it with me on trust, on consignment. I was desperate to get the art out, and didn't have the money to pay Maurice the $38 000 he said I owed him in back rent and lawyers' fees. I forged a banker's cheque. I went into my Citibank and withdrew a certified cheque for $38. Then I added three zeros to it. I thought it would buy me enough time to be able to restore the artwork to its rightful owners. A judge in the civil court had made an order that I should be allowed to take out my medication, my clothes and identification from the storage.

I had added the words "and personal possessions" although I am not sure what I hoped to achieve by that. Everything in there, not held on consignment, was my personal possession. I wanted to get out the paperwork which would show that the artwork didn't belong to me, so I could return it. Tim Lefens and Christian Brechneff, another artist I agreed to represent had got wind of the bailiffs clearing out the loft. Quire rightly, they were anxious to get their artwork back.

I lost all respect for the Manhattan DA's office after the first encounter, years ago, surrounding the death of Larry. Someone in their press department was leaking stories to the gossip columns about my predicament and when I hastily moved the location of the gallery to a townhouse in the East 60s, a rash of articles about me appeared on Page Six, Richard Johnson's gossip page in *The New York Post*.

I am as sick as my secrets, those things you don't know about me that you couldn't have read, here they are. I felt ashamed, that I had taken my eye off the ball and lost myself, yet again in a destructive relationship. I was sick of my own lack of judgment when it came to men.

When the cheque bounced, which of course it did, Maurice called the DA's office and I was arrested and indicted for uttering a forged instrument. The altered Judge's order came back as another indictment for tampering with a legal document. It's hard to feel dispassionate about what I did.

I was drinking and drugging again, Myles did cocaine recreationally. I was bored with the persona I was with him. I was pretending to be interested in which premier cuvée blanc grape best complimented a poultry dish, and which full-bodied red would bring out the flavour of a beef fillet.

I preferred the company of old friends, the Valium and cocaine I had started to take again, in order to zone out enough to be able to take being with Myles. I needed to numb myself against the chaos I had created. I am not passing the buck for my actions, I just didn't relate how the crime and illegal shenanigans were a way to numb out the pain and create chaos so I didn't have to look at the dystopia I was building around me.

Christian Brechneff was a fading talent who begged me for a show. In me, he said, he saw a young Mary Boone, the self proclaimed Queen of the Art Scene. He had not had an exhibition of paintings for a few years and I needed a show, which would sell. His paintings were pretty and commercial.

The relationship between a sexual young woman and a homosexual, middle-aged failed artist could only end in pain and tears. I thought I was tough enough to ensure that they wouldn't be mine. I used to read a lot of Capote but was oblivious to his personal life and they way he mauled his female friends. I should have looked more closely at Truman.

Christian wanted to reform me in some Galatea-like fantasy. I wore my hair long and loose. There was a certain look that Oribe, the café-society hairdresser had built his reputation on: the mane of just-got-out-of-bed hair that he nurtured for his clients radiated like a halo of wealthy sexuality. Long hair needs constant grooming and the late Eighties launched ranges of products specifically for growing hair by titans of trichology such as Charles Worthington.

It was all part of the illusion of excess and having time, the rarest and most expensive commodity. But Christian informed me that a woman approaching thirty (I was twenty-seven) shouldn't have hair below her shoulders, he told me what to wear, with whom I should be seen. He had acquired a socialite friend's mailing list to invite people to his opening. On that list was Terry Kistler.

There was something inherently insidious, even cancerous about the relationship between Christian and me. Every friendship is on some level transactional, whether it is based on love or sex or mutual interest, but being involved with Christian was soul destroying. His interest in make-up and clothes and men, which was such fun and great gossip to begin with, soon became annoying. A man can't know, no matter how much he fantasizes about what it feels like to be a woman, he can't know what it feels like inside her body. He can't see the world from her mind.

Straight men take on that challenge as part of the journey to know a woman, but for a gay man there's no end prize to make an effort try and understand her. The unnaturalness of the situation sets in and the rot starts to stink. The friendship became a burden I no longer wanted.

He didn't have any innate talent but he was well connected through his long-term boyfriend, Tim Lovejoy and he hyped himself up, all the time, to everyone he ever met. His art was soulless and mediocre. The barren snow-covered landscapes, or empty unpeopled beaches with rows of wooden posts, weren't art in the way Clem had spoken about, they were decoration.

Later, when I trusted my own eye a little better, when I had some experience in what I liked and what resonated, I understood Clem's warning. A landscape could be moving, like Andy Moses', he made heavily layered work; he mixed his own paints with pigment. They glowed, and were windows into his personal vision, which, as a dealer was one that I could believe in and sell.

I didn't actively court controversy or the media, but I didn't have the savvy to use them in a way that would be beneficial. I was a painfully private person, in spite of the polished and confident guise that I presented. That was my public face. I certainly didn't want the intense glare of the media spotlight on me because it highlighted the cracks I knew were there. I didn't need further dissection and examination to make me aware of them. I didn't want to face my own past or what had happened to that nine-year-old child, I wasn't ready; I was still a pre-fabricated creation, a reaction to my history.

Christian had a friend who was a hack at the *The New York Observer*, Jeffrey Hogreiffe. He had a high-pitched nasal voice and was determined that he was going to write the first in-depth piece on me, which Christian encouraged. It was meant to be a sycophantic character profile which would provide an easy backdrop for Christian's upcoming exhibition.

The situation with the DA's office festered for over three years and took tens of thousands of dollars to defend. Christian's was the first exhibition on East 65th Street and because he was nagging and persistent, he dragged in a few clients and it sold well. They bought because they thought they were buying a society painter's work, someone they could boast about to their mutual friends. They didn't buy out of passion or because they wanted to be a part of that vision. There are as many different reasons for wanting to own a piece of art as there are for selling one.

Victoire Bernbach was the wife of the advertising mogul, John Bernbach, who was then one of the B's in the advertising agency, BBD. She was Swiss-French and on her way to lunch with Christian she breezed in to look at the exhibition.

She liked one of the *Fallen Angels* paintings, elegies in burning red and gold acrylic paint. They depicted torsos in the ravages of AIDS but we didn't tell her that, it might have offended her Swiss sensibilities. They could pass for something less specific, perhaps a Dantesque cleansing hell-fire or something purgatorial. But she didn't like it enough to write out a cheque for it on the spot. His 40th birthday was coming up that same weekend, couldn't she try it at the house and see what he and their friends made of it *in situ*? She needed her choice to be validated.

The party went well, Victoire said she sent in a cheque, Christian, who lived beyond his means and hand-to-mouth was pleased he would soon collect half of the $13 000. Two weeks elapsed and Christian was desperate for his share of the loot. No cheque had arrived. I called John's office to ask them to stop payment on the first cheque, which we hadn't cashed or received and to send in another one, rather urgently. They sent a second cheque and I cashed it.

A gallery has huge running costs. Our rent was $6 000 a month, we had to keep up appearances and had fresh flowers weekly, and the space had to be spot painted after every show. Then there were the costs which came with each exhibition, printing catalogues and invitations, mailings and the cost of the opening party, the wine, the canapés, the bar staff. I have never been good at juggling finances but that time was sheer hell. I'd never had to learn or been taught how to balance a chequebook, and I was falling deeper and deeper into debt. The first cheque arrived, after the second one and I banked it as a temporary measure to keep the wolves from the doors.

Victoire Bernbach went to the DA's office to inform them she had paid me twice for the painting, she had been encouraged by Christian. He had been a strong support for me when Myles and I broke up. He and his lover, the technically accomplished painter, Tim Lovejoy had looked after me. They used to take me for weekends to Tim's sweet house in Connecticut.

Herb wanted nothing more to do with me. The second time I was arrested and arraigned, he told the kindly solicitor who was representing me that he couldn't help me. I found out later that the powerful privileged bankruptcy attorney might have been accused of tax evasion just around that time; naturally he wanted to stay well away from any heat or attention.

When Hogrieffe's article about me finally came out in *The New York Observer*, it was a mixture of fantasy and venomously narrated truth. I saw Christian's hand in it; he'd filled in gaps about my past, which he hadn't known about, things about my family, with nonsense about being related to a Middle Eastern royal family.

The cartoon image which accompanied it made me look like a hybrid of super-dealer Mary Boone and the singer Michael Jackson.

Friends in high places had tried to stop the publication, but eventually it came out, it was just delayed. It hurt only because Christian had instigated it and because it was a lot harder to ignore or brush off than a silly Page Six item. It was essentially an extended gossip piece, one-sided, salacious and unchecked. Christian had me firmly in his sights; he was out to destroy me because in his mind I had betrayed him. Nothing was out of bounds now and the gloves had come off, he ran and ran with the story until it had run out of steam.

It's taken me fifteen years of bad and good press to come to terms that the media will take out of a story what they want from it. All the damage and the pain that today's papers may cause, make a good liner for a puppy's pooping corner the next day. All the column inches we struggle to gain or to lose mean nothing. Journalists lie. At best, they distort the truth. So much of what has been written, printed and published has been hard.

Even with retractions and nodding apologies from hacks I've known, even after publications that have changed what I have written so it is no longer mine, and have delivered apologies with fresh bouquets from expensive florists, the truth remains that journalists aren't interested in the honour of the story. I have long ago stopped reading articles about me, and more recently, I have stopped caring.

I think about where it came from and what the intention behind it was (flog newspapers) and then along with all the other pieces that have been written, blogged or whatever, I can throw it into a bucket out of my life, where it loses its colour and representations of truth and lies. There it all mixes, out of sight out of mind, into one shapeless, senseless mass of gloomy mess.

There is no greater pleasure than rejecting someone's version of me and their words. They don't know who I am. How could they? At the time I was so lost, I didn't even know. What I did know was that I was not the sum total of my actions.

The Poet Speaks

In the words of the bard, (Heaney or Horace, you choose) shit happens. Horace said it in poetry and Seamus put the Blarney spin on it with his uncut brogue. He looked old when I met him, past his prime. But he was old. I was back on my bread and water diet of meaningless affairs with meaningless men.

There were few possible contenders with whom I could envisage embarking on a serious relationship, when William L. Kistler appeared in my life. The poet, banker, Renaissance man stepped into the three-storey townhouse on East 65th Street and carved out his space in my life. With a lot of encouragement and support I had become a proper art dealer.

Internally, I was drowning. He told me later he felt my soul slipping away and that was why he had hung onto me. Sometimes, during those dark days, Terry was my only link to sanity. I'd seen every creed and colour of therapist in New York, I was seeing one then, but as soon as it became uncomfortable, I stopped.

My core problem stemmed, as in the case of most classically fucked-up daughters, from that first relationship with my father. The problems with my mother have evolved from the way she lets herself be undermined and bullied by him. She is afraid to stand up to him so her anger comes out sideways, she screams, hits and rants a lot. She's too comfortable now, to leave the life and luxuries he provides. Any thoughts of Akbar are just a distant musing. I cannot approach my father with any sense of equanimity, he's impossible and if he doesn't like what he hears, he hangs up the phone or walks out of the room. My friends always found him charming, hip, approachable and there is that side to his personality but in each other, we see only the void of unfulfilled potential. I am the daughter that might have been, who sees the father she used to adore. But he couldn't protect me from the abuse, and so by his silence, became a party to it. They don't acknowledge it. I embody his worst failures. I never did become a lawyer and I didn't go back "home" wherever that was meant to be. My family's dynamic is more Bollywood filmy than epic Greek tragedy. So far we have let each other live.

My rage rotted me. It was corroding me from the inside out. My temper was like a genie which possessed me and fed off my fury.

I couldn't stop, it was like fuel or oxygen, stopping was worse than not breathing. It was a dance on hot coals in bare feet. But anger is addictive, the fuming adrenaline rush that explodes with passion is hard to abandon.

We, my dad and I, are still locked in an adolescent tug-of-war. He has never completely let me go and let me be. There have been endless times when I have been disinherited and disowned and in the same way I have told him he doesn't exist as a father to me. His is the voice of the nay-sayer who whispers in my ear as I lie sleeping and the lead in the chorus of "I told you so" when my life goes awry. I have needed chaos to sticky-tape over the cracks in me. It felt as though the more noise I could make, the less I would have to deal with the darkness within me. The more combustion and fireworks I could inflame, the further away I could push the shadow. I believed that it had to recede. All the while, the bigger I made the chaos, the harder and faster I danced, the longer and closer the shadow crept, towards me.

Terry was an oasis of calm. He started buying art from me straight away. I was twenty-seven and he was thirty years older although he was sprightly and healthy. It was always hard to write about him, now it is impossible, I feel as I am reaching back for the hand of someone who was never really there. Maybe he is the closest I have ever come to loving someone. It all started innocently enough, he took me out to dinner, nothing fancy or glamorous. I couldn't understand the fuss Christian was making, this was just going out to dinner with a client, but Christian was insistent that I should nurture the friendship, I should let it grow into something more.

He had been an important player in the art world and he was still well connected. Christian's eyes lit up at the thought of how much art Terry's investment fund could buy. I didn't see him as my personal piggy bank, not in the beginning. I had dated older men but certainly no one as old as Terry. To me, he was the funny, kind man with a light in his eyes. Life was written across his face in deep lines that gave away so much, but he was still handsome. I loved his face. He smiled a lot.

It started out as a clandestine courtship. He took me to lectures given by his friend Robert Thurman at the Open Centre on Spring Street. Thurman had recently published his translation of the *Tibetan Book of the Dead*. I learned about dying and the temporal nature of everything in our early days as a couple. He surreptitiously held my hand during Bob's effusive talks on Bardo. We started our romance in the dusk of inevitability, how could we last? Terry was a Buddhist and a big donor to Tibet House, The Dalai Lama's New York outpost.

Our first, serious date was to a fundraiser in a Manhattan theatre on the Upper West Side which wasn't far from where he lived. He had failed to mention that he had a girlfriend, a deeply neurotic Jewess, a modern Esther-artist. She took photographs of idylls, which she manipulated by painting and decorating them. He had had an argument with Susan who had heard about me.

But that night, the proper first date to announce our relationship to the world, I met other wealthy donors to the Tibetan cause and Natalie Merchant sang *a cappella*, without her ten thousand maniacs. He invited several of the artists I represented whose works he had acquired.

Terry was relaxed, he had done the wives-and-families cycle of his life. He came from an old German family which had settled in Oklahoma, his father had died when Terry was still young. He had left his widow, Ruth Hardman, to remarry young. He had been a hippy, of sorts, and had spent time around Jack Kerouac and the other Beat poets in San Francisco when he attended Berkeley. His first wife, Anne had produced a quick succession of blonde babies. When he left, he left them well provided for and the family moved to Santa Barbara, a rich, white enclave for old wrinklies south of Los Angeles. He lived daily, in the guilt of having left his children when they were so young. Two had ended up addicted to drugs, although one of them, his daughter, gave him a beautiful granddaughter called Elizabeth.

Maybe he thought he could redeem himself if he could save me. The second wife was also called Elizabeth, she was a poetess. The marriage didn't last long and when I met her, I liked her. She had left Terry for another woman but she was interesting and alive, which is more than could be said for the first Stepford wife, who sported too blonde hair and a carcinogenic suntan. She was brittle and raspy. Elizabeth treated Terry with the right amount of mockery and deference. She represented the strength a woman needed if she wasn't going to be swallowed up by Terry's larger-than-life, God-like presence. It was hard to maintain any small sense of self around him, he shone so bright, his charm, his gentleness and his wealth all conspired to make everyone around him fall in love with him.

Imagine a neon light, something trashy, designed by Donald Trump's principal decorator that flashes above the head of someone the first time you met them. It would indicate, by the intensity of its flashing, how important that person was going to be in your life. If we could, would we wrest with the hands of time and force them back so that we could avoid the people we wish we had never met? Or would we sigh, a little resigned to our destiny, and accept that the teacher comes when the student is ready for the lesson? Should we believe that we are never dealt with more than we can handle? Bill O'Reilly, when he was being polite about an artist's work would say with a wry smile, "What's not to like?"

Terry was a bit like that, there was nothing about him not to like. There wasn't a good enough reason not to go into it.

We were in the back of a yellow cab, having just seen a life-affirming film that moved us, *Bandit Queen,* the story of Phoolan Devi by Shekar Kapur. Terry was obsessed with India and all things oriental. He used to hold my hand and caress it through the length of the arty films we watched together, but the long, lingering kisses that night, on my hand, in the back of the yellow metal chariot, were different.

A strange tingling of longing started to stir in me and I stood on the edge of this feeling, daring myself to do something different. I had never been with a man this much older than I was and this blurring of the line between the known and taboo added to the adventure. The taxi snaked through Central Park to the exit on East 66th Street. As the taxi was filtering out of the park, he asked me in his husky voice if I wanted to spend the night with him. He ordered the cabbie to turn around and gave him the address of the smart building in which he lived on the Upper West Side.

His broad arms felt like a safe place then. I felt far removed from the chaos of my own world. The cabby's eyebrows shot up but he didn't say anything as he made a u-turn to cross the park again. We threaded our way towards the looming towers of the Dakota building. She remained always distant, in mourning for her favourite son who had been shot dead on her threshold. Every corner of New York City holds a million beginnings, ours started at the intersection of Columbus and 79th Street where his large bachelor pad was located, in a shiny new building.

He used to live in the same prestigious building as Jackie Onassis, a green-canopied, brass-pillared, quiet Fifth Avenue block. That was a lifetime ago, when he had been dating a young art impresario called Frances Beatty. They had been the centre of a convergence where downtown and uptown collided, they were the loves of each others' lives. I reminded him of his younger self. They lived out their romance through art and artist friends. She helped him put together a considerable collection and when it all went pear-shaped she went to work for Terry's doppelganger, Richard Feigen, the inscrutable dealer in Old Master Paintings.

The apartment was on the twenty-second floor with views over the park and the Westside. The view was the south of the city, from midtown to downtown. It offered itself up like a prayer and it felt as if anything was possible. Our hopes nestled in the city's cradling arms.

When I was a lot younger I used to have a dream. I was curled up, sleeping inside a giant palm. When I woke up from this, I would rise calm and fresh and as if there was a shape, something of God in my life. Those first few months with Terry offered the same sense of sanctuary.

In the beginning it was all honeymoon perfect. The first time, I was sober and nervous. He played Gorecki's Fifth Symphony, the *Symphony for Sorrowful Souls* on the stereo. It filtered into his bedroom which was painted deep red, like the inside of a womb.

Afterwards I slept peacefully beside him in his old wooden bed. I never expected to fall in so deep with him. Love is a terrible chase, when he was ready to renounce everything and make a new life with me, I wanted nothing of it, and when he spoke about having children together, of creating a new family which he wouldn't fail, I laughed out loud. I had other younger, charming men in life; they dared me and excited me. He was my gentle giant, he was my best friend and my lover who wrote beautiful poetry in the second bedroom of the apartment, which he had converted into a study.

Sometimes I would wake up in the middle of the night, and, disorientated by the blackness of the room and I'd reach across the bed for him, but there would be only space. Where he had lain, there was a question mark in the crumpled sheets. I wrapped myself in my Victoria's Secret silk robe that hung in his bathroom and padded sleepily out of the bedroom.

I would find him, sitting upright behind the desk, his face lit up and craggy by the light of the desk lamp. When he looked up his face would break into a smile.

"There you are!"

He was a serious poet, everything he did was with gravitas, whether it was buying millions of dollars of stocks and shares during his day job, or stretching his long muscular limbs in yoga asanas every morning and night. This is who he was to me, this contradiction of a man, shark-like and shrewd by day, who gave into his world of words by night. He carried on the long tradition of working poets, such as Pound and Eliot who had not been ground down by diurnal demands. He was like a stream, or that place where two rivers meet and go off in another direction.

He held his Buddhist beliefs devoutly but also dabbled in Sufism, through Rumi and other sub-continental mysticism through Tagore. His strict Protestant upbringing made him careful with money but generous in spirit. His was smorgasbord spirituality. He told me the first night he loved me in that mad, magical way that poets possess. His poems painted the colours of my dreams. He told me he had loved me from the moment he'd seen me.

The morning after, he made me sit down at a glass table overlooking the park, and watched me eat breakfast. All I wanted to do was leave, make a run for it back to the safety of the Upper East Side. He fed me homemade *kicheree* with honey, nuts, raisins, and bits of salmon at the bottom of the bowl. It tasted foul but I didn't say anything. I swallowed it, trying not to gag all the while. When I left I didn't know if I would see him again.

There was no last look back at the building. It had been a lovely evening, he was a nice guy. Nice was never enough.

"What's not to like?"

I curse you Bill O'Reilly for casting your infernal spell of doubt into pleasant situations. Love depends on timing. We grew closer and closer, we seemed to fill something missing in each other's lives. He encouraged a solo exhibition of the work by Bokhara Legendre, the much hyped and lifted San Franciscan socialite, who was an ageing Archimedea. Her flat acrylic paintings depicted amateurish smudges of paint, which were symbolic of various Buddhist and Hindu deities. The figures were distorted, demon-like and they loomed like smashed zephyrs, not really paintings, more smudges of paint sitting on canvas.

I wasn't so sure but he told me a solo show of Bobo's work would pull in a name check crowd. The secretary and chief lawyer of the Metropolitan Museum of Art, Ashton Hawkins, Bob and Nena Thurman, Josh Berman and uber-agent Lynn Nesbit attended the opening. They were amongst Bobo's three hundred closest friends who previewed the exhibition that night. She went on expensive and exotic trails for rich, bored people into places like Tibet and Bhutan. That was where she had met Terry. She wasn't a bad person; she's not malicious, just wasted. She was pure old Hollywood glamour, with her voice like an ashtray and sweet southern ancestors who had been something important in the Civil War. Andy Warhol hated her, I could see nothing to hate.

She was like a little bird, tiny, with unlikely auburn brown hair. Bobo looked good for a woman pushing sixty. She bought some of Christian's work, over the years and he was salivating at the possibility of getting his grubby paws on her exclusive address book which he thought he had first dibs at, after all Bobo had come through him.

Soon after Terry and I had started seeing each other, when he cleared the way and broke up with Susan, he went to a conference which was being held at the University of Dublin. Monks from Tibet were in the process of creating a sand mandala that depicted different Gods in their pantheon. They worked all day and pilgrims from all over the world would come to watch them in this active meditation. Terry had taken off on a cold February morning with slush melting in the streets. He left me with promises to call everyday and he did. Gradually he was installing himself as part of the furniture of my life; he would plan our evenings, with poetry or book readings, concerts at the Lincoln Centre. We might venture downtown into the psychedelic glow of the art-house Angelica cinema.

Terry acquired people and cultures, he had planned the trip to Dublin well before we met and I was glad for the space. The first thing I did, was go out to the neighbourhood boutiques on Madison Avenue; Cashmere Cashmere, where I bought a burnt orange sweatshirt jumper, and the Pucci emporium, where I bought a pair of leggings in pinks and greens. Bobo remarked how much younger I looked in my new get up, now Terry was out of town. Maybe a part of me was more subdued when he was around, it wasn't something I did deliberately.

He phoned me everyday but his voice sounded so distant and old. He was always enthusiastic to tell me what he had done in the fair city and I dutifully listened. Some of the poems he wrote about the beginning of our relationship found their way into his book, *Poems of the Known World*.

I went on preparing for Bobo's exhibition while he was away. Inevitably I met up with some of my old crowd. It was difficult, I couldn't see them as much as I used to but it was awkward being around them. They were the progeny of Park Avenue families. My new, old boyfriend had known most of their parents in another life. I had completed the customary social initiations required of me. I lent my name to invitations, along with lots of other bold-face gossip column fixtures, for Eurotrash parties so Marc Biron and Michael Ault could promote trendy venues. There was a hardcore Brit brigade in New York City. There was Simon, my wanker-banker neighbour downstairs on East 16th Street whose unsuspecting English girlfriend came over once weekend a month oblivious to the sexual shenanigans that went on while she was not there.

Later the London bad boys, the downtown city-slickers in their handmade Oswald Boateng suits with flashy silk linings came to roost. These were my favourite boys, they were like proud peacocks in mating season. If I had been born a man I would have been just like them.

Clive and Garry were two London traders, barrow boys who had made it big in New York with their successful bi-continental company. We met through Alessandro Alessandri, who was another lost first-worlder who had come to America to find himself on the new frontier.

Clive was handsome and dangerous. He had bought a new build house on the wrong side of Southampton, not too far from Terry's rambling barn conversion, which had been shipped from Vermont to the potato country of Sagaponack. Clive bought art from me.

He was slightly olive-skinned and had big, brown eyes. He was a modern Gatsby, an orchestrator and an observer; he held lavish parties at his "new" house, during which he would sit back and watch. He registered everything, who was talking to whom, and who wasn't. Coupled with other illicit substances, the champagne and Pimms flowing, social interaction was made easy with copious lubrication.

They threw a bachelor party for a friend who was getting married. They had started at a restaurant and I met Clive and his gang at a restaurant downtown, to catch up and have a drink. Terry was away on business but was tolerant of Clive, he was sure there was something going on between us but there never was. I had confessed to a few fumbled kisses, one night when Clive had dropped me off in a taxi, but that was before I had started to see Terry seriously and when the spectre of Susan still loomed. That night, we ended up at someone's flat, drunk and cocaine-glazed. Clive dared me to stay. They had invited some call girls to service the soon-to-be-married friend and he said that it might be a laugh.

Clive looked such the English gent, he played the part to perfection but sometimes the foul language that came out of his mouth in his London accent could turn the air indigo blue.

He was in fine fettle that night. He dared me to push myself to live large, like he did. He liked Terry, but he let me know that we bemused him, and he thought the relationship was a farce. He teased me about how I was living out a Jocasta complex. In his eyes, Terry was the easy choice – he didn't challenge me. I thought he was wrong.

Clive's world, in which he worked and played ruthlessly, was dark, sweet and irresistible. We were friends who didn't fuck, but the thought of him with someone else was repulsive and compelling, even if he was paying for her time. He had no idea about my Bel Air days. That wasn't the issue; he could have had any one of a dozen women there, in minutes, ready to sleep with him for the unspoken promise of all he offered. I wanted to fuck him, he was so much like me. It would be the closest I could come to making love to myself. I thought if I watched him, I might be healed of the urge. How great could it be? The idea and anticipation of sex with someone often proves better than the actual act of grinding groins.

Our worlds were littered with people who wanted something from us. From me, they wanted exhibitions, encouragement, art sales, help with acquiring good young artists for their noteworthy or budding collections. Everyone wanted a piece of me. From Clive they wanted whatever he could buy for them. Foolishly for them, they wanted him to fall in love and stay faithful to them. We both knew restriction, we had to: our currency was in holding something back of ourselves.

He was polished and sophisticated. I had watched countless women fall under his charming spell as he hunted. He was a lesson in modern anthropology, like a young Rake. He liked beauty, he liked surrounding himself with the most beautiful possibility and his women were the same. They were colt-limbed and perfect, like kewpie dolls. They bared teeth like the Fisher King's pearls but they were accoutrements to his image in the same way his Tateossian cufflinks added some flash to his wrists, or the Hermès cashmere and wool horse blanket artfully thrown over the kudu leather sofa in his den gave him instant class. All of it was inconsequential.

Terry's Buddhism intrigued Clive. He was, although he protested otherwise, naturally spiritual.

Although he lived for the next reckless experience on the edges of Alphabet City, which had been planned and plotted from the safety of his penthouse in Trump Tower, he could fly away on a whim. He would jet off for a weekend in London because he missed the taste of a proper English brew. But he craved something else, something bigger than all of this. I encouraged him to paint, almost as a joke and bought him a set of acrylics and some brushes. He was a good friend to me. He was honest and saw through the bullshit I projected, perhaps he felt something of it in himself.

I saw, through men I have known like him, that sex is about power. It's the thrill of the chase and essentially, stripped away of all the romance and flowers and candlelit dinners, it's the exchange of a commodity just like Robert Wylde's copper futures or Terry's stock trades. It's all wasted motion in pursuit of the final prize. The night at that flat downtown reinforced what I already knew about men and women. But still, a part of me wanted to hang onto the fantasy that what Terry and I shared was sacred, different and somehow above the messiness of the way that other people loved.

When the prostitutes arrived, he asked me which one I thought was the prettiest, that I should pick her out for him. They were all pretty and interchangeable. He asked if I wanted to watch and if I was up to it. He wouldn't do it, if I didn't want him to. I didn't want him to, but I had no intention of stopping him. Clive was my friend and I had no proprietary claim on him. I felt challenged, as if I should stop him and offer myself up, but I wouldn't. I cared about Terry and faithfulness was still important.

The eroticism that comes of watching a couple have sex, live, is strange and disconnected. It's pornographic but watching him didn't elicit the jealousy or discomfort I had anticipated. It was transactional, I thought as I was watching her head bob up and down between his legs.

His hands were tangled in her long hair as they guided her head, pulling and pushing to the rhythm he needed. It was like watching a film, but I already knew how it ended. After he satisfied himself, he lit a cigarette, threw the girl another hundred-dollar bill from his wallet and told her to go next door and take care of his friend.

We both watched as she slinked off in her lacy underwear, which she hadn't removed and I noticed the tension where the garter pulled at her stocking. Just a scrap of frilly elastic held up her sheer second skin. We teetered for a moment, as if we were balanced on the point of her stiletto, both of us – we had crossed a line and couldn't go back. Neither said anything for a while.

"So, what are you thinking?" His voice sounded curdled and thick, and he was lying on the bed with a towel draped around his waist, as if he was a great athlete who had run a long race.

I tried to stay deadpan but the scent of his sex and her perfume that filled the room, was stifling.

"I don't think anything my darling." My voice was slow and steady and I dared him silently to meet my eyes. When he did, they were blank. He pushed himself; in the same way that he pushed me, to the outer edges of ourselves. This sexual encounter had been a purchase, a stress reliever, in the way another man might use Radox in his bath. Where others might meditate, Clive would copulate.

It was my own fault for putting myself there, no one forced me to stay but I might as well have watched him masturbate. The woman's mouth was a sperm receptacle.

She dutifully swallowed his seed whereas a non-paid for girlfriend might pull away, or spit it out. This isn't the neo-feminist in me come out to play, no one had forced her to be there either, it had all been politely arranged over the telephone in the same way his secretary would have booked his weekly appointment for a trim at Bumble and Bumble.

This was the mean city, even the streets were for sale. The first summer we were together, Terry took me to his house by the beach, every weekend, a great barn with a double height sitting room. The space that we found for ourselves there, helped to shut out the ridiculousness and the reality of the situation. I could pretend, when we went for long bicycle rides that he wasn't really thirty years older than me.

We walked along the deserted Sagaponack beach, far from the summer tans and corrected smiles of Gin Lane. We were miles from these other lives of expectations perfected. The house was broody, too big. We slept blissfully upstairs, in his bedroom. It was minimally furnished, Shaker in style. An old colourful Tibetan textile hung over the bed and I felt a bit like it must have; an expensive trinket which bore testament to his exotic tastes. We were more things that could bask in his light.

His presence affected me, he was tall and slim and softly spoken but when he lost his temper, which was rarely, his voice boomed and made the timber frame of the house shake. There was a pool in the back garden, black and cool because it was lined with quarry slate and I would swim laps and look over the box hedges at the neighbouring potato fields. This is how I wasted my life. He shut himself off and wrote and rewrote.

Every time I passed them, the silver olive trees that lined the driveway up to the house would tremble and sigh. He needed a lot of time with his work, if we stayed out on a Sunday evening, he would be up and on the phone, calling in his trades at seven in the morning on Monday. He didn't keep photos of anyone in his family, around the house, but lots of art by friends from his past. Susan's strange pseudo-paintings cluttered the study and I made him move the one in the bedroom downstairs.

Although it was a big house, there was a paucity of air. He had turned the bedroom next to his study, over to me to use as a den, this was my space. I kept a step machine and an architect's drawing board in it. Neither was used much. I played the part. We had a few close friends we would see over the weekends, for a movie in East Hampton, or dinner at Match Box or in Water Mill.

Artist friends came to stay and paint and Terry was always the perfect host. He was affable, generous and funny. I cooked using an Italian cookbook that Detroy Kistner (the only good thing that came out of the brief encounter with Leigh Keno), had given me. I was playing wife while I followed meticulously thrown together recipes by a Tuscan princess for the perfect saffron risotto or a spring leg of lamb, with garlic and rosemary sprigs cooking in its juices. I thought I enjoyed the narrow domesticity our lives together gave us. It was a cushy escape from my own.

There was another side to Clive, far removed from the anaesthetized and searching soul he presented. I went over to his house to help him hang a Doug Rice painting he had bought from me. It consisted of forty-two, five-inch square panels. Clive was a perfectionist and I had been up and down the ladder more than a few times that morning. For reasons known only to the collector, only I could hang this particular installation, which Doug had called *Forty Second Street*. When we had finished hanging the last square, on the wall of the double height stairway that gave out onto the sitting room, he helped me climb down from the scaffolding his handyman had installed for the task that morning.

He handed me a glass of Pimms. He led me, gently, by the elbow to the pool outside. He wanted some advice on patio furniture. I sat down and swung myself so I perched on the low, brick wall that bordered the perimeter of the decked area. I could feel the sun-warmed bricks on the backs of my thighs. My feet were swinging, some ten inches above the ground. They were liberated from the strappy Chanel slave sandals I was wearing.

Clive was as brown as a nutmeg, he was just back from the Caribbean and his hair was longer than usual and sun streaked, it was glinting gold where the light was trapped in it. He was doing his impossibly Englishman caricature, in a white, light linen shirt which he wore undone at the cuff, rolled a few turns upwards. I could see the muscles in his forearms straining. His light khaki, cotton drill trousers, the carefully chosen alligator skin belt and sandals finished the look. It had been hot and hard work getting the six rows of seven paintings to sit perfectly, at the right height and I was thirsty.

He came over and stood close. Gently he shifted my knees apart and made a space where he could stand. I tried to sit back on the wall but it was too narrow. I had to get back to Sagaponack, we had people coming for dinner, but he leaned forward and he kissed me. He tasted of summer and gin and I kissed him back. His hands held me around my waist to steady me.

I wonder what might have happened next if things had been different and if I had been alone with him. Terry had insisted on coming, he wanted to see Clive's new house. He had been engrossed in conversation with a pretty thing Clive had invited out for the weekend. I heard his voice from inside the house,

"Far, are you there? We better get going, baby."

"The old man's calling you. Tell him to piss off." He stepped away a little but still held onto me.

"What are we doing, Clive, I better go…"

"We are kissing, you idiot."

"I know, but I can't. I better go, really."

"Stay with me." His eyes begged the question his voice uttered and I wanted to.

"You know I can't. I'm sorry."

I pulled myself down, feet firmly once again on the stone paving; the large white parasols that were littered like giant mushrooms all over the deck had obscured us. They pandered to Clive's fear of being sunburned. Like most mad dogs and Englishmen, he chased the sun and then suffered for it.

"I'm here, Terry, Just a minute." I was sitting on the ground doing up my sandals which were complicated contraptions of soft leather straps.

"Come with me." Clive said. I didn't look up. "Fuck you. Wait here a minute then. I'll be back."

Clive crossed the path towards the pool house, which we had been talking about converting into a bar.

"Clive I don't have time for this right now, my darling. I said I would think about it this week, I've called for brochures, we'll catch up next weekend…"

He was out of earshot. He emerged a few moments later with a navy blue square under his arm. It had bright brushes of pink and turquoise and yellow, it looked like a painting of a bird in flight. He handed it to me, his arm straight out, like a little boy, proudly handing over his homework. I was stunned.

"It's beautiful; you shouldn't buy me things Clive…" "I didn't buy it, I painted it. For you." He took it from my hands and showed me the back of it where he had written in his round, boyish writing:

"For Farah with love and gratitude for the inspiration and the encouragement."

I was aware of Terry's gaze, his wrinkly blue eyes looking at us some thirty feet away. He couldn't have heard what was being said but the intimacy between us was unmissable. Clive had me trapped in his inner world, this gentleness was what I thought I had glimpsed before, but I wasn't sure it was real. He'd told me he had started to paint and I had encouraged him. Too many people around us had burned bright and then extinguished like super novas. I said nothing.

I hugged him and kissed his cheek, I inhaled the smell of the Penhaligon scent he wore. That scent can still draw me back to that Southampton summer afternoon, one passing waft of it, and I am back in Clive's arms and his Gatsby world. I whispered thank you in his ear, I had to stand on tiptoes to reach him and I felt his arms around me, almost carrying me off the ground, I didn't care any longer what Terry saw. I wanted to treasure this side of the man I loved. We let each other go. I turned and walked towards Terry.

For a moment, I was aware of the love of two men, both very different. They were both watching me. One was pouring his desire into me and the other coolly observing, safe in the knowledge that I would always come back to him as I approached him, coming closer with every step.

Every second of a person's life is a choice. I wondered, as I took another step whether I was making an irrevocable decision, and whether it was the right one. Terry drove on the way home to Sagaponack. Where we lived had become an elite artists' enclave, we were worlds away from Clive's flashy lifestyle. Our neighbours were the artist Robert Dash with his Madoo, the beautiful living artwork of his garden and Freddy Plimpton, George's first wife.

Terry declared Clive's house ugly, Clive was new money, and Terry despised the ostentatious show of wealth. I wasn't drawn to Clive's houses or the fleet of European sports cars that were lined in phallic salute as we drove down the gravel drive; I craved the life that surged from him.

Although Terry looked like he could have been in his late forties and he was in good shape for a man of his age, I still felt like I was walking into dusk falling. As much as I wanted to deny and disbelieve it, he was settling into his twilight years. Whether it was Clive or what he represented, or whether it was an inevitable sadness that I felt because I knew I was closing the door on a lot of years of my life I still had to live, I don't know.

Then, settling down with Terry seemed tragic, inevitable. We had terrible fights, which I usually initiated. I felt angry and abandoned; the adolescent in me was reliving all the past pains that had been inflicted on her. He fed my feelings of constant rejection that reminded me I could never be enough. But it's difficult to conduct a relationship, or an argument, from behind a closed door with the writer barricaded behind words and volumes.

I found out I was pregnant, we had gone to Santa Barbara for Christmas and a short hike had left me breathless. He had tears in his eyes when I told him. He talked to me about how our child might look, but I didn't want to know. I didn't want a child. When we got back to New York, we attended a benefit at Nell's. I was hormonal and having violent mood swings although I was only a few weeks pregnant. I wore my new black velvet DKNY long dress with spaghetti straps and a slit up the side. It was still chilly in New York and a chiffon Mizrahi silk stole, six feet of sheer fabric, was wound around my shoulders.

I had given a painting to be auctioned at the benefit, I can't remember the details of it now but there had been some altercation with an idiot about the painting and Terry was trying to calm me. Terry had followed me into the basement of the club. I was angry and tired, more from being pregnant than what had happened to cause the ruckus. I didn't want to be pacified, I wanted to rage. He was always stifling me, I felt him, gently holding my arms but it felt like a restraint. It was the wrong thing to do and he should have walked away. I reacted violently, pulling my arms away, more forcefully than I had intended.

The sound of the fabric ripping made us both stand still. He held a piece of my gauzy scarf in his hand and he looked shocked. I tore the rest of it from my shoulders and threw it at him.

It landed in a soft heap by his feet and I ran up the stairs. He looked up at me, bewildered, holding the remains of what left behind of me in his fingers. It was cold outside, my shoulders felt the wind first. I stopped a yellow cab and between sobs, told him where I wanted to go. Home.

The moment the stole unravelled, as the fine fibres of silk were exposed, so the story of our love began to come apart. Things were never the same after that, although we both tried. Of course he said he would support me, whatever I chose to do but I knew he was clearing a space in his life for the great American novel he had always wanted to write. He had published several successful collections of poetry and I knew he didn't do family man particularly well.

The pitter-patter of tiny feet would be tormenting for him. I didn't want that for my child, I knew what absence felt like and I had promised myself I wouldn't recreate that hole in my own children. I had an abortion. He had a vasectomy and made sure I went for the three-monthly contraceptive injections. Just in case.

We tiptoed around each other's fears and desires. When we made love, we did so with Gorecki or George Harrison's *Hare Krishna* playing. We thought that the notes in the music that had joined us initially could bring us back together. When that failed, there were the poems.

Pictures of the Dying

There are some artists who shake the earth as they walk on it. They consume life as they live it with the greed of a starving child and then they regurgitate it in their work. These are the ones who raise the dust. That is their proof that they are the living.

Gods and angels make regular appearances in my life. I've lived like a lost butterfly that flutters this way and that, seeking warmth and nourishment. I sought shelter from the sun that burnt my wings, yet I craved her warmth. I wanted the light. Other people lent me their strength and their eyes when I was too weak or too blind to see where I was going.

Madame Blavatsky predicted that the last twenty something years of the millennium would bring about a mass awakening of the conscious, it was the dawning of the Age of Aquarius. She predicted the rebirth of the final Buddha, Maitreia. As we crept towards the middle of the 90s, a fin-de-siècle angst and a midnight sense of doom had begun to settle in. Perhaps it was the realization that the Era of Excessomania was going to end that made that particular winter particularly grim.

I had gone to Nairobi, land of my childhood holidays to defrost. I sought out the comfort of my kindly father-figure in Mohammed, Gulshan's light-eyed husband. He embodied the qualities of the father I didn't have, he treated me like his own daughter. He was everything my dad could have been, if he didn't have the disease and the self-loathing. I was back in New York in mid-January with the image of the love in his eyes still shining at me, when we said goodbye at Jomo Kenyatta International.

I'd locked myself out of the house in East 65th Street and I was waiting at Nello's on Madison for the friend who held a set of my keys to make his way uptown and let me in. Nello was a moon-faced, kindly Yugoslavian. The restaurant was still in its early days and no one was sure if it would catch on, but his die-hard closest few hundred friends visited regularly and I was one of them, it was exactly half a block from where I lived.

The food became more edible as the weeks progressed. I took a seat at the bar with my Louis Vuitton suitcase on the floor by my feet. I was having a drink, and chatting to the friendly barman. There were only a few people about, back from wherever they had fled for the cold snap of Christmas, so the restaurant was deserted.

He wore torn jeans, but not the artfully ripped Rock and Republic denim that fashionistas sling off their snaky hips. His were ripped with age and wear and tear, old jeans. They were covered in spatters of what looked like coffee, dried blood and ink stains making spidery old runes up and down his faded blue leg.

He sat at the other end of the bar, under a halogen halo; its neon blue spectrum flickered at the edges of his blonde head, making it appear that the edges of his curls were alight. He wore a weathered face, Peter Beard was fifty-seven, his voiced boomed when he laughed and he filled out the whole room. He was larger than life.

Peter is a necromancer, he's been described as a lot of things, some not pleasant but it is impossible not to fall in love with him. He was deep in the final stages of the kill, of this skinny prey. He promised modeling pictures to the young blonde cokehead that was hanging onto his every word, caught in his gaze.

Peter had been a part of my Africa. It was strange to bump into him; hours after I had come off a plane from Nairobi, I'd met him there years earlier. It was incongruent to see him here, in the northern hemisphere with his face made angular by down lights. He should have been bronze-torsoed, muscular and back in his element at Hog Ranch, the fertile swathe of land he owned outside Karen.

He dazzled outside the gloomy stare of Najma. She is his much younger Asian wife, who was always there somewhere in the horizon, hanging on like a patient camel. Peter was our Dionysus. To know him was like putting yourself, voluntarily, through electric shock therapy, daily. The pain and the inevitable drama that he brought with all his adventures and misadventures are soon forgotten and I willingly took up my front row invitation-only seat in his life, for a short while. He saw me, staring at him, fascinated and he introduced me to the girl with the googly eyes and explained his latest project, Living Art, and he called it.

It was every red-blooded male's brown on white fantasy, gazelle-like beauties in the mud, having sexually charged play fights with each other at Hog Ranch. He cackled as he described the scene, circling his prey again, savouring the life in her eyes for a final second. He would soon consume that light.

Peter has always introduced me as "Farah, my friend from Kenya." He survived as a remittance chum with handouts from his wealthy, waspy family, which had inherited old steel and railway construction money. He also relied heavily on friends and the kindness of strangers who came under his spell. There were many.

153

There's much mythology about him which he watches as it spins, seemingly with a life of its own, like the wicked elf in Rapunzel, he knows how to create gold, to further the unknowingness about him. He cultivated his image as the archetypal bad boy. Chuck Pfieffer and the others who tried to do the barefoot in leather loafers and navy blazers were one-dimensional facsimiles compared to Peter. They didn't quite get his louche chic.

The creation story, the one on which he discovered Somalian-born beauty Iman in the bush, was pure fabrication. He brought her to Eileen Ford, the high priestess of the modeling world and omitted the detail concerning the Nubian goat-herd was really the daughter of a diplomat and attended Nairobi University. She was on the edges of the ex-pat crowd, at the centre of which was our PB. The stories that followed him about courting other iconic beauties of the 70s such as Lee Radziwill and Bianca Jagger furthered his reputation as the playboy-paparazzo, who became a celebrity.

My friend arrived with my keys and I kissed Peter. We said bye, or what passes for it in New York, a slang goodbye which is an air kiss on either side of the face, he held my shoulder in his gnarly hand as he planted a proper kiss, that touched the skin on my cheek. The blonde was as malleable as wet sand by now, I wondered if I would see her again.

Life at Farah Damji Gallery was precarious. I was digging a deeper hole of debt and although we were doing well, it was a bottomless pit of money I didn't have. Terry was supportive, he would buy something from each show and he helped financially, but I didn't like asking him for help. There were strings attached to every act of kindness.

He got a buzz from helping with the installations, once he helped to paint the walls when we couldn't get a painter in on short notice. He enjoyed visiting artists' lofts with me and the fresh scent of new paint transported him back thirty years he'd wasted gathering power and prestige. Terry looked to me to regain some of his lost innocence but I didn't have any to share with him.

Christian and his cohorts were making my public life difficult. I had a profile; I was on a couple of junior committees that helped to fund raise for the museums. I was there by invitation, not because I could grease the hinges of access by paying large donations to ease my way. Christian was the consummate gossip, he and Myles had spent a lot of time together, Myles' finer feminine sensitivities resonated with Christian's fake polish and worldliness. Christian had been an important part of the relationship with Myles. Terry couldn't stand him, he saw through him straight away and kept him at arm's length. Besides, Jane Stubbs, the dealer who sold Tim Lovejoy's work, had been part of Terry's old social set, the ones he'd fled when he ran for cover on the Upper West Side. He didn't want to go back there.

154

Amanda Ursell was a Jewish Park Avenue Princess and Melanie Seymour was the opposite, she was a friend of Clive. They both managed the press relations for the gallery. The scion of Howard Rubenstein's PR institution, Richard Rubenstein, whose girth matched his generosity and enthusiasm, was a close friend and helped out too. I had moved premises again, this time because our absent landlord, who lived in Aspen most of the year didn't think that he should make necessary repairs.

Carolina and Ronaldo Herrera rented the third and fourth floors of the same house. Bill, the errant landlord, was unreachable; I was responsible for tens of thousands of dollars of other people's paintings. The building had leaking pipes and I refused to pay anymore rent until they were fixed and he was in no hurry to fix them so we played chicken to see who would blink first.

He did and in that second I decided to move. We owed him money that I withheld because I knew I might need it if we had to leave. We found a similar space on the same block as Frank Campbell, the fancy undertakers in the low 80s, between Madison and Fifth Avenues.

Bianca Jagger is a lot smaller than I had imagined she might be. It was four o'clock in the afternoon, the day of Peter's opening, at the new Downtown/ Uptown Gallery which was what I had renamed the space. It was a tribute to Peggy Guggenheim's Downtown Gallery. She was the first dealer to exploit the potential for bringing the vibrant downtown art scene to the wealthy streets of the Upper Eastside.

Peter hadn't had a New York exhibition since the 70s and I needed something big and brassy to detract from the increasingly awful publicity I was attracting. We agreed on a limited edition of six issues of seven of his best-known pictures. These were reproduced from the original negatives and printed in black and white onto paper using a colour process, so they had a sepia tone. They were then heat mounted onto canvas, which gave them a textured, painterly effect. We also picked out some pictures that we could have produced as platinum prints and C-Prints, which he would collage onto, in his trademark style. As they sold, he signed them off with a flourish of his faithful fountain pen.

Peter loves scandals. Najma was fed up with the endlessly public indiscretions and that he had installed himself with Rekha, his long-term Danish girlfriend, in Andy Moses' loft downtown. She was suing him for divorce and custody of their darling Zara, Peter's daughter. It was becoming progressively uglier. What does a woman like Najma expect when she marries a man like Peter? She goes into it a fool if she thinks she can change his ways. I received a call from someone on her side asking if I would testify for her, stating what everyone knew to be true, that Peter was unstable and promiscuous. I cared about him and as exasperating and annoying as he could be, there was no way I could say a word against him. Part of me might have been scared of him, I had watched

155

the way he devoured people who had crossed him, in reality or in his own mind, like a hungry cannibal.

Najma Khannum was the daughter of a Nairobi High Court Judge. She came from respectable stock and she thought she would exact her revenge for what she perceived to be Peter's betrayal. Evil lies were circulated about how he had molested Zara.

Peter B was staunchly anti-establishment. But the establishment respected him for it. He wore falling-apart Jesus sandals that exposed his big toes and feet that looked healthier when they were sole to sole with the red earth of his beloved Hog Ranch. He'd gone native years ago. He was indeed an encyclopedia of perfidy; there aren't enough words in Roget's Thesaurus to describe his philandering, but that was how he had decided to live.

She knew what she was getting into. The darkness in him, the burden of self-destruction, was what allowed the art he created. There was nothing else like it. To want to try and control Peter was like splitting an atom and not expecting the explosion. She wanted Peter to become a domesticated pet, from the wild beast that he was. He would never become benign, like the tranquillized animals in the zoo that he railed loudly against.

It was hard to feel any sympathy for Najma, the wronged wife. She was much younger and attractive but she was still a long way from beautiful. She had black, straight hair and hooded, close-set Arabian eyes. Her Pashtun pointy nose and her complexion the colour of light coffee were insufficient guarantors, in the modeling career she tried to pursue.

She was slim and tall and clothes hung well off her rake-like bones and she had followed Peter expecting his luminary New York connections to open the doors in the cloistered world of fashion. She was bitter and disappointed when the agencies didn't beat a path to Giorgio St Angelo's door, where she was staying. Najma was light years away from recreating the personality of "Peebs" as she insisted on calling him in her whiny, little girly way. Most of us accept we just don't understand him. We wouldn't dream of trying to change him.

My local neighbourhood butcher on Madison Avenue had fulfilled some strange requests in all the time he had been purveying meat to the city's wealthiest residents, but my request for cows' blood, in pint bottles, managed to raise a quizzical brow. He pretended to be unfazed, as he wrote the order down in a little spiral notebook and tore my copy out of it. It was for the adornment of the canvas prints.

Peter Beard had taken up with an oversized, hyper-inflated, investment banker called Peter Tunney, who was financing his life and the court case against Najma.

He had a large downtown gallery called The Time is Always Now. Perhaps he named it that so it could serve as a hopeful antidote to the permanent state of procrastination in which our shared Peter thrived.

Watching the process of Peter creating art was like watching a painting unfold. He scavenged detritus from his life and that of those around him, and he collaged them with tabloid headlines with matchbooks from downtown restaurants. Then he would write in his distinctive handwriting in ink the colour of dried blood, passages from Pliny or *Out of Africa,* chilling ancient and contemporary prophesies.

Thus, the collages would build up, on an original print, and that's how they have become part of the history of the depiction of fashion and conservation. He was in the midst of a revival, his art had come around again, these snapshots of moments that are daubed with blood, spit, ink and rubbish represent a life in art. He decided to do an Yves Klein on one of the canvas prints, but not with paint and nubile young women, because Peter is never derivative. He daubed himself with the recently acquired cow's blood and lay down on the giant print so a corpse-like bloody image was printed on the top frame of the picture of two cheetahs in the Taru desert. He floats, a spectre of him, in that empty desert sky. That afternoon, in the basement of The Time is Always Now was another of those art history moments. The stink of fetid blood, of Peter's sweat, are all infused within that image.

It's part of the tacit ritual that Peter B comes with a retinue of hangers on and hopefuls, people who hoped he might graze their little lives with some of his gold-dust. Rekha, much younger, perky, had been working at the Karen Blixen Museum in Denmark.

Karen Blixen had been his introduction to the Old Africa he knew. His portrait of her, old and syphilitic, shows a woman whom Africa destroyed, her dreams, her love, her coffee farm, she lost everything and still she couldn't help herself, she loved her Africa. She wrote in her book, that she knew Africa, because we do, those of us who have been bitten by her, it infects our souls.

"But what," she wrote, "does Africa know of me?"

Peter dealt with Africa the same way other ex-pat conservatives dispense their own brand of neo-imperialism. He believed in culling and his stark book *The End of the Game,* which depicted the mass elephant graveyards in Tsavo is both a testament and an indictment of the country he loved. It is also a bold accusation by a *farang,* about the mess that the Kenya Parks Authority was in at the time. He paid short shrift to the idea of the noble African, although he had taken on some of Blixen's old retainers at Hog Ranch, which was an act of philanthropy, not necessity. Peter believed that Africa couldn't work if it was left to the Africans.

Thirty years later his diabolical prophecy has proven true. TIA, he used to say. This is Africa. It is the sad mantra of all of us who have lived there for any length of time. Peter didn't Disneyfy Africa in his portrayal of her, he showed her loss and the melancholy that makes her, and in this way he drew from her beauty and captured her impermanence. This is life on the edge of death in a frozen frame. Terry bought that bloodstained picture.

He also bought a picture of Connie Cooke, the equestrian, which had been double exposed on an old American Confederate flag and Peter wrote the words *Poems of the Known World* for him on it. Terry used it for the cover of a collection of poetry, which was published while we were still together. He dedicated the book to me, and the author's photograph, on the inside back flap is one I took of him. He needed a new author's picture for his publisher and this Poseidon-like image, of him in his blue jeans and a dark t-shirt, with thunderous grey clouds above, captured his mood. He looked as if he might walk straight into the sea with his silvery hair ruffled in the wind. Terry was after paradise but it receded further away from him as he came closer to the horizon.

It was taken on a rainy afternoon in Sagaponack, at the end of a long summer we had spent living on the edge of Occam's razor, trying to find a way back to a simpler place. We both knew the truth of our situation but we preferred to circle the edge of the precipice, trying to find another way and to step into the romantic phase again. We were the happiest when we were looking at art together. He loved the Old Masters, Caravaggio, Tintoretto but he also liked modern masters such as Dubuffet and De Kooning. Something came over him, when he was in art.

He revised his poems by hand, dozens of times, each version was then carefully typed out on an electric typewriter by his secretary who came to the flat a couple of days a week. He made notes in pencil on the margins, to find the perfect mitre, and to par down to the essence of what he wanted to convey.

He had become heavily involved in the gallery. He had friends who were painters and artists, such as Barnaby Ruhe, famous for his fifteen minute Abstract Expressionist portraits, and David Hatchett, the found object sculptor. Jeff Wright was the founder of the Nuyorican Poets, and self-proclaimed king of the stanza was a master wordster, who had been inspired by the Beatniks and the rocking and frolicking of the *On the Road* generation.

They didn't recite, rather they screamed their poems and they were as slick as the thin layer of oil that collects on the surface of rainwater puddles. We held poetry readings at the gallery and Terry got to know other poets from the downtown scene. He was already established uptown, he had been one of the founders of Poet's House.

Peter's exhibition had given me the boost I needed, as it gathered momentum and news of it spread, many different sorts of people made the journey uptown to see it. Many shiny, interesting people came to the opening, including Peter Riva, Marlene Dietrich's nephew and the designers of Madison Avenue.

We had held a successful party at the newly re-opened Studio 54, which its original pioneer Steve Rubell had refurbished to its original decadent glory, complete with the man in the moon with the coke spoon. For that evening, Michael Ault restored the place back to how it had been, a decade ago. Some of the old Warhol crowd, whom Peter used to know showed up for the party and the anticipation and all the hype around the exhibition called *Uncut,* took on a life of its own. Andy's old art-world friend and the elder statesman of the contemporary New York art scene Anthony Haden-Guest came to the launch and the after-party.

There is a famous triptych of Peter, painted by Francis Bacon which is now in a private collection in Switzerland. Bacon climbs into Peter's rabid soul, and Peter is exposed. He seems to writhe as if he is trying to free himself of the structure of the paint and the constraints put upon him. Both Bacon and Peter's art speaks of death. Peter's photographs in a room are like black glitter, glamorous reminders of dying.

We had chosen the best-known images from his archives but also some of the personal pictures that hadn't been shown before, for gossip column fodder. One of these was the picture of Bianca Jagger, his Big B. We had printed it large in its original black and white format and she was sitting with her back angled to the camera. She is clearly topless and the firm outline of her breast can be seen in profile. Although it wasn't full frontal, it was provocative. Her muscular back was animated by the gestures she was making with her arms.

The press had written extensively about the exhibition, prior to the opening and they had mentioned the Bianca photo, which was described in the press release. She called and asked to preview the exhibition before the preview, in her usual diva way.

It had been a difficult exhibition to hang. The pictures were vast and fragile and Peter had managed to collage and complete only one full set of C prints and a couple of the canvas pieces, and this after much bribery, screaming and cajoling. Envelopes stuffed full of cash helped. I had decided to circumvent Peter Tunney, I didn't like the Svengali he was playing to Peter's talent.

I rushed back from Marni on Madison, where I quickly paid for the first outfit that I saw that might suit me for the evening, a pair of butter-soft black leather jeans and a camel coloured skinny sweater. My style had changed, as had my shape and although I was still quite compact, I had shrugged off the Chanel constrictions for softer, flowing styles. I was in a hurry, the opening was in less than an hour and judging from the way the phones had been ringing off the walls, we were going to have a crush of people.

As I fumbled to find my keys, I wondered where Peter would be and where I would have to send a cab and probably a gallery assistant to go and fetch him. I needed to get downstairs and shower and change. The alcohol and bartender still hadn't turned up. I dumped my shopping bags on the floor of the main space and called out to see who was still there.

The gallery was spotless, Terry had sent Leandra, his maid to come and clean it. The doorbell sounded and I cursed. I had kicked off my shoes and padded, barefoot, to answer it, it could only be the bartender or a delivery of flowers or alcohol.

Although she was tiny, she was still stunning. She was about fifty then, and she wore her wavy hair to her chin so it grazed the collar of the smart long jacket she wore. She is one of a handful of people I have met who can freeze a room just by being there. Once you are in their range, your eyes see them and only them. I wasn't sure at first, and then she spoke, with a deep, heavily Spanish accented voice that I knew from the phone earlier, "Hello. I am Bianca Jagger. I have come to see the picture."

When she had called earlier, I said I would call her back, to arrange a time she could come up. I needed to speak to Peter to see if he would agree to the sale before the preview, that wasn't likely. She was slightly incensed that she hadn't been invited and I explained that her invitation was probably still in the post, New York mail was so unreliable. We had never sent her one. I told her again, I would call her back and then I was distracted doing the ten dozen things that have to happen to pull off a successful opening.

About an hour later I had her Park Avenue attorney issuing guttural threats down the phone line at me, about injunctions. I tried to stay calm and called Peter, if I became flustered over it, he would pick up on it and that could only spell further trouble. If I told him that Bianca didn't want us to show the picture that she wanted to buy it and have it delivered straight away, he would flatly refuse. He wouldn't be bullied in this way and, like him or loathe him, there is no manipulating Peter Beard. However, there was one way to get through this situation which I relished as much as handling a stick of dynamite. He was mercenary about money; he always needed it, just as I did.

"How much is it?" I told him what we had priced it at and I could hear him drawing in his breath and sucking in on his Camel unfiltered.

"You can get ten times that, FD."

"I know, but I can't change the price now, she knows what it is. And I've got her attorney breathing down my neck..."

"That's fantastic," he snorted derisively, pleased his art could still elicit such ripples.

"Maybe from where you are sitting but from here, it doesn't look so good Peter."

"Yeah, she's going out with that politician from New Jersey, Robert what's-his-name. She needs to straighten out her reputation, doesn't need nudie pictures getting out, does she."

"Robert Torricelli, the Senator." I said calmly. I prayed silently, I knew how much potential mischief Peter had in him. Bianca's political ambitions extended beyond the shores of the East Coast and its politics, she was positioning herself to be the next president of Nicaragua. She'd tell anyone who would listen and it was common knowledge, but I wasn't about to enlighten Peter any further. I had promised to call back the attorney after I had spoken with Peter.

"Ok, she can have it but I'm not signing over any rights to the negative, it's mine. You can sign whatever you like but they got nothing on me."

They had asked for an undertaking that we wouldn't reproduce the photo or use the original negative again. And when I had told Peter, I left out the bit about the negative. His pictures were his babies. He would never agree to such impositions, which in his mind would concede to killing his art. I agreed to sign whatever they wanted and deftly avoided the subject of Peter's involvement or lack of it. I was only his dealer and I could only be held responsible for the work I had in my gallery, they accepted that.

They still made me sign some straightjacket, life-restricting paragraph when I went to pick up the Big B's cheque and promised that the photo would be delivered. After the opening night.

She brushed past me, her heavy perfume scent making a way for her to follow, and went straight to the corner where the black and white picture was standing on the floor, waiting to be hung. She went and stood in front of it and I lifted it onto its fixing, so it could be viewed properly. It needed space to breathe.

I was standing behind her, staring at her back and her friends on this long-ago boat trip. I watched her expression, over her shoulder, on the half of her sculpted profile I could see. She is flirtatious and charming.

Whatever she did with the rest of her life, she pinned herself, like a poster, onto the mind's eye of a generation of women, she was the first footballer's wife. She turned to me and said in that unmistakable voice, as sexy and dark as her eyes, that she would buy it. She made me promise to take it down and put it away so it wouldn't be on view and she told me to try and make Peter "behave."

161

As if. I was in a rush and I needed to get Narcissus out of the gallery, so I promised and lifted the picture off the hook and rested it on the floor again.

I explained I would need someone to help me carry it downstairs and she looked down at her heels and smiled almost apologetically, beneficently. She wasn't going to offer. Before she left, she slipped on a pair of big black sunglasses that covered most of her small face and she wished me goodbye. She stepped out into the early evening and slid into the limousine, its door already opened, waiting.

The picture stayed on the floor and Peter reveled the whole night in the story of how Bianca had tried to ruin his big night. She knew I would leave it there. It was because she felt she was worth it, even if she wasn't physically there, she would remind us all how bright and beautiful she had been. She granted us the privilege of access to that moment in her life, when it had criss-crossed with the amazing Peter B's, decades ago.

The Empty Dreams of Exile

The question of my identity didn't consciously concern me; but it was always there, like a mild headache. I felt like a spy, drowning in international waters. Often, I felt as if I was a spectator in my own life, that events were unraveling elsewhere. There was the illusion that although my life was happening, times crashed forward with birthdays and the change of seasons, I wasn't involved in it.

AD Coleman wrote a positive review in *The New York Observer*, it was perceptive, but then critiquing photography was his métier. After the glowing piece, which was an in-depth on Peter's, life and the way in which he worked there were two sentences, which pinpricked my initial euphoria. They described how I was still under investigation by the DA's office.

There are people, more than events that I regret about the time and as I was going through the motions, I knew I would regret them even more later. The whole horrific encounter with Colette, the performance artiste is one of them. She was neurotic, screaming. She begged and bullied me into showing her work, and I knew I shouldn't have. Her frilly concoctions of pink, confectionary, girlie pictures, which depicted her in different outfits, were decorated with glitter and gunk.

She made a photo portrait of me and Terry, with one of her ghostly Colette effigies in the background, leaving the frame of the picture. I am sitting in a gilded armchair, looking sad and sophisticated in a black Donna Karan tuxedo, with a silk grosgrain collar, my legs are crossed so the silk stripe down the length of one trouser leg is visible. Terry stands behind me, his hair swept back. He wears an Andersen and Shepherd suit, charcoal with white chalk stripes. We look serious; we are the cool New York couple, the dark-maned Islamototty and her protector behind her. Colette never finished the portrait or returned the $10 000 she charged Terry for its commission.

I was still being swept along by the hubris of the case against me and Brechneff and his friends made sure I didn't get too far ahead of myself. He had invented a vivid back-story about me, which he had concocted over too much wine and with every time another newspaper retold it, the story grew. I read more anecdotes of how I was related to Middle Eastern royal families, or that my father was a maharajah from India.

The more I shut down and refused to discuss my family, the louder the whispers became. It wasn't from a sense of shame that I clammed up, but a desire to separate from them and from my history. The men I picked, who were deeply imbedded in American society, were an easy solution, with them, I could share the life. Or take what I needed from theirs.

Part of being an exile, because that is what I am, is living out Agamemnon's sorry prophecy about Orestes, about how he lived on empty dreams. The king said he knew, he had been there. I have also been there. An exile seeks to settle her soul in the shifting landscape of wherever we happen to be. We don't seek to grow roots, we only seek comfort in the shade.

Growing up Asian in the 80s in Britain was fine. We were immune to the riots and the racism. I knew about Mrs. Thatcher's exclusive Maharajahs' club, which brought together the rich and influential Indians and East African Asians, but we lived like polite guests, not taking up too much space or making an excessive amount of noise. Our parents lived lives of quiet desperation; they didn't know the language of the song they had left behind or its tune any longer. It was soon forgotten, it belonged to another place. We, the children of the initially dispossessed had been regurgitated by Africa.

She no longer wanted us, thank you, she said, the ungrateful mother, for the years and generations of labourers and of pioneers, for the freshly laid railways that crosshatched the continent and made it accessible. Thank you, but now you have to go. And we were pushed out too soon. Like baby birds expelled from the nest, we weren't ready. We were the proud prodigal children, we couldn't go "back" to India, there wasn't a back to go to, and she was only forty years from partition and struggling to find her own shape.

India was ancient but new in the world and was finding her place in a post-colonial, post-war order. Besides, in the late 70s, India wasn't the fledgling super-power she is today, she didn't hold the chic, shimmering glamour of Bollystan and bright ideas. I am described as first generation. I wasn't born here, and England has never felt like home, but I can't lay claim to that title. My parents were the first generation of my family to settle here, with their parents in their old age. My children would be the hip 2Gs, which leaves us three, the siblings as the one-and-a-half generations, somewhere in the mists of the in-between. In America I was able to just be. It is a new culture that is self-obsessed and too introspective to care what anyone else is doing, or where from where they hail.

Anyway, even old is new in America; one look at the scrapbook skylines of any city reveals how she both reveres and despises tradition. The skyscraper is inspired – it's like a Canaletto Capricci – it evokes one of his fantasy cityscapes of styles crowded together from different historical eras. There is nothing in America of her own. And yet she owns it.

164

Not all Americans belong. Some Americans from the great-name families don't fit in. Margot Hemmingway was the granddaughter of Ernest and came to the gallery with Amanda Ursell. Everyone knew her when she had been a successful model and actress in the 70s.

Now, in 1994 she had freshly returned from a stint in rehab. She was six feet tall, and scrubbed looking. She wore her hair scraped back from her freckled face and very little make up and even at forty-one, she didn't need it. She radiated a soap-and-water, natural beauty. I expected her to be arrogant, still riding the crest of her former fame, she wasn't. She was humble. She laughed out loud and covered her wide grin with her long hands when she giggled.

I was dubious about her, she was another in the long procession of Manhattanites who were frantically recreating themselves in the new shape of their personal deity, and I wasn't sure whether to trust the charm and the spontaneity that tumbled off her. I was also wary as she made no bones about how much she liked Terry, and he, ever the knight in shining amour, saw another opportunity to reach back to the younger version of himself, just as he had tried to with me.

Margot was hard to resist. She had given up drinking and cocaine and had put on some weight so while she was still stunning she was a little zaftig and in New York, in order to be a model then, you had to be Twiggy thin, or voluptuous in the way Cindy Crawford and Christy Turlington were. But Margot wanted to get away from her old life, the modeling and the movies, she said were triggers for her addictions. She had changed the spelling of her name, from Margeaux to Margot to get away from her legacy of drugs and alcoholism.

She liked the peace and quiet of the gallery. She meditated in the still space and she used to sit cross-legged on the floor, her shoes, kicked off to the side. She chanted, a low, Native American song, casting spells and fixing light around her to ward off the demons that frequented her life. The family had Idaho American Indian in their blood, Margot's sloping cheekbones and her upright posture gave the secret away.

She was like a squaw in the city. She formed her own spirituality, this was her moveable feast, a pinch of Hinduism and a dash of Buddhist inevitability plus her own brand magic gave back to Margot what the modeling world and the early abuse at the hands of her godfather had yanked from her. She had latched onto these mystical security blankets, for protection. She used them in a way that they worked for her.

Amanda, our PR lady was orphaned young and lonely. She went into PR because laying the foundations of someone else's fame was easier than examining where she came from. We had lunch at EAT, a delicatessen with a café attached to it. Margot was shy. She covered it up with exuberance and the light she shone out at the world, but the ghosts of her old life stalked her, they were just around every corner and Amanda was helping her to overcome her irrational fears of being judged and disliked.

Margot asked me, in that wide-eyed way of hers, if I noticed something different about Amanda. She looked as she always did, well turned out, her glossy brown bob combed and groomed. Could I have missed something momentous, a deeper shade of chocolate mousse on her already gorgeous hair or a new pair of spectacle frames, which perched elegantly on the end of her reshaped, retroussé, ski slope nose?

I settled into my chair, on my side of the beveled glass top table and then I could feel it. Amanda's stillness came as a shock. The frenetic energy, the circling, rushing thoughts that chased in her mind, those whorls that drowned her in their vortex of words and ideas, they were calmed.

"Oh no, what have you given her?" I was suspicious that Amanda had downed a diazepam, but her chill didn't feel chemically induced, her eyes weren't glassy. They both laughed, I had become sanctimoniously sober, drug free and drank little and occasionally. Terry hardly drank and though he never tried to stop me, his healthy life was beginning to rub off on me. Clive told me I was getting old and boring.

"No, Margot gave me a treatment." Amanda glowed; I had heard a lot about Margot's massages and so far had managed to beg off being subjected to this spiritual, physical facsimile that she had learned from her latest shaman.

She was eager for willing victims on which to practice her newfound skills. I murmured something about doing it when I had a little more time.

Vogue's stellar astrologer Shelley von Strunkel recognized Margot and came over from a nearby table, so happy to see her after so long. All eyes were fixed on this tortured beauty from the much-mythologized Hemmingway clan and I wanted to protect her. We all did.

Her sister Mariel had settled down with her stable husband and opened Sam's Café on the Westside, which was doing well. Margot had inherited the sadness in Papa Hemingway's soul. She knew she would give into the seed of self-destruction in her; she talked about it, openly, what she called "the other side." It was simply a matter of choosing her moment.

Maybe we all knew what she would do but didn't want to believe it. Too often I haven't heard the pain in people's stories and lived to regret my deafness. I agreed to let Margot work her magic on me, it had clearly done Amanda some good.

I couldn't stop giggling, initially. I lay on her masseur's table in the back room of my gallery. She was breathing in and out, deeply, resonantly and her hands were hovering just above my bare back. Like Madame Sosotris, she wore a special shaman's shirt that helped her to channel. Then she stated making low, nasal sounds, like the voice of the wind, if it could speak.

Margot lifted the grief and the doubts from inside me, she absorbed them and then she spat them out. I felt set free, like I was newborn at the end of the hour. My skin glowed, whatever Margot had done, her belief had spilled over into me. She refused to take any money from me although I knew she didn't have much cash and was being supported by her ex-fiancé, a financier called Stewart Sundlen.

I told her I would get Terry to make an appointment and that she must charge him, and me, the next time. She handed me something from the big leather saddlebag she always carried. She had her own Boho style, part Audrey Hepburn elegance and part ethnic-chic, in the shape of silver hooped earrings, leather fringes and turquoise beads on her clothes.

Her height gave her a beguiling gawkiness, she described herself as "five foot twelve inches," it's just as well she was too tall or she might have been perfect. I thanked her and we kissed and hugged. Margot came the closest I have ever had to a friend who was a woman. She didn't expect or require anything of me, just for me to be myself and I was comfortable around her.

When she had gone and her afterglow had faded a little, I unwrapped the present she had pushed into my hands. It was loosely wrapped in white tissue paper. She had given me a perfect, polished rose quartz orb, a littler bigger than a tennis ball. I held it up to my cheek, and it felt like a cool breeze on a spring day, just like she did. Rose quartz will always remind me of her.

Of all the beautiful and extravagant things I have been given, the handmade platinum and diamond engagement rings, the extravagant Chanel suits in their tantalizing mausoleum-like black boxes with serious white lettering, as much as I loved the thrill of receiving these, Margot's rose crystal, which Terry commandeered, in the name of safekeeping, was the most special.

Life appeared to be turning a corner for her, she was staying at Stewart's flat not far from me but things were difficult with her family. The way she described it to me, they always had been. The addiction had made her burn bridges with some of those closest to her but those of us who knew her now, as she was, bare and honest, we loved her completely. She was in talks about doing some plus-size modeling and had started filming a series of wildlife and outdoor programs. It was a future perfected.

Some people are too pure for the darkness of this world. Margot's unlined pixie face needed Idaho sunshine; she had been raised on her grandfather's farm in Ketchum. She couldn't survive the grey consumption of New York. She tried to shine her light, to tell the truth wherever she went but the gloomy episodes, which had robbed her in the past, possessed her future and they were clouding her present.

It's not for me to say if I believe her stories of abuse and isolation, whatever happened to her as a young girl, stripped away any chance she had of having some self-esteem or any vestige of a normal life.

She tried so hard, to put it all behind her, to heal herself but how do you, when your innocence is blown out and those around you, the ones who are meant to protect you, the ones you trust, all they can do is to turn their faces?

Margot had brought positivity to my life, I saw just the goodness in her and she had tried to teach me to see it in others. Ironically, she brought Terry and me closer. It all seemed so much simpler in the quiet pause of her gaze.

She entered my life and ever so gently, she shifted the axis of my path and as quietly and mysteriously as she had descended on us, Margot disappeared, just like an angel.

If I'd known she only had a year left, I would have spent more time with her, I would have loved her more. I would have basked for hours in the light she cast that brought something to all of our lives, to anyone who knew her. I want so much to know you now, Margot. I have thought about you so often, since the news of your suicide. Finally the secret from the other side of the grave robbed you of your grace and your desire to live down the demons.

Peace wherever you are my angel-friend.

The Summer of 95

Robert De Niro's character in *Taxidriver* prays for rain, to wash away the scum and the sleaze of the city. But the humans, stained, aren't cleansed and the lightening vices which flash in the sky highlights the flaws and fissures, and then it embeds itself in us, like varicose veins in an old hag's limbs. We are the purified filth of the city.

Snow is deceiving, it is described by the narrator in *Ugly Betty* as being a heavenly blanket which falls and "makes everything beautiful." But beauty fades and snow melts and life is all that it is again in a shallow china cup of experience, one in which Swann might have dipped his Madeleines. We seek succour from the bitterness of reality. We want a guarantee against its determined tragedy of our little lives, like something sugary, dipped in icing and topped with glacé cherries that we think might take away the stark realization: this is all there is.

In the summer of 1995 I opened a gallery on Route 27 – the main artery into East Hampton – with Thomas Lok, who was an unreconstructed hunk of a German, all Sephardic eyes and flowing black hair, longer than mine. We called it Downtown/ Uptown Gallery LOK, He had a loft space in the as-yet-untrendy meat district, but his art parties were circled dates on the calendar. Mary Boone had her driver wait outside the converted slaughterhouse as she climbed the rickety stairs in impossible shoes, to show herself and her support for the next generation of super dealers. It was good to be seen there.

Thomas' approach to dealing art was diametrically opposed to mine, perhaps that is why we got along well. He painted too, and would sell his oversized abstract canvases once in a while to maintain his lifestyle. He was like a deer caught dancing in the strobe lights, captured by the glamour and the glitz. A stream of fawning art groupies had increased his rating on the shagability index, it was all part of the bonus package. He was calm and sensible and there was a side to him that knew not to bask too long in this glory. The sun has a natural tendency to move.

We made a success of the space, which was an art emporium in a cultural wasteland. It was located in a newly built shopping mall, ours and the surf shop next door were the only two tenants of about fifteen units, at the beginning of that summer.

169

It wasn't far from Terry's house and if I didn't take the blue saloon car in the morning, he would drop me off, with a smile, like a proud parent leaving his offspring at the school gates. He must have been relieved I had something else to do; he pretended to get on with the great American novel, which he still hadn't started.

There were many haters who let it be known that they thought I should have kept out of the public eye and kept a no-profile while the criminal cases against me were untried. I should have sunk into gravity and blandness. But, much to their chagrin, whatever I did, I did it with noise. Terry and I were a popular couple amongst the literati crowd. We were amongst the set of people who decamped to Long Island for four-day weekends, which started on Memorial Day and went on till Labor Day.

There were two weeks at the end of August when the skinny island was all but deserted, anyone who could leave, did. Like robots, we waited at pre-designated stops, for the green and white Hampton Jitney, to collect us before we sailed noiselessly, in air-conditioned comfort onto the I95.

There was nothing and no one left in the city except the sweaty skeleton of people who had to stay. They were the backbone that kept New York working, the doormen, street sweepers, taxi drivers, domestics and decorators whose function in life was to service the elite of the city. Air conditioners sweltered, drip-dripping condensation from their window perches. The humidity sprung, every year like a trap. Spring had us basking in warm light, ankles barely had time to feel the dew in the new grass, and then, one morning, summer dropped like a lead balloon. It was like trying to breathe through a hot wet sponge, the heat and the humidity were too much.

That summer was a long one, like the space between two empty speech marks. It was a breath I couldn't take, out of fear and anticipation of what the autumn might bring. The carousel of the social world had started up and I was busy with the day-to-day running of the gallery and making believe that all was well with Terry.

He shut himself away all day in his study, writing and rewriting on those neatly typed squares of text, fiddling and rearranging them until they were perfect. That was what the poet needed, divinity, and a spark of immortality that would ensure his safe installation in the hierarchy of American culture. At night, we were quite social, we went out, but we were both just hanging on, I was too scared to let go of my end of the piece of string, he was too kind and worried to release me.

Herb Ross purchased one of Peter's pictures, a giraffe, floating like a smudge of charcoal mist against a creamy sky. It was a large sepia toned canvas print and on it Peter had written Blixen's words, "a giraffe is like a lady, one must refrain from looking at her legs," in his distinctive script. It was framed in a heavy, simple oak frame. Ross bought it for his wife, Lee Radziwill.

We arranged a date and a time over the phone and I promised I would deliver it myself as he was private and a little difficult; he was after all, Hollywood royalty. Their house wasn't far away, in East Hampton, a beach "cottage," which was still substantial. A long drive lead up to the pretty double-storey house. A housekeeper unloaded the picture for me and showed me where it was going to hang. It's one of life's great unfairnesses that women do not age as well as men. Experience and pain make men grow into their bodies, they spread out, emperor-like, letting their stories and the years fill them out. Women fade, something of us leaves, our luminescence grows softer, skin becomes crêpey, even in the most beautiful fifty-year-old. Perhaps it is something to do with the pain of giving life. Only women bleed.

Lee Radziwill was a wisp of a woman, thin-boned and elegantly fragile. She glowed, like an opal that's been left in the light. She came into her sitting room and I didn't notice her. It was a classical American version of English country chic, framed Redouté originals in grids on the walls, overstuffed sofas dressed in their summer slipcovers, casually strewn on bleached maple floors. I had my back to the door as I balanced the photo on the ledge that had been constructed by their handyman especially for Peter's picture.

"Hello." It was an affirmation, not a greeting. I turned around. I was struck by how petite she was. I always imagine famous women will be like goddesses in their stature. Her features were finer and softer than her famous dead First Lady sister. She didn't have Jackie's angular beauty, or her perfect proportions. The stark contrast of jet-back hair and her ivory skin was missing, but she had the aristocratic Bouvier look. She was pale and this was barely covered over with a slight tan.

Her light brown hair was cut to slice her square jaw, it framed her strong face. Although she was slight, like a bird, she exuded calm. She wasn't meant to know about the photo but I couldn't very well hide it, it was five feet square. Herb Ross had told me she would be out the whole morning, at a planning meeting for an upcoming fundraiser.

She was delighted; her face had the creased up expression of a child who sees the Christmas lights go on for the first time. Her pale grey eyes glittered and focused on the picture.

"That is perfectly beautiful." She sighed, Lee Radziwill, princess, socialite, style icon, whose face remained calmly stoic, even in the rude popping of the paparazzi's flashbulbs, looked like a young girl for just a moment.

She hugged herself with her arms, wrapping herself in her own embrace, a cream cashmere kiss and she kneeled on the sofa in front of the picture, getting up close to it. She was much more delicate and pretty than in the pictures I had seen of her, and she didn't look at all old, especially in those few moments.

The room, the house, the seemingly scattered arrangements of tea roses in Moroccan glass vases seemed uncontrived, but there was an artful appreciation for beauty and for living, which was reflected in the way she had decorated it. It fit her perfectly; she wasn't an ornament in it that didn't belong. She looked as if she might have been there forever and as if she planned on staying for a long time. She remarked what a lovely birthday present it would be. She perched herself on the edge of the sofa, barely making a dent in it.

"Has anyone offered you some tea? Some fresh lemonade?" I pointed to the empty glass in front of her, on the coffee table and she smiled, "Well, you'll have another won't you?"

Peter had been close to Jackie who had bagged him for Random House when she began her last career as an editor. I knew Peter was fond of Lee, he was sweet about her but in their New York world, although they inhabited the same one, they sat at opposite sides of the table. If they saw each other it was over a crowded room, over seas of people. They only shared the feigned intimacy of a passing greeting or a quick exchange of words.

She poured us both a glass of juice. She asked me about the exhibition, how it had done, had it been a success? She seemed genuine and interested and then I noticed the sadness. In spite of the wealth and the style that radiated off her and everything around us, in spite of all the accoutrements of a life well lived, she seemed forlorn and the house felt lonely.

When Herb Ross came in, we had been sitting for a while. He was a tall, broad, big boned man who wore his world on his sleeve. He looked at the giraffe and he looked pleased, it seemed to float off the cream wall, then he shifted his gaze to her. She was still delighted, beaming and his eyes swept over the picture and then over her, proud he had been able to make her happy. He didn't live up to my image of him; I had been warned that he was meticulous and boorish, but here in this room, soaking up the last of the fading light and long, sighing afternoon shadows, he was docile.

She patted the space on the sofa next to her and he came around, carefully sitting next to her. He was proprietary, she might have been a piece of prized porcelain and he didn't want to brush into her and break her. I stood up to leave, a little star-struck by the movie magic perfection of this glamorous couple, well into their middle-age but still alive and clearly in love. They thanked me for bringing the painting over myself and said I should come and see it again, when it had settled into its new surroundings. A plot was brewing in my head.

The best way to get anything by Terry was to let him think it was his idea. He loved to play the perfect host to the bright and the beautiful. Peter and Terry got along well, and when I broached the subject of a dinner party to boost the interest in Peter's work amongst the summer crowd, he suggested we have it at the house.

Peter had aged well; he had no intention of becoming graceful in his dotage. David Hockney once said the ones who control the images and the lens control society; Peter did that.

The wealthy in Manhattan had only two choices, when it came to catering their events. Strangely, the accumulation of money narrows the possibilities available. We chose Glorious Foods. The choices became still more constrained when it came to flowers. For every event from christenings and Bar Mitzvahs to the final shirking of the mortal coil, there was only Renny. Terry called the caterer appointed to our cloistered court and they arranged a menu. There were two tables set up; we had about two-dozen guests. Terry, effortlessly hijacked what should have been my evening with Peter shining.

Hundreds of flickering votives brought the flaming orange of the sunset inside. They were set in clusters, on the tables. Posies of wild flowers stoked some movement and colour and it was an evening of rustic sophistication. The menu that had been selected was simple, he spent a lot of time choosing the wine, trying, yet again, to recreate something from another part of his life, something long lost.

Lee arrived on her own. Herb Ross had been called to LA on business but sent his apologies, she looked relieved. She dressed simply, in a silvery column dress, probably Armani as she was one of his sartorial ambassadors. Peter scrubbed up well for the occasion; he wore a navy blue single-breasted blazer and a thin white cotton shirt. His twill khaki trousers were laundered and freshly ironed.

He beamed when he saw her; he had seemed a little anxious leading up to her arrival but the shadows fled as soon as her slight frame stepped through the door. Peter had brought Rekha, his girlfriend and when it came time to sit down for dinner, Lee and Peter naturally found their places next to each other, they turned their chairs so they were half-facing each other. Thus they enclosed their private space. Her face looked young and her cheeks were flushed by Terry's fine wine.

Peter's gnarly feet were planted squarely on the floorboards but besides them occasionally grazing the fabric of his trousers, a pointy, silk slipper danced on tiny painted toes. They laughed, and in no time twenty years had slipped away.

The evenings grow long in the summer amongst the potato fields. The rustle of cornstalks and the ripple of the water in the pool drew me to stand at the edge of the French doors. I leaned up against the wooden doorframe, feeling the soft sheath of sand-coloured silk dress against my skin. I wore an Armani Fortuny inspired jacket over it, shades of peach and bronze. I spent ages getting myself ready.

That night everyone was beautiful, including Terry's grey banker potentates who were there solely because they were prospective buyers. Andy Moses had come to dinner, we had one of his shimmering landscapes in the house, next to the wall where I stood, and it glistened with particles of diamond dust when the light caught it.

He was a good friend to Peter, Bitten, his Swedish model-girlfriend, had been one of Peter's many muses and there were naively erotic pictures of her and Najma stuck to the fridge at Peter's house on the tip of Montauk. He came and stood next to me, he was spiritual and calm, a Buddhist. He stood by me in all of my turbulence.

"Hey." Andy was a surfer but looked Mediterranean. His brown wavy hair and brown eyes gave him a sensitive, soulful look and his hands were stained with pigments.

Andy was a normalizing influence on Peter's insanity – he was loyal.

"Hey, back." I answered, not looking at him.

He stood close to me and I felt grounded, he felt real. He worked successfully as bond trader to maintain his loft in Soho but painting was in his blood, his father Ed was a successful painter too.

"You are a million miles away," he said softly.

"At least that," I smiled. It was past eleven o'clock and the sky was still light, and night's sleepy hand was brushing darkness onto the edges of the clouds. Flat fields, furrowed, lay as far as I could see.

"Everything all right? It's a great party."

This was one of those moments in my life when I felt myself slipping into one of these "out of body" states, it was as if a part of me had stepped a few feet away to observe. I was no longer the protagonist in my own story. Behind me, the slim goddess in the silvery waterfall of a dress held court and those who listened to her sparkled like tropical birds, when they caught her attention. They were in their own, cocooned world.

I should be happy, I thought, I have it all. But the fugitive in me gazed at Terry who was smiling and shining. He was in the middle of a toast to Peter and his impresario, me. He had a crystal glass poised in the air; I smiled back, still outside of myself.

174

I felt lonely and disconnected, he couldn't reach me. None of them could. I realized I was living the dream I had always wanted, I wasn't yet thirty and I had a life charted out that promised only greatness. The mess I had made involving the DA's office seemed a long way away.

That night, we left the dishes and the glasses and he followed me upstairs, a sprightlier version of his usual tired self. The guests had gone and it was well past midnight. Lee and Peter had lingered long, I didn't realize how close they had been or how many stories they had shared together.

The next day was a Sunday but the caterers arrived at ten sharp to clear the previous night's mess away. They took away all the evidence. Terry was already buttressed in his study, I answered the door bleary-eyed and towel-tongued, and the daylight seared the back of my head, deep into my brains. I must have had more to drink than I could remember. I felt guilty for not being happy. I had it all, yet my desire was my downfall.

We all have these clean slate moments when we can rewrite our history and take control of who we want to be. In the same way I had removed everything that reminded me of Susan Brockman to the other end of the house, it dawned on me, in the haunting taunting words of the narrator of *Desperate Housewives*, that "the truth is a nothing more than a previously agreed upon set of lies." These were the lies I came to draw upon when I tried to define who I was and where I was headed. None of it made sense, none of it mattered.

On the Wings of Hummingbirds

Every young artist worth his salt who wanted a decent investment portfolio was tied up in an ego-breaking contract with a major dealer. This Faustian pact of a promise ensured the artist would provide a certain number of paintings for an exhibition, that he would take on commissions and not to go to rival dealers for fear of punitive penalties. In return the hyper-inflated 80s art market was given wings as collectors queued round the corner for a new painting by Ross Bleckner or Eric Fischl. When they inked up with the Mary Boones or the Gogo Gagosians they might as well have signed with their own blood. They were signing away the next decade of their life.

In the Hamptons, the rules were more relaxed, like waistbands in the summer, it all loosened up a little. Top buttons were undone, and shirtsleeves were rolled up in a determined effort to acquire an informal look. Artists could invite prospective clients to their summer studios in the time-honoured tradition of this age-old artists' enclave.

I went to see Ross Bleckner's pictures; his elegiac hummingbird paintings sang to me. I bought one directly from his studio downtown. It is on a midnight blue background, and the bird is caught in mid-flight, in linear striations of oil paint. Ross was affable and owlish, he had learned to paint properly, the old art school way, and from there, using his academic knowledge and learned technique as a springboard, he had ventured off to find his own style. There were no shortcuts in his art.

Terry bought two smaller hummingbird paintings and another friend, a deeply neurotic Manhasset psychiatrist who put me on Zoloft and was married to Sixtus, one of my artists, bought one too. But the ten-foot squares, on which dozens of hummingbirds appeared to move and flit, out of the corner of the eye were inspired and humbling.

He had started his flower paintings in the same massive format, armfuls of cascading flowers, looked as if they had been randomly tossed onto the canvas and were captured in detail worthy of an Old Master. Some were whole and perfect, others bruised and fading, some had settled and others were still mid-trajectory, hurtling their way through space. Terry wanted one of these flower pictures and commissioned one directly through me. But Ross was bored of painting flowers and was looking for new subjects. Even flowers that cost upwards of $60 000 can lose their bloom.

Terry's deposit went towards my escalating legal bills. They saw themselves as the new Young Turks, they were the de Koonings and the Pollocks of our day; we had Eric and April, they had Jackson and Lee. Ross was a quiet decanter of soul and spirit.

The old homesteads had been turned into the fort palaces of the good and the great. Julian Schnabel, the plate thrower, had purchased Andy Warhol's old estate. Jeff Bergen the dealer from ACA galleries in the city and his gentle wife Dorian and Jeff's father, along with their two bright Steiner educated boys lived in a rumpled house in Amagansett. Terry was suspicious of Jeff. The Bergens were spiritual but he called it cultist, and for all his embracing of the East, at least in the comfort of his bed, the Bergen brand of Orientalism and mysticism was a step too far.

This hero worship of a guru, particularly a barefoot Indian one was unsettling for him. Andrew Harvey had entered our lives through Bobo and we bore the full glare of his born-again dependence on the diminutive Versace deity, Guru Mai, through to her inevitable descent, in his eyes as his disappointment in her grew to match his once fervent faith.

She demanded absolute obeisance and *puja,* or service. I visited her ashram in South Fallsberg, in Upstate New York and was intrigued by her. She was wrapped in orange silk, like a crepe Christmas cracker. Her big eyes were kohl-rimmed and her pupils dilated, in ecstasy. Another friend who brought some calmness in the storm was Josh Berman. He was easy to be around. Being round Josh was comfortable, like wearing your favourite loose summer kaftan. He was a gentle spirit who got on with whatever it was in front of him, without a fuss. These were my friends and this was my world.

My legal case was stagnating; Terry helped fund it and would encourage me to speak to my lawyer everyday in order to stay on his back to see where the case was and what had happened. He told me to broach the situation, not to bury it or run from it. The resolution was as inevitable as the summer drawing to a close when the beach houses were to be closed up again for the winter months.

Barry Slotnick had gained a reputation as a people's hero, he was a maverick in the stiff world of the law. He had successfully gained an acquittal for Bernhard Goetz, the notorious New Yorker subway shooter. His status reached that of cult hero, in Miracle Gro. His actions and fearlessness, the inherent rightness of shooting at the subways muggers poured warm comfort on the fear-frozen hearts of his fellow residents.

New York's subway system had become the symbol of lawlessness in the city. At last someone had stood up for right to live without fear. Slotnick brought the issue of human and civil rights into the public forum, he became the archangel of the faith and the defender of the Yankee spirit. His connections and his insider's knowledge of the workings of the judicial system and all its major players, offered hope. I retained him at the end of the summer to cut me a deal with the Manhattan DA's office.

We went through the charade of getting a pre-sentencing psychiatrist's report done, which described what I already knew. It said I was able to "split off" from myself, to break away from the inner moral compass and values in order to commit my crimes. It all read well, it had to; it had cost a lot of money and was written by a leading court-circuit psychiatrist. Barry and his colleague Keith Watanabe never lied to me.

Orwell said that telling the truth was a revolutionary act in a world that thrived on deception. My truth, what was happening to me and what was unfolding with the legal mess is an untold story. It's been mythologized. Sometimes, it has been useful, I can pass under its shadow unnoticed, unremarkable. I am not what people expect: I can slip away, as did Lawrence of Arabia dressed as a Bedouin in the sands.

Slotnick knew my Honourable Judge, Franklyn Weissberg of Court 37 in the Supreme Court well, they played poker together. He told me I would be extremely lucky to be given a community-based sentence, that I was probably looking at some time inside, but I hung on to my delusions that I deserved freedom.

It was Halloween, 1995. All the ghosts and the ghoulish were out. On the way downtown to the courthouse building, the sky felt too close, it was leaning in on me. It even felt as if it had crept inside the cab that was crawling down traffic jammed avenues. I was counting on a miracle, Barry was a rainmaker, and I was visualizing myself on the Number Seven train, after the sentencing back uptown.

After all, such foxhole praying had always worked up till now. The traffic made me late and when I arrived, we had only a few minutes left to consult. He asked me if there was anything he wanted me to say in mitigation, he was going to make a plea for leniency but he was expecting no mercy for me when he tried to explain in his summing up some of the stupid things I had done, out of desperation to keep the gallery going. He told me sometimes, he couldn't reconcile those actions with the person he thought he knew, sitting in front of him. He asked me if I had wanted to be caught, I knew I would be, and that it would all catch up with me. I didn't answer. There was no longer any point in explaining, I couldn't find sense in any of it.

We agreed that I should plead guilty to some felony indictments and that others would fall away. Everyone was relieved. Terry who had posted $30 000 in bail would get it back. It must have hurt; the City paid no interest while it sat in their coffers. Slotnick's impassioned plea made me sound like the victim of circumstances and prone to bad judgments. He described me generously as an important player in the emerging art market and held up the sheaf of over thirty letters of support and character references which I had obtained from clients, friends and artists. He did an impressive Atticus Finch to my downtrodden Boo Radley.

No one had ever came up to me and confronted me with the mess I was making of my life. Instead they gossiped behind my back. I wouldn't have heard them anyway, I was not ready to hear.

Judge Weissberg was weary of this courtroom saga, although he listened attentively, perched behind an impressive oak paneled barricade, he seemed to have made up his mind. I didn't notice the restless press reporters and photographers in the gallery behind me. I wasn't aware of them till the flashbulbs went off in my face a few minutes later.

Weissberg was done listening. He folded his hands in front of him and said he had heard everything that Barry had said and appreciated his efforts. Barry looked up at him from the advocates' pit where he was sitting and bowed his head again, deferentially. I was disassociated from the process, I had no voice, Barry was my voice and the People of the State of New York wanted blood and restitution.

Without further ado, he sentenced me to six months in prison and a five-year probation supervision order. Then he made a restitution order for a fantastically overblown amount and the court sheriffs took me away. In as much as I was the business of the day, I was done. Barry's plea to defer the sentence so I could take care of my affairs fell on deaf ears. Weissberg thought I had had plenty of time and enough of his indulgence.

I was taken by the arm and lead down to the tombs and only when I physically passed them with their outstretched spiral notebooks, with pencils ready to pounce because they were waiting for a quote, with their cameras shoved in my face, did I become aware of the flurry of hacks and photographers around me.

Keith and Barry came to see me downstairs, I can't remember whether Terry was there, and we made hasty arrangements. They told me I would have to serve four of the six months, at Rikers' Island. If I had been sentenced to longer, I would have been sent to a Federal Penitentiary, a much better option according to Slotnick.

The Rose M Singer Centre on Rikers Island was meant to be hellish and he prepared me for the worst. There were various schemes that might offer early release and he promised to look into them for me. Then, he hugged me, he used to call me kid – which he did – and he said goodbye. They turned on the sole of his hand-made leather brogues and went back into their own world, above the surface where the real people lived.

That night, I regarded the view from my new residence. The moonlight was caught in the fangs of tangled razor wire and high fences. I could see guards with guns circling the perimeter and the lights of the city, teased me. They were a breath away but just out of reach, a hand-span across the sparkling fairy-bridge, which led back, taut with anticipation, to my other life.

I read a lot, even Rushdie, even books he wrote after *Midnights Children*. Terry sent me the cutting from *The New York Times*, which appeared the day after I was sentenced. I am pictured leaning over the gallery, flanked by a court orderly on either side. My eyes are glistening and filled with tears. I don't remember crying. I look dazed. In the picture I am wearing the same black leather jeans and soft sweater I had worn to Peter's opening and a black and beige Gucci blazer.

When I got to Rikers', Terry had all my smart clothes put into storage, along with my sense of who I was. Everything was held, on ice. At the end of the cutting was a quote from Peter, "I know Farah from Kenya. I don't know why everyone is so down on her."

It was a sweet thing to say, it sounds like someone caught Peter on the hop, but it helped to prop up the house of cards that I had built on lies. I wish someone had taken a match to it and burnt down all the deception, forever. But I know only I could have purged myself, only I was not ready. Denial was my comfort zone. I received dozens of letters and many people came out to visit me. Bill sent me two hardback books on classical sculpture but they arrived jacket-less, in case he had soaked them in heroin for my personal use. The books were a salve to Bill's earlier comment when he realized I had been less than truthful with him about the scale of my problems, he had said pointedly,

"Thank you for your perspicacity and your tenacity."

I felt smited. He had only wanted to help but I wasn't ready for anyone to help me. I didn't want to rely on anyone, so far, whenever I had, I had failed them and pushed them away. Dependence, intimacy, these were feelings a step too deep into murky waters.

Four months later and twenty-five pounds lighter, I emerged. The late February sun bounced off cold curls of metal atop glistening fishnet fences. A municipal bus came to the gate. I used the token the prison had given me for the fare and went straight to Slotnick and Shapiro's offices. Terry had carefully conspired to be out of town on my release but he had left keys for the new flat he had leased for me on East 91st Street with Barry's office.

Barry and Keith were solicitous, they had done a search of all the debts I had accrued in the Civil Court and said we should make a plan on sorting out the monetary judgments awarded against me. They spent a lot of time that day trying to make sure that I was all right and that I was in touch with people and had maintained a network. They had tried for early release but Judge Franklyn Weissberg had sentenced me shrewdly, it was too short a spell for a Federal Pen, which would have offered a lot more privileges, think Martha Stewart, and a six month sentence did not qualify for any kind of reduction on any of the Correctional Departments programs. The point was I had to suck it and suffer.

Terry had been nothing but a gentleman during those four months. He had shut up both galleries and made sure that the artists received their paintings and whatever money they were owed, he had arranged for everything else to go into storage. He had paid off my outstanding debts, those he knew about, with his own money.

When I emerged from the greyness of Rikers' Island under still skies, I felt as if I was coming out of hibernation. I had managed to compartmentalize the whole experience. I had kept my head down and because they were worried I might be set upon again (I was put to sleep so a gang of girls could steal my Rolex watch, which I had stupidly kept on my wrist) and I had done most of the four months in a secure wing.

It wasn't real, it had happened to someone else. The only thing that was mine in the nightmare was the pale grey hand-knitted Krizia cardigan I always wore, it reminded me of another life, elsewhere.

That was whom I had hung onto. The image of me that you built up. Why should I change what you took so long to create?

Leaving the Grey Behind

Leaving prison is a bit like dying. I thought I could leave the intrinsic greyness and the no-colour anaesthetized self I had become and step into the sunlight, fully restored to my former glorious self. They say humans make plans and god laughs, but it was impossible not to feel more than just a little foolish when I came out and quickly stepped back into the intricate network of social relationships I had left behind. Something had changed, it had all moved along a little. I had thought it would all stand still without me.

Terry had decided we had broken up. He had installed me and all my things into a flat on East 91st Street, a whole floor of a grand brownstone. He had removed my furniture from storage and it had all been thoughtfully put in the flat. He planned to be away on a business trip the day I was released but Sixtus met me in Manhattan, when I had finished at Slotnick and Shapiro. We took the subway uptown together, to my new home in Harlem, I called it. It wasn't. The East 90s form a good neighbourhood of families and young couples but it still far from the madding 60s where my art world had crashed.

There had been some descriptive angry articles when I was sentenced but the artists who still believed, commandeered by Terry, wrote a joint statement to the papers expressing their hopes for a future with me as their dealer. Dan Ratner the proprietor of the seedy *Dan's Paper*, a poor relation to Randy Schindler's glossy *Hamptons* magazine printed it, as did a few others.

My dad flew over when I was released, he was kind and supportive, and there was a lot of love. I wish I had grabbed onto it with both hands at the time. I maintained that I had learned my lesson and that I was fine. But still, I separated the entire experience from myself, it had happened to someone else. I just told them what they wanted to hear.

The first night out was frightening, I hadn't imagined how it would be and I hadn't prepared myself for it at all. My dad was tired, he went back to the hotel he was staying at and we agreed to meet the next day. Looking back on it now, he had shown up for me, in whatever way he was capable of, whenever I had been down on my luck. That's all a child can expect. He's been there since, chequebook in hand to bail me out of whatever I have got myself into, but that was never what I needed. I needed him to tell me it was ok, it wasn't my fault, and now it's just too late.

But he hadn't been there the one time it had really counted, when I was stolen, years ago. All the countless other times he did show up will never redeem him for that one failure. For what they did to me emotionally, those men that took me might as well have murdered me. Then they could have chopped me into little pieces with an axe and buried me in the woods.

They wrenched my childhood and all the nascent trust that would have bloomed into something tangible, something on which I could have anchored myself and my sense of who I was. They shredded the promise of my future. Those that were meant to protect me, they couldn't, and they came undone. Worse, they denied it. They didn't have the words for it. They never could reach me after that. It took a long time for anyone to be able to reach me again. It's never left me.

I was terrified of black men for decades afterwards and living in New York, it was awkward not to get into an opening elevator if I saw a black guy inside, he could have been wearing a $5 000 dollar suit, been a doctor in a hospital, still, I felt unsafe and untrusting in a completely irrational way.

I couldn't help but register the disgust my father felt for Terry, but my mother had flown over to see me in prison, and Terry had taken her out to dinner, he had been very kind to her. She wasn't fooled, she couldn't understand it, and he was older than she was. I wouldn't listen then, I couldn't explain the attraction.

Perhaps it was just hanging onto something familiar. I was looking for daddy-love. It was never there. And I've looked for it in men, I've always been with much older men. The only thing that has changed is that I have grown older and I know what I am doing. That awareness doesn't help to break the pattern. I don't want to be "saved." I've needed to create chaos in order to stay alive, don't you see? I play Russian Roulette because I don't have a sense of self. I invite the bullet. I can fuck all I want, not to feel, I can take every substance imaginable and accumulate people, friends and things, like I do. I'm tired of hurting. But I don't really want intimacy. It would burn me alive.

I am so hard to love. I'll push you away because I don't want to get close to you, I can't trust you. I'll lie and cheat on you, to make you hate me, like a three-year-old having a tantrum, I'll kick your ankles and spit in your face until all you can do, for your own sanity, is walk away.

I loathed Terry for being away. I needed the immediacy of sex, a substitute for love. I was meant to step into this new life, accept it and be grateful for the clean slate. I was, but I felt needy. Anything would have been better than being alone. With the exception of a single piece of hate mail (which I believe it was sent by Colette), I faced only an overwhelming welcome back, and generous gestures of support.

I called Jonathan, to come and stay with me, the first night out. I wanted copulation without consequences. I wanted to show off my new skinny body, he had always teased me that there was a thin woman dying to come out of me. Jonathan Cousar had gone to prison for four years for a mortgage con. I had known him briefly through friends, we had had a brief affair, after his affair with my friend Robin who had been a very married married Junior Leaguer.

Jonathan had just come out of prison when we met and was recently humbled, he felt fragile. When we had dated, he no longer wanted to keep up with the trips, the dinners and the premium tickets that membership of our select tribe require. Prison had made him look for more, and he had found God. He had started an Internet hosting service called Lazy Lizard and he was enjoying making a success of himself, on a smaller scale. After months of ascetic living, I craved the nearness of a man. Any warm body would do. He had written to me in prison and he'd been kind. He knew where I was emotionally and what I was going through, after all he had been there.

Shakespeare's Viola said, "I am not what I am."

Wanting to be close to a man that night, needing the warmth of a body next to mine indicated how broken my sense of self had become. I refused to feel the despair, I wanted friction to block out the pain. I needed someone living who I could reach out to in the night, from the depths of my self. I felt as if I was spinning out, it was so dark in and around me. The sex was perfunctory, perhaps neither of us expected it to be anything other than that, it was just part of the unspoken contract. He spent the whole night which was quite an accomplishment as he had always left to go back to his own apartment previously. We slept with a night light on.

Everything was different. Terry threw himself into the two books of poems he was trying to finish so he could clear the way for the great American novel, which he still hadn't written. It was his fantasy which consisted of part autobiography and part social commentary, and I passed the time by going on extravagant shopping trips with his American Express card. Because he was a man of the people he insisted on keeping to the most basic card, every man's green but he had an unlimited credit line, much to my delight and his injury.

Although he had moved me out of the house as well, he would still call me and we would see each other most weekends. Sometimes it felt as of we might slip into the old, easy comfort of the life we had shared but neither could give into the "us" that had existed before, he loved my new shape and enjoyed the recently sculpted body I had become. I didn't regret the $60 000 bill I racked up on his Amex. He deserved it.

He started to spend a lot of time in Santa Barbara, that winter but he still couldn't shake off the greyness or the winter pallor that had seeped into him. In his own head he had been nothing less than the most perfect gent. He had told me over tears and prison tea that he had felt my soul slipping away and he had to hold onto me. He had felt me descending into a dark place and he didn't feel that he could walk away. I wrote him long pleading letters from prison asking him to forgive real and imagined infractions, but the whole time he had been factoring away, moving further, ridding everything in his life that reminded him of me. I thought I would die if he left me, not in that Bollywood heaving bosom dramatic fashion, I thought I would curl up into a ball and expire, as easy as letting out a sigh. So much of who I was remained tangled up in who he thought I was. I thought this thing we had was love. I always fell too easily. I had never invested as much of myself or as much energy in a relationship and I didn't want it to end, I felt I would come undone. But he was resolute.

Terry had a coming out party, catered by a company which employed ex-cons called Fresh Start. They cooked up a delicious spicy jerk chicken and rice dish and served it with simple style to the thirty people Terry had gathered.

I had found some meaning in art and it brought something to my life. Friends encouraged me to look for another space in East Hampton, where I could recontextualise out of the city. I found 75 Main Street. I thought I still had the residual strength to kick-start my life and get myself going again. I did, but I didn't count on other people trying to undermine that tiny bit of resolve I had left. But at the time, they felt justified.

I decided to call the second floor space Farah and Company. The sign was elegant with hand painted gold leaf lettering on a Hunter green board. Most of the young and glamorous emerging young artists I had had before agreed to let me have another chance. I appeared to have emerged whole from my mess. I agreed a rental for a year, with David Fink, the appropriately named New York attorney who owned the space. David took the money but kept on delaying the signing of the lease.

The same weekend that we signed the lease, Dan Ratner printed a three-quarter page black and white picture of me in his eponymous paper. It was a photo Peter had taken a couple of years earlier. Underneath, he recounted the story of a contessa that had summered in East Hampton and passed bad cheques. The following year when she rolled up in her limousine, people were more careful of her. He implied, without saying as much that I should be dealt with in the same way.

It's a lie to say that once a person has served their time and repaid their debt to society that they can return to the life they knew before. Everything shifts, seismically. It was expected I should be ashamed, broken, that I should hide away in a corner and although I didn't court Page Six or the *New York Newsday* columnists, I frequently saw spiteful articles about me in them. I used to read

185

them at that time. They hurt but they also showed me I existed, because I was there, written about in black and white.

I met Richard Johnson, the harbinger of bad news, only once, at a party at the Guggenheim.

I went up to him and held out my hand. I beamed a megawatt smile his way.

"Richard. So lovely to see you."

Automatically his hand reached out for mine, and he raised it to his lips. I had never met him though we had spoken on the phone often enough, usually one-sided conversations with me pleading with him not to print something nasty, or him trying to draw out information on some salacious tidbit about me over which he was feasting. I deferred to his kiss politely enough all the while keeping my gaze fixed somewhere in the middle distance. He noticed the aloofness.

"Do you know who I am?"

I watched the mental Rolodex cards flip over in his mind,

"Yes, of course..." his voice broke off, he hadn't a clue. He should know my face from the number of times his silly minions had published pictures of me but he was grasping.

"I am Farah Damji. Supposedly pregnant by my tycoon boyfriend and pining away in my Chanel suits. Do I look like any of that to you?" I stood sideways so he could get a good look at my flat stomach. He looked at the floor.

"Oh you know we don't mean half of what is printed in the paper, it's all just for fun...to amuse people. You know they say there's one thing worse than being talked about..."

He smiled and twitched nervously, he was looking for the emergency exit out of this situation, I could almost feel him leaving my space. The light was leaving those dancing eyes.

"You don't know me then?" I persisted.

"No, but it's lovely to see you."

I wanted to spit at his affected use of the word lovely, he strained his eyes through his horn-rimmed glasses to catch a glimpse of someone he did know so he could beat a retreat.

"And you. Lovely to *meet* you. "

I thought he looked sufficiently chastised, little beads of perspiration had broken out where the frames of his owlish glasses met the bridge of his nose and his cheeks, so I dropped his hand, the way I might drop a soiled piece of tissue paper and I turned on my heel before he could say anything and before he could leave.

I resented that they all thought they knew me, they thought they could write about me. They claimed to know how I functioned in this Moschino heart-shaped, lipsticked version of Machiavelli. In truth, I was floundering. I ploughed ahead with the opening of the gallery regardless.

It was the big night, the gallery looked so beautiful. Each room had a different look and feel, it was like being inside someone's home, I had found old furniture from the junk shops which I had restored. Muted green and sun-bleached blue paint set off the art on the walls. There was a lot of noise about the new gallery, not just because it was me. Main Street was in East Hampton's fashionable main drag.

Tommy Hilfiger and Ralph Lauren, the godfathers of Hamptons hip, had stores close by and the Barefoot Contessa, which was an organic deli that sold every fancy delight a Hamptons hostess might long for, was located across the street.

The police came.

David Fink had let the space to a set of architects as well as to me. He told the police that he had never signed our rental agreement, although he had indeed taken the deposit and three months rent money. I had shown the police the deposit slip into Fink's account and the signed courier's bill, showing another cheque he had received and cashed, which had been left at his office reception. I had also shown them a signed tenancy agreement.

Fink had seen the picture and the article in *Dan's Paper* and decided he was going to keep the money and renege on our agreement. As I had been in prison for theft and deception and he was a pillar of the local community, obviously everyone would have no choice but to believe him.

Bertrand Russell's nice people came home to roost on the grave of my future. I had tried to reason with David but to no avail. I had retained a local solicitor who was trying to unravel the mess with the police, but he just saw me as a meal ticket. He was always in waiting, for his next $1 000 cheque. The last thing we expected was the swat squad circling the gallery, tonight of all nights. Steve, the gangly attorney, came and shut himself in a room with me. He told me police cars had circled the premises, both front and back entrances were secured, in case I attempted a Lara Croft style escape.

The pictures in the following Sunday's Hamptons' papers show me looking gaunt. I am being led out of the gallery and down the stairs by a police officer.

A swoop of black hair hides half my face and the glint of a Chanel chain strap rests on my shoulder. I was taken to the police station and charged with forgery. I, not David, was said to have signed the tenancy agreement, and so I was put in front of the District Judge.

She was surprised; she had received an invitation to the opening and had planned on attending. Her disbelief was reflected in the low bail she asked to be posted. Other charges emanated from my investment banker "friend" Maria, whose house I stayed in and whose car I was permitted to use. She had been having an affair for years with her boss and one day in a mild fit of pique I decided to tell her unsuspecting husband, Tom, about it.

The artists who came to the local nick were sympathetic but didn't want to get involved in another round of legal dramas. Terry was still fuming about his Amex bill. Sudsy, the manager of another local gallery who had been a friend at some point, kept the gossip going through his column in the *East Hampton Star*.

When the Judge remanded me so my bail could be paid, she told me not to worry, Suffolk County Jail was going to be a playground compared to Rikers' Island. The next week passed in a flurry and a blur. Stanley Cohen, art collector and social stanchion said he would pay it but never got round to it. Mohan Shah, an Indian friend with his own agenda, finally did. It was only $1 000.

I went back to Manhattan and I hung out with Abby Hirsch. She had attended the party Terry had given me and given me all sorts of soaps and salts, smellies for a clean start, she said. She and I were friendly. Abby allegedly had friends at *Vanity Fair* who supposedly wanted her to write about me, an in-depth profile to tell "My Side of the Story." She encouraged me to join the new Reebok Gymnasium on Columbus Avenue where she was a member and she'd grill me over lightly sautéed vegetable lunches at the airy café on the seventh floor.

She confided in me that she ran an upmarket dating service, Godmothers. For a fee of $5 000 she fixed up Manhattan's most eligible bachelors with their dream girls, for serial, serious and meaningful relationships. This was Abby, whose alter ego was that of a serious writer. Abby aided and assisted my paranoia. She was a lot older and had an improbable crush on Terry; I was just her way of getting closer to him. She had inveigled her way into my life and I was desperate for someone to hold onto.

I had been bailed to return to court in Suffolk County in the second week of May and I was frightened. Fink had shut the gallery and taken everything, all the paintings, my clothes and furniture. Once again, everything was gone. I had no stamina left to fight him or the system and although Steve assured me we would win, I gave up. America drew first and final blood.

On May 8th 1996, I flew to the British Embassy in Washington DC to claim my passport had been stolen. I was issued a new one the same day. It wasn't stolen, I had surrendered it to the Supreme Court in New York as part of my bail conditions but I hadn't yet retrieved it.

I flew back to La Guardia the same afternoon and Abby insisted that my flat was probably being watched so I should let her pack up my belongings. She stole some of my favourite clothes, a brown tissue silk Dries van Noten dress, embossed with gold block printed roses, a Bengal rose coloured wool jersey Armani suit and a favourite slouchy mud coloured one and that Calvin Klein silk charmeuse dress that I had worn to the dinner we hosted for Peter and Lee Radziwill. She also stole half the canvas prints for which I had paid Dave Duggal, when I was released.

They ended up at her B+B on the Vineyard. When I contacted the local police about it, they knew her well, she was being investigated for harassing her "boyfriend" on the island by stalking him and sending abusive messages and threats.

I booked a First Class American Airlines return ticket to London on the same night, which happened to be my mother's fifty-sixth birthday, on May 10th. I touched down at Heathrow, in a country I no longer knew and could never call home, but somewhere I could, at last, breathe easy. I could stop looking over my shoulder; the fear had been left behind, on another continent.

Act II

Inside Me

I want you like I need crack cocaine. I don't want to savour you, like a fine glass of red wine, I want to inject you, devour you. I want the mad rush of lust that hits me, like a broad slap when I think about you; I need you every second of every minute. You are like light, I grow towards you. But you reside in the dark side of me.

Listen to the wickedest thing that I ever did. I want to tell you something crazy that will take you inside my mind so you step into the space between my thoughts. I want you to need me, let me seduce you. Breathe me in, swallow the flight of my words so you are left without a choice. I'll entice you, so you have to read what follows so you understand and can be a part of me. Inside me. Let me feed your addiction to my thoughts and deeds like a junkie on smack and watch me as I mainline myself straight into your empty veins. I become the abscesses in the crevice of your arm, which you watch, powerless as they perforate so you can take in more of me. I will lend you my eyes. My sweet words kill your pain.

I live by different rules, not yours. Mine is a different crowd and caste. I have Excessomania. There is a motto, like a cushion on the sofa, of the family home, a tattered hand-me-down of an heirloom, "Never Apologize, Never Explain." These were the words that were crumbled into my baby formula. These were the last words I saw before I shut my eyes and surrendered to Morpheus' sweet promise. Empires have been built on the rhyming-chiming innocence of these four little words. I was brought up to believe I can. I'll take what I can and what I want. I don't answer to your ownership. I will never belong to your world. Yet mine is the anthem of the capitalist, every step I take to move my frontier further into your territory is as invisible and essential as each tiny stroke of a pencil which gives itself over to form a part of a letter which forms a word. First there was the word.

Like another scented protagonist elsewhere, I am too close to my own perfume to smell my sweet putrefaction. My crimes are the sum of me, to discern where the truth is lying in me and where it is real, that is for you to show me. Show me who I am. I am bigger but less than the sum total of my legend, the catalogue of stories, fantastic fitinas of chaos created across continents, like cicatrices on my skin. Which shall I pick at so it oozes its secret sickness across the page and sublimates into your mind?

I could tell you how I used my feminine wiles to betray men with sex and conquests? That's commonplace, mine are no more interesting than yours or his. But women aren't supposed to spill the seed once it has been implanted. I fornicate, holding onto the mad delusion that I will be rendered immortal by this exchange of fluids, this vacuous motion, the tiresome tangle of limbs that exists between pleasure and necessity.

Should I tell you I am a thief, that I will steal your soul? I took people and things, the way I'm taking you now, with my long brown fingers, with the Pied Piper's tune of distance and dreams. You know all about me. Yet still you follow. But what's left to tell, every scenario has been played out in creeping column inches over tabloids and broadsheets; enough to wallpaper the sides of the tomb in which my dark secrets lie sleeping. They tell me that there is freedom in telling, the baring of the soul to sunlight in some self-flagellating Opus Dei way, that the shame will slip off my shoulders; I will feel lighter, more in the world and not outside it. I am a recalcitrant child, being forced to make nice. I don't feel shame any longer. I am the woman I was born to be. My crime has unleashed me.

If I tell you and not explain what my thinking was, then you might think me crazy. Do you have to be mad with me, to understand that your judgment means nothing? Do I mean anything to you? Is there more than skin deep to me, the sloe-eyed brown-skinned woman who stares half-smiling at you, from behind big dark glasses?

A con is a con, by sleight of hand and a clever trick of the light I can make you see in me what you want me to be and I use that to my own advantage, to get what I think I need from you, some words, your body, your heart, some physical or emotional experience that I have to have and if you don't give it to me, I'll steal it.

Cool Britannia

London didn't fit. Isn't it strange how we imagine that we can just step into a place we left a long time ago and that it will comfortably meld itself around us? I harboured the delusion that I could resume my old gait, step into the rhythm of my stride in a pair of old shoes.

It was the time when the economy was re-finding its feet but still on wobbly legs, the recession was over, the Blair Glory Years were in full swing. It was a sticky-back plastic veneer, something that could be peeled off and that was not built on solid foundations. Britain was fighting to find and define a new identity.

Imran Khan, the human rights lawyer, was fighting for justice for the family of Stephen Lawrence, a young black kid who had been murdered by three white boys. Witnesses came forward, the same three names kept cropping up still the police refused to do anything about it. The investigation into the police's handling of the affair and the findings of Lord MacPherson's Report, determined that the Metropolitan Police was institutionally racist. It put Imran on the map as the champion of the underdog and defender of all of our freedom.

This Brave New World that was dawning highlighted the cracks in the wall of the establishment. We wanted to believe everything was just fine, after all that would never happen to a young Asian boy, Asian youths didn't get themselves into such situations. But the 2 and 3Gs, as the second and third generation branded themselves, had different expectations of what Britain should provide, as "home."

An ocean's space creates a lot of longing. Terry came over, he decided he missed me after I left. Since I was no longer just across the park at his beck and call, he thought he had lost me. I came to realise how much under his grip I had been, I had traded my father's shackles for Terry's dog collar. But it was comfortable; it was what I had grown used to.

We booked him a room at Blake's, but he stayed with me in the garden flat I had rented in the wrong end of Chelsea. We tried to recreate the spark, thinking that it could come alight again, but what we once had went out long ago. We stayed with it, in the same way that you want to reread a book, which is an old favourite from a long time ago, but this time, you know the ending and there is little pleasure left in revisiting old stories unless the writing engages you again, in the same way. It didn't.

He fantasised about moving to London, he could write and mange his investment portfolio from anywhere in the world, maybe this was the escape he had sought to leave his New York gilded cage. He left London after a week spent basking in the renewed romance promising to return. We planned a trip to Kenya. I had spoken to him about my memories of Kenya often, he wanted us to visit the land which I considered as much home as possible, together.

In the Autumn of 1996, I felt freed. I had kept the weight off and was still slim, I exercised like an addict at Holmes Place on Fulham Road, where the young Paula Froelich, before her Page Six days, worked as a receptionist. I found the new life I had wanted. I took no time off at all; I didn't stop to consider what I had left behind. In true entrepreneurial spirit, and, following in the giant footsteps of my dad, I bought an old warehouse off Lots Road in Chelsea. The parents lent me some money for the deposit; I flew straight in there.

I had always wanted to have children, somewhere in the back of my mind I had decided I would have them when I was thirty. Life has always been like that; events transpire exactly the way I had envisaged that they would. Nothing has been random. By my thirtieth birthday, I was pregnant. I called to tell Terry, it wasn't his, and he came to London.

We had planned a trip to Paris, he wanted to see the Peter Beard exhibition at France's National Photo gallery. That was our last weekend. While he was still passionate, something in him had grown old. Later he told me he had met a Long Island estate agent who was much more suited to his life then, being with her didn't entail upping sticks and moving continents. She was a bright light socially and Terry has always liked women who have power address books, filled with the names of the rich and famous in order to gain entry into another, readymade world. I realised how lonely he was, how few people he had in his life that were really close to him. I noticed how little I knew him.

It was wonderful to see Peter and his daughter Zara. Najma brooded over them but Peter had been badly trampled by an elephant and he had gone back to her. We always go back to where we think we can get away with the most.

Terry cancelled the Kenya trip. He paid off my exorbitant spree on his Amex card and we ceased to have anymore contact. I can't remember what happened, if it was really a fight or if he dealt with me in the same way he dealt with everything else he couldn't control, by shutting me out of his life. There was so much about his life I didn't know, he had bought a place in Santa Barbara ostensibly to write the Great American Novel, which to date hadn't been written, and to be close to the children.

My parents were remarkably liberal about their impending grand parenthood. This would be the first grandchild. I remember going to a dinner party with my father and vomiting in the toilet he held my hair back as I leaned into the bowl. There are moments in my life when my father has been alarmingly tender and affectionate. I don't remember those times because he has obliterated them with later acts of cruelty or vindictiveness. If I didn't know better, I might tell you that there are two of him.

They had moved to Cape Town, to start a life there. Thirty years of England and covert racism had made my father realise that no matter how much money he had, there would never be a place for the displaced in this country. South Africa had come of out Apartheid and he saw in the birth of the nation, a new start for himself. My mother dutifully followed, after all she needed to maintain the lifestyle to which she had become accustomed for over thirty years.

I suffered morning sickness for most of the nine months that I was pregnant with Imran. I am not one of those women who took to being pregnant like a duck to water. My beautiful body grew distended and distorted, my clothes stopped fitting and in the end all I could wear was forgiving Ghost, I never bought maternity clothes.

All the time I was pregnant, I worked on the warehouse which I converted into a three-storey house. Fights with builders, frequent disruptions in my domestic life, I didn't think about how these would affect my unborn child. Neither did I for a second, think about how my boy would grow into a man without a father.

I didn't give the man a second thought. As my own father had been largely absent even when he had been present, I thought I could do it myself. All I have from my father is a long hallway in my memory of empty promises in gold-leaf frames.

I started to have cramps and called the Chelsea and Westminster hospital, where I was being monitored as it was a few minutes from my house.

The duty midwife told me I must have indigestion and we shared a laugh, as I had eaten a curry, about the old wives' tale that spicy food will bring on labour at the end of the term. She told me to have a hot bath which would help the cramps. The next morning, the pain was still there and she told me to come into the hospital and she would do some tests. I walked myself there, it was a beautiful June morning. There are days in London when the light hits it just right and it sparkles.

I had set up a home in Kenya as I wanted to live there with my son, I couldn't see bringing him up alone in London and I was still close to the Fazal boys, I thought they would be good default father figures for the unborn child. My plan had been to go out there in early July as Imran was not supposed to be born till the end of June. My mother had planned to come and stay with us for two weeks after he was born. He was born that afternoon, as it hadn't been indigestion I was feeling but early labour pains.

I had passed a series of bad cheques just before he was born, and a week later, when he was still new in the house and I hadn't even become used to the idea that I was a new mother, the police arrested me. I have put my family through a lot, and most of it, I don't feel much remorse about. But this time the earnest policewoman decided to search poor Jena's flat as well.

By the time we reached Ealing, she was fast asleep in her bed and she had no idea what was going on. The police did a cursory search of her tiny one bedroom and, once they were satisfied that they had meted out enough humiliation, they left. I was given only a caution for that episode.

There are so many times in my life I look back on, now, with the generosity of hindsight and think, God, I wish I had got it then. Why didn't I learn my lesson from those four awful months at Rikers' Island? What was it in me that kept putting myself in those high risk and illegal situations? I couldn't fathom it, I wasn't even aware of it, I needed chaos not to feel the screeching pain in me that I had tried to bury for the best part of twenty-five years, and I needed to create turmoil to exist. I could only flourish in flux. I thought a change of hemisphere, a geographical flight to another place might empty the garbage in me. Maybe I could leave it all behind.

We did move out to Nairobi, to the little house I had rented from the ex-MP John Keen. Those were still the days of bandits and barons in Nairobi, we lived first of all in a house belonging to an Asian businessman, distantly related through a second cousin, Lutaf Keshavjee. His houseboy-gardener stole a lot of Imran's baby clothes while we were away and Keshavjee refused to do anything about it.

I soon learned that it paid to stay friends with the local Police Sergeant and a little money went a long way in staying on her good side. Bribery wasn't even discreet. Everyone did it. Only the poor were locked up because they couldn't pay to get out and the richer you were the more power and influence could be bought. But Karen was a lonely place. We moved further away from the heart of the village, which was already in the middle of nowhere, outside Nairobi, into a house on John Keen's compound.

Blixen's sorrowful tears had seeped into the land around us and there was heartache everywhere. The Ngong Hills, clenched like the knuckles of a fist glowered from my bedroom window and every morning cow bells would wake us up as the herd passed the fence which closed off my compound. But Imran was sick a lot. The farm children, including John Keen's grandson, were a hardy bunch. Living in that rural environment had inured them to regular infections.

Imran caught everything, his half-white genetic disposition made him susceptible to even the slightest little cough or cold and he would get it badly.

I tried to live out the *Out of Africa* dream, growing flowers and vegetables and learning to paint. I took yoga classes and Imran had a wonderful African nanny with whom he bonded and who loved him as if he had been her own. We were the archetypal rickety ex-pat family, with a driver who took us to and bonfire nights at Karen Country Club amongst others who had no place to call home except the pretence of here.

One night Imran became very ill. I couldn't find my driver as he had sloped off somewhere to drink c*h'anga*, the illegal and lethal brew the locals make and consume, from sugar. The road to Nairobi from Karen is long and dark. I stopped in Lavington, the suburb outside Nairobi at my aunt's house. She has always been good at crisis management, and I thought she would know what to do. She took one look at Imran and his watery eyes; she felt his sunken fontanel and immediately shouted for Aziz to take us to the hospital.

He was severely dehydrated and the Aga Khan Hospital put him on a drip and made arrangements for him and I to stay until he was out of danger. Lying next to him, so tiny, with tubes coming out of him, all I felt was powerlessness and pain. My mother flew in from Cape Town, which reinforced my feelings of uselessness because she is good at that. Slowly as the light came back into his eyes and he started to look at some of the new toys I had bought for him, I realised what a gift a child was.

Being a mother started to make me look for an acceptable definition of who I could become. For years I had tried different versions of myself, re-launched and restyled like a periodical but in this tiny life I could see the best of me, he was like a tiny angel-mirror.

It's as an act of pure narcissism, having a child. It was another misguided way of believing I could cheat life and immortality. We procreate to replicate ourselves but this mini-me only extends the legacy started by our own dysfunctional origin. For a long time it was just him and me I thought I would live out the rest of my life with him. He was a bright child who delighted in entertaining people. Something about a boy-child represents a blank canvas of potential in a mother. He reflected all the latent love I never had been able to show. Imran was always very protective of me, which is nourishing but I never realised I could love someone or something so completely and without choice, it's just in me.

John Keen, ex-MP had a complicated life. The estate on which we rented our house was ruled by Mama Keen, the oldest, dominant and first wife. Rumours of his antics with his other wives and girlfriends were making their way back to the old lady's ears and she grew more and more irascible. I couldn't last in Kenya. The oppressiveness of the Fazal boys, who were coming undone

197

now that the regulating presence of their recently dead father was gone, was annihilating. When I needed them, such as for Imran's fist birthday party, they failed to show up and when I didn't, they were everywhere. The heat, the unrelenting monsoon that year, the mossies, all served to make me irritable and homesick for elsewhere.

I took Imran to Cape Town, for Christmas. My father had mellowed in his semi-retirement and my son was the apple of his eye. He seemed to be drinking less. She had started a course with Lifeline, the suicide phone line mentors and was busy in her own world, which I though would give her less time to interfere in mine. We went back to Nairobi in January with a view to moving back to Cape Town permanently; his grandson's young life had given my father the impetus and the inspiration to build what he called his second fortune.

He was doing well, he bought old and dilapidated houses in luxury areas and would then renovate them to a high specification. In Cape Town, a little money goes a long way and he was a big fish in a little pond. My son gave him something to live for and he took to bigger and more expensive projects.

Initially I stayed in one of my father's flats. He is defined by his work, he can't do nothing, although frenetic bursts of activity are followed with days in bed, as if to regain or recuperate his energy, in the way an army might as they prepare for the next onslaught. My father treats life like a battle and in the same way, you are either on his side or his enemy. It's very much his way or the highway.

Friends of my mother told me later that she was envious of the choices I had made, that I had gone out and done my own life. What she didn't see was that it wasn't a life based on conscious or pragmatic choices but one based on reactive behaviour. Much of what I did, I did to rebel, to cause anxiety and anger in my father. There were no choices, only reactions and anger followed by prodigal homecomings.

Cape Town was a short lived dream. I don't like the Afrikaans mentality which is a mixture of aggression and self-loathing. We didn't fit in, yet again, we were the outsider as we were clearly not Coloureds or Durban Indians but my father had built his house on the hill, which was invisible to the rest of the world because all around it, fortress-like there was a ten-foot-high wall which enclosed it. There were panic buttons in every room that would alert the local security company in the event of an intruder.

These rent-a-cops maintained the delicate status quo in post Apartheid South Africa. They were run by gangsters, who in turn ran the crime in the cities. The mobsters from Russia and Europe had nestled into the comfortable no-questions-asked lifestyle of the Western Cape. Naturally I found the dissolute lot and wound up in trouble. I started to do cocaine again, word of which reached my mother, but when she asked and I denied, she didn't pursue the problem any further. That is her mentality, she would rather not bother.

It is practically impossible to be deported from South Africa, due to the rights enshrined in the new constitution. It was the same litany of stuff I had done in New York. I had started a decorating shop, which imported furniture and accessories from all over the world. We also created bespoke pieces with local design houses and manufacturers.

My thirty-first birthday, my father gave a birthday party for me at his house, to which we invited dozens of people for a sit-down dinner. When I did well, he spared no effort or expense to show off his brilliant daughter. I couldn't sustain the shop, it cost too much money to run and Cape Town's wealthy community is close knit and gossipy.

In the two years I lived there, I didn't make a single close friend. It was all about getting things done for people and soon I found myself entrenched in the vacuous hole that is the life of an interior decorator with clingy clients and unsatisfied suppliers.

In November 2000 I came back to London, agreeing to be deported (at my own expense) and I left exhausted and spent. My advocate agreed to a clause that I would not return to South Africa, although at the time he expressed some concerns as to whether that agreement infringed upon my Human Rights and the Geneva Convention, as it clearly hindered my right to enjoy my family life, unobstructed by the state.

In November 2000 I left Imran with my parents with the agreement that he would join me in London when I was more settled. The news that a young Asian boy had been killed in a racist attack on the night before he was due to be released in Feltham Young Offenders' Institution rocked the community. Young Asian boys didn't go to prison. But a malaise was seizing our boys, they didn't fit in, although they had tried and unlike their first generation parents they were not prepared to shut up and play nice houseguests. They wanted to claim a place in the country they called home. If anyone had paid any attention to them, if we had entered into a dialogue, maybe they wouldn't have become disenfranchised.

I came back to London, which was undergoing another incarnation as the capital of cool. It was trying to be a smaller version of New York. The transition towards being a cultural melting pot had started. Some of the old friends were still around and I supported myself from income generated by the flats I owned, which I had refurbished and rented out. At one point there were five flats, all around SW3 and SW10, the trendy Chelsea area.

I met Julian Marshall at a bar called Bardo on Fulham Road. I had a new set of friends. They were the Chelsea crowd who represented something of life on Kings Road in the new century, they were interested in ethnic cultures and attracted to bars which were kitted out in pretentious versions of what a Buddhist temple might look like if it were to become a night club. Bardo was one of those places.

Julian had the watery look of someone who is worn out by life. He described himself as my ghastly Ulsterman and the relationship was short lived, purely sexual and meaningless. I discovered at the age of thirty-five that I was pregnant. I didn't want another child, I didn't think that there was space in my life or in my heart for another life. Looking after Imran was hard enough although I had a full time au-pair.

I had rented and then bought a converted grain tower in a field outside Petersfield. This was home, this isolated, Rapunzel place. Imran loved it, in the winter it became part of a dark fairytale and in the summer, the field came alive and he was free to run and plant seeds and be in nature.

I was overextending myself financially by buying this property but I fell in love with it the moment I set my eyes on it. It was different and eccentric. I could see growing old in it, tending the wilderness of a garden and keeping the foxes and rabbits off my flowerbeds. It was where I had a life.

I had serious doubts about whether I could love another child as much as I loved my son. Being a mother is emotionally exhausting, there was no room in my life for another relationship, which is why these meaningless sexual liaisons were attractive. Everyone got from it what they wanted. When he took his first steps I thought my heart might break, as he faltered and fell down. But kids are resilient and determined, as often as he fell over, he got up and tried again and when he finally walked unaided, when he first started to show his own personality beyond the bland mask of babyhood, I was filled with pride. I didn't know if my heart could expand any more to take in a child I hadn't planned, although now I understand that she was always wanted.

Yehudi Gordon was the current star in the firmament of London OBGYN. He has a holistic approach to childbirth. Imran had been born in a hurry, with hardly any labour pains, he was born an hour and forty minutes after I walked to the Chelsea and Westminster hospital. Marina was different, I knew she was going to be a baby girl, I could sense it.

There had been problems with Julian throughout the pregnancy and to compensate I wanted candlelight and aromatherapy oils, to counteract the anger from the litigation we had put each other through. I wanted her to be born in a birth pool and to be eased into life. Imran was excited about the prospect of a baby sister. I had made up my mind that she was going to be called Jehan, after a glamorous ex-Lycée friend but those were the days of a Captain Scarlet revival and he had decided she would be called Marina.

I had gone in for a regular scan, she was a little small so I had to go in often and recently there had been problems with rising blood pressure. St John and St Elizabeth's hospital is in St. John's Wood and Yehudi runs his neo-natal and birth unit from a private ward within the hospital. The scanning department was a few minutes walk away, in a converted church.

I couldn't miss the look of alarm on the radiologist's face, it contorted for a second and then he suppressed the grimace. There were renovations in progress in the church and I thought maybe it was these dusty surroundings that were making him uncomfortable. Plastic sheets hung in the air to try and keep the small x-ray area dust free and heavy cloth blankets protected the delicate and expensive machinery that he was using.

He handed me an envelope with a note inside and told me to go straight back to the main hospital. Yehudi was away, he told me, in Morocco for Christmas, but his deputy would see me straight away. In the five minutes it took me to walk back to John and Lizzies' a welcome party had gathered and was in a flurry of activity.

Marina had stopped growing inside me and there was only a little amniotic fluid left which left her in grave danger. They had decided that they would have to operate that minute. Doctors and midwives lost all their holistic and calming training and flustered around me. They were hunting down an anaesthesiologist. The unit was operating on a skeleton staff, it was just two days after Christmas and not everyone had returned from holiday.

There was no way I was ready to lie on the operating table. There were things I needed to take care of. She wasn't due for another two months and I had done no shopping at all. I imagined she would wear Imran's baby-grows when she was newborn and that we would go from there. I had done nothing to prepare my house in Hampshire or my flat on Kings Road for the new arrival, perhaps it was all part of my denial.

Julian had distanced himself completely and told me to get in touch after she had been born, through his shark-like lawyers as he wanted to confirm his paternity. I had stayed small throughout the pregnancy, from not eating and because I really didn't want to be pregnant from this drunk and dissolute man who was not capable of being responsible for himself, let alone a child. I had made no arrangements for Imran, he would probably want to stay with my sister and her boyfriend, who live in Twickenham.

I persuaded them to let me go home and get together a bag of clothes. The kindly Westminster Council for overstaying in my parking bay, had given me a parking ticket. Memories of Zarah bringing absolutely everything infant from my house to the Chelsea and Westminster after Imran was born were too frightening to think about. I wanted to control this birth. I also had to tell Imran that I would not be home for a few days. He would want to hear it from me, not from his au-pair; we were very close, he was more of a friend and an equal than a child.

Later they told me that the Iraqi doctor, Yehudi's number two, had followed me home, driving at a discreet distance, behind my Mercedes. They were not letting on how serious the situation was, my blood pressure had been rising and I was dangerously close to being in full-blown pre-eclampsia. I had bought a small blood pressure reading machine at Yehudi's request and I had to phone in my readings every couple of hours. When they stayed high, for more than a few hours they would ask me to come and be monitored on one of their more sophisticated machines.

When Imran came home from school, he was excited, he asked if he could come and visit me and his new sister in the hospital, so we made all the arrangements with the au-pair. She was lifted out of me a few minutes after four in the afternoon on December 27 2001. I had an epidural and gas and air, but still I could feel the strange sensation of a doctor pushing down on my belly, trying to put pressure on my ribs so she would move down from, the space where she had lodged herself.

I was awake during the procedure though they had put a sheet between me and the knife cutting the Caesarean section, I don't think I could have watched them cutting me open.

This tiny thing, the size of a chicken in the supermarket's poultry section, was handed to me. She looked startled and blinked a few times, adjusting the light as it entered into her almost violet eyes. Her hair was light blonde and she was as white as a sheet, she didn't cry till they started to do the mandatory tests on her to ensure that she was healthy. She spent the first few hours of her life under red heating lights in a salad box of an incubator, as she was still too tiny to maintain her own body temperature. She weighed less than 2 kilograms.

If I hadn't watched her being lifted out of me, if I hadn't actually felt the weight released as she rose in the hands of the surgeon, I wouldn't have believed that she was mine. She didn't look as if she came from me. Those first few days in the hospital were very difficult.

Yehudi made me confront a lot of my demons, that is his secret and why he is successful. From within the comfort and approachability of his fatherly concern and in the slightly South African tinged accent, he can say anything and still it comes out gently. Counseling from this gentle wizard is part of the antenatal care package he provides. He was the first one to put a name on what had happened to me as a child.

More than twenty-five years after the horrific episodes, Aziz called me, he was in England with his wife and I tried to talk to him about it. I was still recovering from the operation in the hospital. I was holding my own daughter, a few hours old in my arms. He just laughed, "It wasn't like that."

He tried to reconstruct our history so it was more palatable. He was in England from Kenya to check that his wife, another Farah, was clear of the cancer for which she had been treated earlier. They had called me at the hospital, to congratulate me. My dad was on a phoning frenzy to close and distant relatives; he loved the idea of a new baby girl in the family. I could hear Farah-Naz's forced laughter in the background. I wonder how much she knew and if he had perpetrated anything like the things he had done to me on their children. They had a daughter.

His voice became lower and harsher; the words came like spit from a snake, down the wire, "You knew what you were doing, you wanted it."

I felt tired from the stress and the scar of the unplanned C-section, from the sad and inevitable ending with Marina's father. I was weary, after fighting this secret, which was finally out. It was older than most of my life.

"No, I didn't want it. And I didn't know." I wasn't the tired, sexualised woman I am today. I was just a child. I hadn't yet discovered the easy, roaring sexuality of Philip Roth, I post-dated his generation of amazing and accomplished felators. I had yet to discover Henry Miller's journeys in Paris which later defined my own.

I was then just a nine-year-old with no voice and no words to say what was happening to me. He cut my childhood out from under me, I couldn't have described that I didn't want that, I didn't know any different.

I put the phone down; there was no point in arguing or talking to him. Then I took my newborn girl-child in my arms and I made a promise to myself that no one would ever hurt her, the way that I had been hurt, because this was the only way I knew how to relieve the mesh of pain and anger inside me, by loving her unconditionally and completely.

I didn't want to breast-feed. I had never liked it and it was even harder to try and do it for a child who had nothing of India, not in her hair or her skin tone. It felt both gross and intimate at the same time. My breasts were engorged and sore. Because John and Lizzies' subscribed to holistic methods, I was given no pain-killers to reduce the aches, only frozen lettuce leafs which I wore under my bra so they soaked up the heat from the swelling.

We went home three days into the New Year. I was depressed and unprepared. I had needed the last two months to get my head around the idea of another child. I hadn't enjoyed pouring over the baby sections of the posh department stores to buy the essentials, in the way I had done for my firstborn, instead Imran and his au pair had whizzed around Peter Jones with my credit card. She was so tiny, even premature baby clothes didn't fit her. The obliging matriarchs at Peter Jones suggested I buy baby-doll clothes and put her in these. The idea of putting a real baby into toy clothes horrified me. She could only drink two ounces of milk at a time for the first few weeks. But she gladly gave a resounding burp as soon as she was set on a shoulder to be winded.

She was a contented little thing, as pretty as a picture in the little skullcaps she had to wear to maintain her own body's heat. When she smiled, she did it with her whole face and she caught the sunshine, which refracted a thousand rays of light when she looked back at me. She gurgled and made baby grumbling noises if she was hungry or cross. Of course I loved her and I looked after her, but beyond that I felt as empty as a shell. She was mine and I would hold onto her, this little warrior baby.

Inside I was sad and tired.

Dangerous Midwives

She was so officious and bumbling, this stupid twenty-eight-year-old in front of me. She had been sent by the local trust to make sure the baby was all right, which of course she was, though she was still underweight for her age, she was only ten days old. They hand every new mother a red plastic book in which we are meant to chart our baby's height and weight increases till they meet along a perfect, idealized arch, so the midwife can go away and tick the regulatory boxes.

As soon as she was born, I had decided that I was not going to immunize her, I hadn't with Imran and he was perfectly healthy. The torture of too many injections persisted in my mind, I couldn't subject my kids to that. I was a firm believer that MMR was responsible for stunted growth and mental retardation. I decided that I would treat them holistically.

"She hates you, you know," came the firm voice of the midwife.

"Who does?" I had no idea what she was talking about and I was counting the minutes for her to go. Surely she had other new mums she could fuss and fester over.

"Your daughter. She hates everything about you. She wants to kill you and she wishes that you were dead."

This was not good advice to dish out to a mother obviously in pain, who was suffering from post-natal depression. I can't describe it, life was just flat. It wasn't really anything to do with Marina, she was just a symptom of it, but I cried a lot and I slept a lot, waking only to feed and change and bathe my baby or myself. My mother stepped in. She wanted to take the baby to Cape Town, where she would find us a nanny and train her and send Marina home with the nanny in three months.

At the time it felt like a good idea. Now, I see it was her way of trying to rewrite her filthy history. I didn't have the same odious non-relationship that I have with her now, barely acknowledging her existence, but she has known she failed as a mother years ago. She wanted to use my kids as a second chance and get another go at the game. Her own son didn't speak to her for years at a time, he was something successful in merchant banking but he had cut off from the rest of the family after too many inconsequential misunderstandings. He drew boundaries which they couldn't cross and never entered. I wish I had done the same, at that time. I regret nothing more than letting my parents into my children's lives.

My daughter's Euro appearance had made me question my own identity. Imran was firmly ensconced in the British way of life by way of the expensive prep school he attended, near Eaton Square. It proudly upheld every aspect of public school life. He looked Mediterranean or maybe half-Arab, he didn't look at all Indian, with his chestnut eyes and his coarse dark brown hair. His eyes were shaped like almonds and his skin was creamy white, he was a child of the new Millennium, growing ever towards that murky gene pool which will eventually make us all look the same anyway. She was resolutely, un-forgivingly white.

I knew so little of my own culture and where I came from. Of course Jena was still there to tell magical stories of the subcontinent, as she knew it, but they seemed faraway in the way she told them, as if they happened at the time of Ali Baba or Aladdin. What of me would this little white child take into the world? As a parent I was most concerned that she had understood the great sub-continent that she could call half her home.

I had worked on a publication called *Ampersand* under the careful stewardship of Andrew Harvey, who is an extraordinary editor. We managed to get two issues out before it was run into the ground by Hitesh, a greedy accountant and Jonathan Kern, the egocentric criminal who was its publisher and founder. *Ampersand* was short lived and high on style but low in values; Jonathan had served a prison sentence for fraud, and shared a cell with Howard Marks, the drugs lord. It wasn't an auspicious start in publishing but it was an experience in everything a magazine shouldn't be. Maggie Vercelli, the amazing woman whom Jonathan had conned into financing the project, was the managing director in the UK for Dolce and Gabbana, in London. When Jonathan resigned, she handed it over to the unscrupulous Indian accountant.

I wanted to start a magazine of my own, but one that targeted the zeitgeist, we were approaching that Indobrit moment. Anjoom Mukadam and Sharmila Karmani were two PhD students who were researching an obscure and pointless thesis for their dissertations. Publishing looked glamorous and sexy to these two dowdy academicians and so the three of us decided to start a lifestyle publication aimed specifically at second and third generation British Asians, a sub-group that we what called Indobrits.

Indobrit was a word Anjoom had hijacked for her thesis, she pretended to have made it up. The word perfectly described the ethos of the magazine and so we decided to trademark it, with the London Patents Office, in all three of our names, to protect it as intellectual property. I left it to her to do, we had weekly meetings, when they were still involved in the idea and this had been one of the few things that she was meant to complete.

They soon realised that setting up a magazine was a difficult prospect and abandoned the project. Neither of them put any money into the project, only air and ideas. They walked away from it when it became clear that they couldn't contribute in any tangible way.

The time was certainly ripe, Farrukh Dhondy had been kicked off *Bombay Dreams* to make way and rudely replaced by his erstwhile protégée, Meera Sayal to write the final book for the musical. I was sitting in front of Meera during one of the first public rehearsals. She seemed agitated and insecure. Selfridges staged Bollywood that summer and Jessica Hines, the archetypal white *firenge* and long-time paramour of another Big B, Amitabh Bachan, consulted on Indian Summer, Channel Four's attempt at mainstreaming Indian Cinema to the masses. Her main claim to fame was that she had become pregnant by Aamir Khan, who later denied paternity of the child.

Marina came back in March and was vibrant and healthy. In her tail came a South African nanny with aspirations of grandeur, because she had managed to escape the coloured colony outside Cape Town, which offered no future. A social worker, Melissa Halliday, was assigned to our family, to make sure that I could cope. She was a wonderful support, we used to look forward to her visits, she'd sit on the floor and watch me play and interact with the kids and we ate cake. Later she told me that she could see no reason why she had to continue her visits, she was sure that everything was all right in our home and she signed off on us.

Indobrit was born in the summer of 2002. The launch party was held at the Cinnamon Club in Westminster, under the shadow of the Houses of Parliament. A lot of interesting media people came, including Allan Jenkins, the Editor of the *Observer Magazine* with my friend Sandra Yarwood. She and I had become friends by default, our sons played together. It was a defining moment for ethnic publishing as it was the only magazine aimed at an ethnic readership, which attracted hoards of white British readers and mainstream establishment advertisers.

It took off, from its first issue, which had a cover depicting Ray Panthaki, who had found some success and quite a lot of fame in *Bombay Dreams* and Rachel Shelley, who had starred opposite Aamir Khan in *Lagaan*. The cover, which has them both staring like frightened deer, was shot in the lounge at the Cobden Club.

Inside, we had not only fashion and films but also issues which affected us as young British Asians. Our writers were cherry-picked either for their

207

controversial stance on a subject or because they were specialists in their fields. Internationally acclaimed writers such as Pico Iyer wrote for us, we were amongst the first magazines to recognise the potential of power broker, Fareed Zakaria. It looked smart, I had used the same format as *Glamour* which had launched the year before, it was handbag size but big enough for serious art direction and to commission worthwhile photo shoots. The British Asian is a strange creature. We are an envious and fearful bunch.

My little magazine was punching way above its weight. With good connections in the mainstream press, we usually managed to have one or two articles from each issue syndicated in the mainstream papers and I was friendly with the gossipistes who reprinted tidbits, such as Guy Adams who then wrote the Spy Column for the *Telegraph* and Richard Kay, from the *Daily Mail.* The magazine "mainstreamed" exotica and another world onto the horizon of the young and urbane. By all accounts, it appeared successful. We had widespread distribution and the publication could be found across the UK and also in India at bookstores. The writing was excellent, the layout was bold and different. It enabled a generation of readers to be proud of who they were and to understand more about where they came from. We always covered interesting stories from India, and I was surprised that the Indian perspective is a lot broader than ours, which is firmly constricted by being stuck in this cold and lonely island.

Anjoom sniffed around like a dog smelling its own shit, she decided she had been hard done by. I came home from one of many trips to India to find legal letters stating that I was using the trademarked word Indobrit without her consent and therefore infringing *her* copyright. I wrote a sharp letter back to her bloodsucking solicitor outlining all of the expenses that I had incurred in keeping the magazine going and that if she thought she was entitled to £10 000 a year for the use of the name, then perhaps she might like to contribute in an equal amount to the running and other expenses which I had borne.

I kept getting increasingly stupid letters from her solicitor, but at the same time, I had printed a rather nasty editorial piece about Ethnic Media Group and how they lied to potential advertisers about their print runs and readership. They had threatened to sue me unless I printed a retraction and I refused. They then backed down, stating that they didn't want to bankrupt my little enterprise as it was still new and posed no threat to them. Later my assertions were proved to be correct. They were busted for inflating their figures with the massive amount of copies they offloaded via "free distribution."

What Anjoom and Shamila didn't realise was that most independent publications, which are not founded or supported by a major media enterprise, are run on elastic and a bit of sellotape. It is all very scarily held together, if at all. It was the original Oz story, the glossy serious revolutionary magazine built on a dream and without very strong foundations.

I encountered some incredible people along the way, as editor and publisher of Indobrit, which had to change its name to *Another Generation* magazine. It was hastily fixed, in the middle of a print run, as Anjoom had taken us to court for violating her trademark. I really never took her seriously. I thought her envy would die down, I asked GK Noon, her mentor, to speak to her and he promised that he would. He was a supporter of the magazine, since its inception; he wrote for us and also gave us an advert, in each issue, which he negotiated to the bare bones minimum rate through his in-house marketing flunky.

We were three, the terrible triumvirate of Asian media, Raj Kaushal who ran a magazine called *Snoop*, an Asian version of *FHM* and Shabbs, who'd trained under Raj then become the editor of *Asiana* which touted itself as the Asian equivalent to *Vogue*, but which went no further than glossy advertorials and Ganesh-eyed, cardboard and lacquered cut-outs of what Shabbs thought Asian women wanted to look like. We vied for the same mainstream advertisers; their magazines were much more obviously geared towards the Asian market.

My approach was subtler. Parag Khanna of the Brookings Institute had defined it as a new genre. He called it Bollystan, the rich mix of Bollywood glamour and India's deeply layered culture had given birth to a fledgling nation. India, far from the impoverished pictures of starvation and drought, had become the new superpower and a force, both culturally and economically, to be reckoned with.

This Indobrit moment was only brief, in the mind's eye of the magazine consuming public, but it was proud and tangible and as soon as it was here, it was gone. There were those that tried to extend the moment, who jumped on the gravy train created by the COI (Central Office of Information) who allocated a huge budget every year to communicate the Government's messages to the ethnic minorities.

Several media companies were given access to the marketing team at the COI and together they worked out where strategically placed ads for ethnic recruitment in the Police, or a targeted diabetes campaign, should go. Media buyers fell over themselves to access this new market, the brown pound and every other week heralded the announcement of yet another Asian Award platform. Imran Khan was a judge for the EMMA's, Bobby Syed's revolutionary concept of an Ethnic Multi Media Award, which gave Tom Cruise and David Beckham awards one year. It was all a big publicity stunt but it made people talk.

The rivalry between the magazines was outwardly fierce but behind the scenes Raj, Shabbs and I mucked along, we were friends. In our world, people pandered to us. But it was a golden moment of recognition, when the Asians in Britain served up success on a plate, at multiple award events, we had power.

We would go along to these events, if we weren't all invited, one of the three of us would definitely be on a guest list and we would get very drunk and obnoxious and laugh at everyone else. We gate crashed Subash Ghai's birthday party. The PR was shocked but she couldn't remove us.

Indobrit carried a review of *White Mughals*, the fictionalised historical novel by William Dalrymple. He called to ask for a copy of the review, he copiously collected all his cuttings and posted them on his web site. I have never been able to finish any of Willie's big novels, although his travel writing is fine and the passion with which he originally fell into India seems genuine enough.

He is one of many who go there and think they can belong and become part of the great sub-continent. A friendship grew out of the long telephone calls and it transpired that he would be in India at the same time as I was, for an event that the British Council were hosting, to coincide with the launch of the magazine in India. He had long wanted to go and see *Bombay Dreams* and we were plied with free tickets as part of an advertising contract with the producers, so I arranged some for his wife, Olivia, and he to go to an evening performance.

Willie also harboured pretensions of wanting to turn *White Mughals* into a play and he thought that Sophya Haque who starred in *Bombay Dreams* would make a good lead. I met up with Willie and "Olive" and a few friends after the show in order to introduce Sophya to Willie. He told me to be very careful around "Olive", that she was very fragile, "like a hurt bird," he said. Details of his many affairs with young Indian or British Asian women always seemed to make their way back to her. Or Willie would accidentally leave an e-mail from one of his little girlfriends open on the laptop for her to find. He knew how to dish out pain, and he did it particularly well, his sadistic mix of revenge and betrayal, onto people he claimed to love.

There were many sycophantic one-novel wonders, such as Justine Hardy who had milked a living out of writing really bad novels about India. They endlessly pestered us with story ideas. I liked the power to be able to say no. I wish I had said no to Willie. Justine was a non-starter. There are many people such as the ex-journalist, Sue Carpenter who eek a fine living for themselves out of being "charitable" through fronts such as Jaiselmer in Jeopardy, the poor relation to Save Venice. However, I find the idea of flying Shekar Kapur in First Class from India to London for a fifty minute talk quite uncharitable, unless she was doing it as charity for Shekar's characteristic languor.

It didn't take long for Allan Jenkins, the editor of the *Observer Magazine* to get in touch. I had heard he was a big Bollywood buff and had sent him films to review. He submitted his elegant pieces, always on time and well written. This arm's length relationship grew into something a little closer, after he started writing restaurant reviews for the magazine. His words flowed like butter through a knife and it was the same knife he used to carve out a space in his life for me, as he carefully neglected his long-term wife. We were often seen at media events together, I was no secret.

It was hot, at the end of June in 2003. Willie was very persistent. His wife and children had gone to Jersey to spend a few weeks with her sister, who had married up, her American banker husband lived tax-free in America by spending the required number of days on the island of exiles. Willie wanted to "see" me, I resisted because the friendship was blooming, and I enjoyed having him in my life with his lisping upper-class accent and his jaded view of everyone around him. He was considered part of the set yet he could still look with a critical eye and disdain. He never felt he belonged so it was easy to pick it apart, the rarefied social strata, which he sometimes inhabited.

He knew Yasmin and her daughter Layla (by her second marriage to a stray Englishman) and one of Willie's children were going to the same summer cookery school. He had mentioned to her as they kissed their daughters farewell at the gastronomical gates, that we had met. She hadn't answered. I told him that there was little love lost between me and Yasmin and he regaled me with stories about how she flirted with him and all the other men at her birthday party a few months ago. He sneered at her. I couldn't help but feel sorry for her, she thought she belonged in this media-luvvie world, she had set herself up as the High Priestess of Left Wing Birkenstock clad lefties. She was still firmly outside the tent pissing on her own leg.

Social luminaries with last names like Coleridge and Fiennes were Willie's best friends and godparents to his children. But still he laughed at them. Willie, for all his pompous arrogance and pretence, was insecure and scared that at any moment he would be uncovered. The whole charade of the writer in the Emperor's new clothes would unravel and he would be caught dancing naked in the streets, and exposed for being the fake he really was. People who have a lot to hide, revel in other people's defects, it gives them something else to hide behind. Willie preyed on Olivia's vulnerability and neediness, the more he hurt her, the more she needed him for comfort and the power he wielded grew.

He hadn't gone to Jersey, he was going to join them a few days later, or they were going to meet him in Edinburgh where another love struck Bharatnayam dancer had choreographed a dance piece based on *White Mughals*.

"Farah-ji, what are you doing later?" He whined like a little child who wasn't getting his way.

"I am going down to my house." The weekends were my sacred space to get away from the dizzy spinning of the carousel I was on and find my peace. And sleep. My children had gone to Cape Town for the holidays. "Look, come down tomorrow if you like, Shenaz Sutterwallah and Azim Azhar are coming for lunch."

"How are you traveling?"

"By car," as soon as the words were out of my mouth I regretted them, I had told him previously that his house in Chiswick was on my way to Hampshire.

"Well there's no excuse then," his tone was final. "If you are driving, you are going to go past me so please come, for a glass of wine under the plum tree. It's flowering, there's a full canopy…we could sit under it and watch the moon. I'll get yummies from the Lebanese deli… The garden is so beautiful at this time of year."

I had heard a lot about the fabled walled garden, the stage setting for so many of William's seductions.

"Don't try anything on. You promise?" I must have meant it because I said it.

Denial seemed as inevitable as the next day, as sure as the next sentence that would come out of his mouth,

"Would I ever? How could you even think that of me?" His feigned hurt didn't deceive me, all I wanted was to get him off the phone and try and sort out the flat-plan for the next issue, which wasn't making sense. There were blank pages where there shouldn't have been any.

I went, knowing full well what would happen. Willie and I are both carnivores. We have to devour the thing that attracts or intrigues us, so we own it, so it becomes part of us. Sex was the next natural turn that this friendship would take. Neither gave any thought to how damaging the consequences might be or to the hurt in "Olive's" permanently hurt heart and haunted black-ringed eyes.

The walled garden was decked out ready for a seduction scene from *1001 Arabian Nights*. Small Moroccan tea candles flickered in the half-light, which was fast loosing the last remnants of the day, between its fingers. He had laid out a woven Indian *dhurrie* rug and scattered cushions over it. A small feast had been set up and there was a bottle of wine chilled in a silver cooler. William had dressed in some Indian fantasy outfit, a *shalwar khameez* which is a long floaty shirt and loose fitting trousers underneath.

As I turned the iron key in the gate and entered the garden, with its immaculate lawn and overloaded flowerbeds, I was touched that he had gone to such lengths. Inside the house, I could sense his unease; "Olive" and the children's presence was still very much there. The rubbish stank because he hadn't taken it out and the house smelt ripe, putrid. He noticed me screwing up my nose at the smell and took the plastic bags out hastily. The Aga was on, though it was the middle of summer, it was a scene of English middle-class domesticity.

I felt the light silk of my dress against my bare thigh as I sat down on the carpeted square he had prepared. The plum tree reached over us, like a palanquin and I noticed a duvet and pillows.

212

"Are you planning on sleeping out here?" It was a balmy night and the mackerel sky had given way to velvet blue. He played *qawaalis* on the sound system, which we could hear outside.

I never wanted to sleep with William Dalrymple, it wasn't part of a momentous plan but when he brushed his hand ever so lightly on my bare thigh, as he reached for my glass so he could top it up again, I was aware of the choice: I could still leave. I didn't, because it was easier and maybe because I was curious.

He professed a deep love for "Olive," he had lamented his betrayals for hours on the phone, I had been privy to the latest round of fights and tears as he couldn't tear himself away from the young Indobrit novelist, Sejal Mandalia, with whom he was sleeping. These exotic women, all so much younger than him, must have been like new toys to play with. Willie is like the child who always wants something more or something else. Superficially, I could understand the attraction. Willie was high profile and he maintained a social and public appearance that gave credence to the idea that he was a great writer. He wrote often for serious broadsheets about anything to do with India, whether it was a new exhibition or some obscure point of foreign policy. The English are generally ignorant of the ex-colony, so when Willie had taken his place on the panel of experts on the mystery of the east, as a posthumous substitute for Edward Said, no one challenged him.

I remember looking up at the plum tree while he fucked me and I remembered asking myself why I was there. I think a part of me wanted to hurt his wife. It's cruel and people get hurt when one is ruled by carnal desire. That was all it was, just lust. We needed to feed on each other.

After it was over, the first fine fingers of dawn started to trace dewdrops on the grass around us. I was cold so we went inside. The marriage bed was carefully done, she must have made it up before she left. It looked as if she had packed in a hurry. Clothes were tumbling out of drawers and a long pink chiffon scarf lay discarded on the floor by her side of the bed. For the rest of that night at least, the bed was ours, not hers. It was about ownership and power, and knowing that I could have this man and then throw him aside any minute, because I didn't want him anymore.

When he woke up in the morning he wanted to fuck again. He turned me over and on the floor, all I could see was the pink scarf, a fragile scrap of a marriage that was over a long time ago. I made my excuses and left as soon as it was light outside, Willie called me a cab.

His gardener had arrived unexpectedly early and we made a lame excuse about me being a writer friend of his. The brown tobacco plants in the flowerbed glared as if they knew our secret and the gardener noticed me staring back at a plant.

"Would you like one? They are quite easy to grow…"

"Oh yes, I'd love one, I'll get a cutting next time."

He looked a bit puzzled, probably unable to fathom why I was leaving in such a hurry if I had just arrived. My Jimmy Choo purple sandals with lizard straps that shone with an opalescent glaze, the light purple chiffon dress which was a little crumpled and the cashmere cardigan I wore, all screamed out.

It was obvious I had stayed the night. But men who cheat on their wives are accomplished actors and as Willie waved me off in the minicab, I saw him turn towards the gardener and lean into the flowerbed to confer upon some floral conundrum he had just conjured up. He lived by thinking on his feet.

Almost as soon as I returned to the safety of my flat in Kings Road, the instant messaging on AOL and the phone calls started. We had once joked that after we had had sex we would no longer be friends. He asked if we were still friends and I assured him that we still were. It wasn't the same though, he had proven that he had no self control.

Willie was like most writers, but he was the first writer whose mind I could see inside, the frustrations and gaping insecurities that most of us manage to keep contained seethed out of him from time to time. Before me there was Sabina Dawan, the brilliant screenwriter of *Monsoon Wedding*, they had seen each other for years. His need for other women was only to feed the lack in himself. As outwardly accomplished as he was, with his Betty Trasker Award and frequent travel and political or comment pieces in the papers, there was still a huge sense of lack in him. It was like looking at an unfinished painting, with a lot of potential that has been abandoned by a great painter to go off and do something else.

Allan Jenkins believes in one thing only: media, the one who has the voice we hear or who holds the pen firmly in his grasp, the elusive one with his thumb on the print button, that one, is, by definition, power. In the same way that people who wanted to publish or write something in the magazine often approached me or who wanted us to cover this event or that book launch, he felt his position was one of "considerable importance." I played the game.

Allan was a gentleman, he built up to the sexual conquest by courting me, with cards and gifts. The cards depicted sexy 50s style college students, in push-up bras and short skirts, with captions like "Teachers Pet". Or they were beautifully intricate reproductions of Indian goddesses. Inevitably, he wrote something thoughtful inside them and finished the thought off with a flourish of his signature initials, AJ x. I was deeply drawn to him but in an addictive sort of way. He told me early on in the affair that at this stage in his life he didn't feel capable of any kind of passion, but why shouldn't he?

He was going to be fifty soon but he was still very sexual, he was a purveyor of the finer things in life. Allan wanted what he wanted and he got it. I was charmed by his persistence which started with text messages:

So how often you thought about me today?

Came his text message when I hadn't had a chance to call him back. He kept himself always in the forefront of my mind.

I was another pretty toy to add to his collection, but for a while at least I was a favourite toy. Allan had cheated on his wife, Henriette Helstrup, for years. It was supposedly a tacit understanding on both their parts. The marriage was loveless, he told me. They were best friends more than husband and wife and besides, she lived half the week in Denmark as the architectural firm she worked for was headquartered there.

He and I saw more of each other than they did and we made no secret of our affair. He told me how she had had her womb removed because of cervical cancer and he told me it left him cold, although he had stood by her throughout the ordeal.

It was strong, our bond, but it was also a gentle, slightly old-fashioned romance, he told me that he hadn't expected it to develop into anything, but it became love. He made me "wait" and we went on proper dates before anything much happened. Weekends were hard on both of us because she was in London and he had to be careful. He couldn't be seen to be absent, physically or otherwise.

I thought it would be one of those affairs that gently fades away, that we would stay great friends but there were others who had malevolent ideas and thought it should end with more of a crash than a whimper.

The situation with Willie had become very messy. "Olive" had found out thanks to his indiscretion in India. The event at the British Council had gone off well but people noticed the sexual spark between us and some of the innuendoes that came from him. I was the straw that broke the proverbial camel's back. Allan started off being the perfect friend, always there, a wealth of knowledge and experience from his years as the editor of various men's magazines and now, for the last decade, at the helm of the *Observer Magazine*. He was always enthusiastic about what I was doing with *Indobrit* and keen to help, write, and look over stuff. And I was charmed and flattered by the attention of a sophisticated, older, sexy man. He was dangerous, like playing too close to an open flame, he drew people in with his pseudo spirituality and his held-breath stories about tigers and doing *darshan* in Rajasthan on elephant back. That was how he drew me in, with stories of a place I love, the continent which binds us, he said. India. He was married, he said he loved his wife. He said he loved me too.

215

* * *

A rainy September evening, I had just finished a shoot for the accessories pages. We have plans to meet for a drink or a bite that evening. Suddenly frantic phone calls from Willie. He and I have agreed that for the sanity of his wife and the sanctity of his marriage we shouldn't communicate anymore. I agree, relieved at the prospect of peace. I don't want to see him. He is obsessed and dangerous. He wants to save his marriage and I can only imagine the dark and ugly picture he has painted. Difficult day, we've been calling and texting each other constantly and I miss you.

I don't want to meet William. I go to the Savoy instead to some book launch I said I might attend. I am way too early. He calls incessantly and texts me that it is for my own good that we meet, he has something to say. I go to the ladies, praying my mobile won't work in the basement. The phone rings. I don't answer. He rings constantly till I do.

"Look whatever it is, put it on an e-mail, tell me on the phone. I don't want to see you. Allan says not to go." You had told me not to go, to wait for you, that you would wait outside or come with me.

"Listen you can bring him if you like but these are things you don't want him to hear."

"Willie, he knows me pretty well. What would I not want him to hear?"

"Farah, this is not a phone conversation. Look I am 200 yards up the road at the …Pub, meet me here. I am waiting."

"No. I can't. Tell me on the phone."

The phone buzzes. A text message from you.

Remember you are beautiful sexy and strong.

OK, he can't do anything to me, it's a public place. I call you and tell you where we are meeting. You have left Jori White's Red Bar launch and are seeing a friend, an old lover, a food nutritionist, who has just adopted an Indian baby. The same one who told you not to see me, the same one who has been counseling you against us since before we even started. She wants champagne. You tell me you are going over for tea. Later you tell me she wants a threesome but that you won't share me.

"Look, I'll get in a cab and I'll come now."

"No. Allan, don't. I'll text you where I am meeting him."

"I'll call you in ten minutes, are you sure you don't want me to come?"

I walk upstairs to the first floor of the pub. William is sitting at a table opposite the door, strategically placed so he can watch me enter. He is bald, fat, nothing like his publicity pictures which he told me were only taken last year. Perhaps the years of lies and deceit have finally extracted their toll.

"You look very elegant, Farah," William says as he takes in the black Prada suit and the corset underneath. Eyes settle a little too long on my cleavage, I try and button up. Difficult to do sitting down.

"Thanks. What is it?" I don't feel like niceties, the hairs on the back of my neck are standing up, I want to run out of here and scream, 'You were a bloody mistake, that one bloody night with you, in your stupid garden. Have I got to pay for this for the rest of my life?' I say nothing, waiting for you to speak. You say that she has had a private investigator look into my background.

"And there's all sorts of stuff. About New York, about you never being married to your son's father, about there being faxes and e mails to your brother's boss, telling him that he was a rent-a-boy…"

"What are you saying?"

My brother and I have not spoken since before my son was born, and he is now nearly seven. He is a successful banker but because of the difficulties he had growing up, he doesn't maintain any contact with the family. I have never sent e-mails or faxes to his employers, I don't actually know where he works, he is so out of my life.

"Yes, Olive has a whole file of information, and everyone is talking about it. Everyone. All the people we know."

"Who everyone?" All the socialite Delhi darlings that decamp to London in the summer? All the washed up blonde lost Sloanes who went to Injah and wrote bad travel articles and even worse books and never quite come back? Those remittance charity chums? They are not my friends.

"Look I am telling you to protect you. I care about you. So keep your head down and keep a very low profile." So, this is all done under the guise of wanting to protect me, like I am some vulnerable colony.

"What are you on about? I don't even have a profile. What is this really about? Whose business is it how many times I have been married or whether I am a serial shoplifter? Please, I have to go."

The phone rings, it's you. "Are you all right? I am worried about you. I can be there in five minutes. I'm finishing my tea. I'm coming over now." There's concern and anxiety in your voice.

"Allan, I'm fine but I'm not up for any big night out. I can't go to your do at the Dorchester."

"We'll have soup and steamed rice; I'll hold your hand." I smile, I'm falling, the affection is beguiling, even a mile away.

"I'll meet you at the Savoy. The Beaufort Room, I think that 's where this launch is."

"Now let's both turn these darned things off and talk for five minutes." William orders. I leave my phone untouched on the table. He reaches for it. I take it away.

"You are very lucky with Allan, Farah, he clearly adores you."

And how many times did I hear that?

I adore you, I love you. I love your eyes and your smile and your face. I love the way your hair scatters on your face. You are beautiful. I love the hit I get off you. I love the smell of you.

Just words from a person who cuts and shreds and dissects words for a living. William's famous green eyes attempt seriousness and candour.

"Look babe," I cringe, "I thought I had to tell you because if there's one more incident, Olive is going to go public with everything."

"What incident?"

"Well she says she has been getting telephone calls at home and she has talked to Yasmin who just confirms that this is how you always behave."

That word. I can't stand the woman, she is the hollow eyed aunty-ji who has made a career as the voice of the disenfranchised Asian "Blacks" whatever that is. She wrote about me in her failed book as the niece who was "too beautiful for her own good." She described her mother, my grandmother as a prostitute and said unforgivable and unkind things about my mother who took her idolised big brother away. My father. This was supposed to be a biography. It was more like a bibliography of lies and character assassination.

She stands for no one, and I personally don't know a single Asian who aligns themselves with her views. Time to get off the soapbox dearie, and put the false teeth away. I saw her at a memorial for Edward Said last week and she looked like an ageing hooker. Short, short black skirt, hair still dyed raven when she is pushing fifty and that owl-eyed liner she thinks makes her cow eyes look sexy. I could almost hear her crooning in that patronising pseudo Oxford voice, "Come over here, love, a tenner for a blow job."

I ignored her. I have no respect for her. She has built a life of complaining and on a pack of lies. She says she supported herself through Oxford, she didn't, my father paid. He also paid for the deposit on the flat in which she still lives in Ealing. And her first failed marriage to her gorgeous Sky. Was there a word of thanks or acknowledgment? No, thank you, we're Asian, we don't do gratitude.

"Willie, I'm sorry, I have to go. Have you finished?"

"Oh I have to go too; I have someone coming to dinner at eight and see what time it is already."

You gather your papers and stand to leave before me. Always the last word, always the first to go. You shake my hand,

"Good luck, you are a good girl. Just lay low. It'll all blow over."

You wilt very elegantly Farah-ji, he said to me once. Now he is suffocating me.

I walk in the rain to take my place in my world again and sit in a crowded room. You see me as soon as you enter. I feel you walk into the room; there is chemistry. You sit next to me and pull your chair closer then, as if you had done it forever, you put your hand on my thigh. Just place it there. I cover your hand with mine, much smaller, unlined. I graze your cheek, bearded and mottled brown and white with a kiss. We can't sit here; we are like two love-struck teenagers who can't wait to get their hands on each other.

"Let's leave," you say.

You sign us in with a flourish at the Adam Street Club, one of your favourite haunts. I want to drink to wash off the dirt I feel inside me, the tawdry mess of William and "Olive." I am given a coat check ticket, funny I found it the other day in my wallet, number 109. We sit at the bar, I drink mimosas, and you drink whisky.

"Don't you see what he was doing?" Your eyes are fiery and protective and you have your arms around me. Strong and gentle. Fierce gentleness you called it.

Hate it when you don't respond to text. Though guess you do respond to words voice and fierce gentleness plus the urgency of my fingers Liking you even more today.

I've told you, told you everything that he said to me and I don't feel better for it. I feel hunted, like an otter in a chase she can't escape. Trapped.

"He has to make you look like the devil woman because you are still a threat to her. What sane person checks out a person's background? I hate this middle-class dinner party nonsense. It's such bullshit. See it for what it is. And as for Yasmin, come on, she is always ingratiating herself. When I was at The Independent she was always trying glad-handing with me. People see through that."

"Oh. Were you friends?"

"No, darling, she's brittle. I like moist. Like you."

I try to take comfort in your words and then you kiss me. And it's not an ordinary kiss. It's a kiss that changed my mind. I felt like something good again and out of the mess under the plum tree away from the gossip and the vicious e-mails. You made me feel good, that's what you said you wanted to do.

"I am here to make you feel better. For as long as you want me." You said.

Want you for a long time. Will miss you more than will ever say, you write.

And you tell me that you'll be different, that you will always be my friend and that you will always stand by me.

Still shaking from the thought of not having you in my life and will use my considerable power to avert that, you write, a few weeks later when I am having doubts in India.

"I'll never leave you; I've decided I am going to be your friend."

"And when did you decide that?"

"When I decided to write for your magazine."

And even then I know those are big words from you. We kiss, you reach inside my jacket, you kiss my breasts, and the bartender looks on amazed. You stand behind me and reach down cupping both my breasts and kissing me so hard I think I will fold into you. We have dinner there, I lose a shoe under the table, and you reach down, get on a knee, kiss my foot and replace my shoe.

When we leave to go back upstairs, you grab me and push me against the wall. I am quite drunk.

"Allan don't." Too many years of Church of England school.

"Why? Why not? I want to taste you and smell you. Now."

I can't do this. This isn't right and before I know it your fingers are deep inside me and as fast, out again, in your mouth, under your nose.

"Fucking delicious."

"Stop it." I feel sober again, there are people all around us, no one looks but I feel naked.

Upstairs, outside Charing Cross , you do it again. Push me hard up against the railing and reach into me so hard I gasp.

"Four fingers," you say in your deepest half octave dropped voice.

This is new, exhilarating. I have never done danger like this. And you are happily married, right? And you love your wife, when I am standing half-naked pressed against you for the whole of Trafalgar Square to see?

In the taxi on my way home, alone, still drunk and dizzy you text me:

Will put my finger in my mouth and think it's in your cunt. Fucking gorgeous.

***

Someone sent me e-mails Willie had been sending out, all comprise various degrees of denial but one of them read as follows:

An email from Tracy Jackson to Nancy Stoddart forwarding an email from Justine Hardy to Tracey Jackson

Tracey,

Sorry I haven't called - too much juggling yesterday - and OH MI GOD - check this out - this is the monster editor I told you about Farah - and Willie is Willy D... read on... we have much to discuss...

And another one, from Willie to Nancy Stoddart

I think it looks as if its going to be quite easy to prove ourselves innocent of all the stuff she has been spreading and show that she is a serial fantasist... But how ON EARTH have you heard about this???? No one here knows-

I think (& hope)

Love Willie

Nancy to Willie

Dear Willie,

When I wake up each day, I start reading newspapers from around the world, including the Daily Mail. It seemed pretty likely one of the two men was you. The real subject is your friend "Alan Jenkins of the Observer magazine" and you are merely a part of the story. Alan Jenkins of the Observer magazine-middle aged guy with grey in his beard or something who doesn't use condoms. It is Alan Jenkins of the Observer magazine sounds like such a psycho creep just like Farah.

I just naturally assume that an attractive, charismatic and talented guy such as you probably fools around as opportunities are everywhere. That's what men do, and some women too but we aren't driven by testosterone so maybe less, I don't know. If you are always on the road doing exciting things and have a stay-at-home-mom wife who, as you told me, wants even more babies, this is the price you both pay.

Remember, we discussed this. I think Olive can use this entire incident to throw aside her guilt about the kids and get out there as your companion and woman in her own right. It's the career for her, not the kids.

She is very talented, beautiful (from pix you sent) and she could have a few affairs of her own as payback. So there is a silver lining. I always find it odd when a man has a "long suffering wife" at home. The wife obviously knows, at some level. In any case, sexual fidelity is highly overrated. Or even a myth. I hope we can continue this when I get back. Or call me. xoxoN

Willie to Nancy

Now Nancy: can't say you're the most popular girl in Chiswick after that last e – Olive read it before me (as its name implies this is a joint account) and is FUMING, and I can't say I'm too thrilled either. I know that what you meant to say is "I know you are completely innocent and that woman is clearly a psycho and serial fantasist' – so lets just pretend that that is what you did write, hmm? All is forgiven, but please realise that there are a lot of bruises in this household at the moment and tact and friendly consolation is what we want from our friends at the moment... Love Willie

***

This was what was going on, in the domestic bliss of the Dalrymple household. Willie was denying and "Olive" wasn't buying it. He was wary of Allan, I had told him about the affair, he had known about it the night we had our one-night fling, it seemed a good way to throw him off, in case he decided he wanted to re-enact Seduction Under the Plum Tree again.

The emails that were being circulated, I still believe by Olivia, said that I was dangerous and unstable. It was in no one's interest, least of all mine, to send messages about my criminal past to hundreds of people in the media and close friends of theirs and mine. It was old news, the affair was over as soon as it started and having seen this man at his most base, I had let the friendship subside. Maybe her way to deal with the damage he had doled out on her was to lash out at me.

When she told him he was to have nothing more to do with me, he couldn't write for the magazine; he certainly couldn't speak with me. I asked him how he felt about that and he looked chastened but told me I should accept it as she would not be calmed. I told William that as far as I was concerned she could tell the whole world whatever she wanted to about me, and that besides, everyone knew. Thanks to the interconnectedness of the media world I inhabited, there was a carefully concocted Wikipedia entry and countless pages on Google were devoted to me. I enjoyed wielding power in the life of a woman I hardly knew. I liked the fact that I could rock her world with one glance at her man, inevitably, she would conceive it as being flirtatious. I was a threat.

There was an event for India Ink in London, a charity which supposedly builds schools and teaches poor Indian children to read and write. It spends more on administration and its glamorous events, flying luminaries in from all over the world First Class, to speak or debate. This evening was to be held at the Sotheby's showroom in St James'. The auction house was displaying some rare Indian jewels from the Raj for an upcoming auction and Willie was top billing, he was debating with Salman Rushdie. Rushdie sizzled sex appeal, he still had hair and wore an expensive Armani suit. His affair with the beautiful model Padma Laxmi gave him street cred, surely someone as ugly and brainy as he was couldn't be all-bad if he had managed to bed such a beauty.

Allan had arrived early. He hadn't really wanted to come; he despised Willie and everything that he stood for. We were going to Benares later that evening for dinner and he suggested we meet at the restaurant. But I was tired of William's protestations of innocence in the tale that was making its way around London gossip circles. He said that I had thrown myself at him, another fawning chicklet, in awe of his writing and his amazing circle of connections. When I got to St James' I was excited to see Allan. But as soon as I saw him, in the gallery room, my heart sank, Allan and Willie had found each other and there stood "Olive," tight-lipped and white as a ghost. She had tried to apply liquid eyeliner, which had smudged all around her eyes so she had the look of a distraught panda bear. In the centre of the circle was Caroline Michel, Rushdie's editor extraordinaire who was there to support her leading writer.

"There you are," Allan reached out both arms and introduced me to Caroline, whom he had known for a long time. She was exactly the genre of classy, refined women Allan admired, she radiated sunny confidence. In comparison, "Olive" seemed to recede into herself, in the way that figures in cartoon films do, to imply distance. She didn't say a word but glared at the embroidery on my antique Annamika Khanna sari. Allan had teased me about wearing a sari and said that he had never seen me in one, and that he probably never would. That night I wore it for him. My uniform those days was mostly Prada and Jill Sander. Severe cut suits with deep splits in the skirts to show off a good bit of thigh. Allan liked the schoolgirls smuttiness of the look. Willie looked anxious and he mumbled something as he guided Olive away from this centre of subterfuge and discomfort to take her place in the front row. She didn't say a word but the hatred smarted off her like a snake about to spit venom.

Allan and I remained standing as we had not intended to stay for the whole debate.

"You look gorgeous my darling." For a boy who had come from the neglect that Allan and his brother had suffered at the hands of their mother, he was remarkably successful and well-adjusted. She used to lock them up for days in the cupboard and not feed them, they were left to sit in their own excrement. When he told me those stories, about how when they were found by care workers and it was reported, it was the worst abuse case ever in Britain, my heart went out to him. I couldn't help but love him more, for the way he had not only survived it but had managed to overcome it. He was a Barnado's boy and suffered the usual torment inflicted on kids in foster homes but eventually, he got out of the hands of the state and learned a trade which was to install high-end floors and fireplaces. He had also run a book shop in Notting Hill, back in the day.

Allan was a true lover of the word. His favourite authors were VS Naipaul and JM Coetzee, who soon became my favourites too. He guided my reading, my consumption of art and fashion, he knew a lot about everything. He wasn't beguiled by the world he was in. He had clawed his way up and become the Food Editor of *The Independent* where he had encountered Aunty (Yasmin) who wrote a weekly column. He was no one's company man. I thought he was centred and strong, I looked to him for support and strength. Willie kept looking at us, nervously, from where he sat on the makeshift podium,

"You are making him nervous, he can't get his eyes off you, my darling."

"I don't think it's that, I think he's afraid…did you see Olive. She looks as if she might fall apart any minute."

He held my hand protectively and whispered in my ear, "Whenever you are ready. It's not Naipaul is it?"

This was our cue to make a hasty exit. I didn't wait for a pause in the dialogue, which was really a Rushdie soliloquy. He knocked the spots off Willie who was sweating under the bright lights and whose stammer had suddenly become quite noticeable.

I felt her bore holes into my back as we left. To her we must have looked like a glamorous media couple. He made me feel like a goddess. With him, this wise, worldly older man, I felt I could do anything at all. He told me when he had first met me at that Indobrit party that I came across as just another socialite doing something to pass the time.

224

The black Ben de Lisi failed to make an impression, he thought I had looked mumsy, in spite of the mermaid chiffon tail and the deep v cut into the silk neckline. Later, he told me he loved the magazine, he loved everything about it and that I had ink, not blood, flowing through my veins. I didn't set out to hurt his wife. I didn't want to sleep with him or to be with him out of an evil intention. Men who had affairs were normal in the currency of my life, it had started with my father. To me sex was at best a commodity; I hadn't planned to fall in love with Allan.

Sexually he was amazing. After he made love to me the first time, he said to me, "My God, you look so pretty."

"Thanks," I answered wryly.

"No I mean it, you look really beautiful, and we should do this much more often."

We used to go back to another furnished flat that I owned in the building I lived in. It was untenanted. After he made love to me, he would hold me for a long time, he was never in a hurry to get back, even when Henry was in London.

Allan introduced me to Maharishi and S and M. He was buttoning up a pair of beautifully embroidered snow-pants, and I told him I admired them, He stopped mid-popper, and leaned over to where I was lying on my stomach, on the bed. He stood over me and spanked me hard on the ass.

"Jesus, what was that?"

"A spank. If I had a whip or a riding crop, I would love to hit your ass with it…"

There's a fine line between sex and depravity. This was uncharted territory for me, but with this man I loved, I would have gone anywhere and done anything. He kissed me hard and deeply, I loved that he kept his intense green eyes open when we made love and then, out of the blue, he would say something silly, he was born a hopeless romantic. I was in India for my birthday, during the time we were seeing each other.

He tried to get the hotel to put rose petals on my pillow and chocolates by the side of my bed. They politely declined, for security reasons they told him, they couldn't confirm that I was a guest at the hotel or even if I was arriving later that day.

He explained to me about "housekeeping." He was constantly asking me for my mobile number. Given the number of text messages and phone calls we traded on any given day, this should have raised four alarm bells in my head.

"You send me such explicit text messages, I can't keep them on my phone. It's called housekeeping."

"Oh, that's what it is?"

"You should send me a completely benign one and then I can store it and Henry won't get suspicious."

This was the same Henry who didn't mind that he had girlfriends who turned into mistresses. He had kept seeing Jane Clarke the well-known food writer for years, after, he said Henry had found out.

My message that day had been urgent. I needed to see him. It was like a junkie needing her fix, I felt so complete around him, because I could only thrive on impermanence. I needed to tell him it was all over, that I wanted to walk away from us and I needed him to allow me the space to be able to do that. We were seeing more and more of each other and the craving was getting worse with each meeting. He was invited to go on a press jaunt to Amsterdam, to see the studios of the Amsterdam Seven. He had asked me to go but I was busy and frustrated with our situation. I didn't want to go, there would be far too many questions asked on such a journey, he was going on the Eurostar with other journalists.

Before he had to catch his train from Waterloo, we went to see the installation of light by Olafur Eliasson, called the Weather Project at the Tate Modern. We met a little way away, near the Royal Festival Hall, and walked slowly up towards the art museum. There was sadness in us that we couldn't shake off, we were in the middle of another one his crises of confidence. Allan wasn't happy and I was impatient. I don't know where I thought it would go, or what might happen if I started to make demands on him, which he just couldn't meet. We stood on the balcony in the darkened cathedral of light. The installation, which was suspended like the midnight sun, had created an awe-inspired hush in the flocks of people who had crowded to see it that grey afternoon in the autumn. It was as if this bleak, nuclear light somehow emanated life.

He stood in front of me, against the balcony and held me close to his back, then he leaned back, in a deep backbend, almost yogic and his eyes were yellow and glowing, but sad and teary. He turned round and wrapped himself tightly around me and said that we needed to take a break.

That we shouldn't speak to each other or see each other for thirty days and after that time, if we both still felt the same way, we should continue, he talked about leaving Henry if that was what I had wanted. I didn't. Even I, for all my foolish arrogance as the mistress in this three-way party, knew that a man who cheats on his wife then leaves to be with his mistress creates a vacancy. I think James Goldsmith said it better.

We lasted about fifty paces. As I crossed the wobbly Millennium bridge and looked at the winding grey Thames which had carried so much of our story, he called.

"Fuck, I can't get you out of my head. It's wall-to-wall Farah."

I didn't know what to do to comfort him.

"What do you want me to say? I need you like I need air. I can't do this, it's stupid, let's just end it."

"Is that what you want?"

But I didn't know what I wanted. He was leaving for Amsterdam in a few hours, then he would be out of my orbit and I could think and breathe unobstructed. A break would do us both good.

He called all the time. He used a pay-as-you-go phone as it was untraceable and is the communication weapon of choice for married men. It leaves no nasty paper trail of phone numbers for an inquisitive wife. He called later that night when he was drunk. He was pissed off, as he had realised that he had over-tipped the hatcheck girl and given her fifty Euros instead of five.

"It's all your fault. I was thinking about you. I can't stop thinking about you."

It was late and I had been asleep with Marina in the bed next to me when he called. She had been disturbed by the phone and the conversation and was now trying to go back to sleep and sucking her thumb very loudly.

"My darling, I am sleeping. I'll see you when you are back, ok?"

Life was strangely peaceful without the tension of having him around, craving him, wondering when we would be able to sneak some time together during the day.

"No. I need to hear your voice. I need to know that I am the last voice you will hear and the last thought in your head before you fall asleep."

"You are. You always are," I murmured, sleepily.

Friday evening, Selfridges is a good place to see the girlfriends of married men on shopping sprees as their weeknight lovers take off to their wives for a restful couple of nights.

My phone rang, I smiled to see his name come up on the screen.

"Where are you?"

"Selfridges."

"What are you doing?"

"Buying shoes."

"Hi-lo?"

"What are you doing?"

"I'm on my way home on the Eurostar."

"What did you buy me from Amsterdam?"

"Oh, did you want a present?"

"I thought about buying you the new Dries van Noten perfume but it's too edgy for you."

Fuck you too, I thought silently.

"Let me talk to the shoe-man."

"What?" I didn't understand.

"Let me tell him what sort of shoes I want you to buy so I can fuck you in them, standing up,"

"Don't be hideous."

"I'm deadly serious."

I passed the phone to the bewildered looking shop assistant, who dutifully took it from my hand.

"My father…wants to know what kind of shoes I am buying."

"Oh right. Hello sir?" There was a pause while Allan explained that he was not the father but the boyfriend, and the clerk went on to describe the shoes.

"Prada, pale salmon silk grosgrain. Strappy with silk rosebuds on the heel and the toes…they are hard to describe but I'm sure you will see them soon…"

He was cut short, Allan knew which shoes they were, we had admired them together, earlier somewhere else.

He handed me back the phone.

"Good girl."

"You old fool." The craving for him was back as quickly as it had left me.

"What time are you coming into Waterloo? I am taking the train to Hampshire, I want to see you…show you my shoes if you ask me nicely enough."

"Oh no." He sounded genuinely disappointed; "You told me you were catching an earlier train so I asked Henry to pick me up at the station."

I imagined her gliding through the city in his sleek Mercedes, making her way from Belsize Park where they lived, to South London. Behind the wheels of his car. Something in my stomach curdled. I didn't think about her at all, only when he mentioned her in passing, to say that she would be away or that she was coming home. But suddenly the reality of her struck me like a smack in the face.

"Oh." I felt small, cut down to size, the excitement and the sexy shoe talk had fizzled out.

"But I can call her if you like? Tell her I will get a cab home? Or I can see you on Monday?"

Taking a cab went against the grain for Allan. He was thrifty because of where he had come from, he thought he might lose it all in a minute. This was a big sacrifice.

"No it's fine, I'll see you Monday. Anyway got to go pay for these shoes…" My voice trailed off and I hung up the phone before we could do our goodbye ritual of seeing who would hang up first.

Later the following week we met at the Adam Street Club, where he signed my name in with his ink pen. He looked admiringly at the candy pink Miu Miu coat and Gucci boots I was wearing but I wasn't in the mood for trivialities. We had come here often, in the past, it was a place that the media world could sink into its need for deep-sprung privacy, as comfortable as the low sofas and their leather cushions. Anything that happened in there stayed strictly in there. It was like AA meetings but with the alcohol.

I told him I thought I was pregnant. He went misty-eyed for a moment and started to gush about the gift of a new life. Marina was barely two and there was no way I was going to raise another child on my own. I had begun to accept that this situation was very comfortable for Allan, it didn't challenge him at all. I didn't want him to leave Henry. I was happy with resigned to the scraps that a mistress in a relationship puts up with.

He had gone to the Boots chemist before he met me and we both tried to sneak into the ladies' room together. He tried to watch as I peed onto the digital oracle that would speak of a baby in our lives, or not. I knew already, I had previously done the test at home, but I hadn't told him, he had asked me to wait till he returned from Amsterdam.

A woman was changing in there and aghast at what she thought she was about to witness. She covered up her naked front with a t-shirt she had just taken off and demanded to know what Allan was doing in the ladies' room. He turned all apologetic but I was having none of it.

"He is my boyfriend and we are doing a pregnancy test," I told her. She went very quiet. The first test was inconclusive so he went out to the Boots on Charing Cross Road again to buy another one. I waited for him in the Club Lounge. The second test confirmed what I already knew. We went silently back up to the lounge together.

"What do you want to do?" He asked me, quietly.

"I want to have an abortion."

"Are you sure? Have you really thought this through, Farah?"

I downed the gin and tonic in front of me and looked at him, square in the face, I noticed his eyes had become grey and looked sunken and tired. Today, in spite of the cashmere sweater and the elegant trousers, he looked old. I felt responsible, I didn't mean to bring stress and chaos to his life, and we were just meant to be a fun fling.

"I have to go, I told you I have to be at Vama at nine to meet Mark Ackroyd."

"Fuck that, it can wait. We need to talk about this."

I got up to move, the last thing I wanted was to talk about the awfulness of it. I didn't want to look into the abyss of no future that lay before us. We walked out of the club a lot wearier than we had looked when we walked in. He still put his arm around me, and offered to get me a cab, he asked if he could come with me, but Mark was a real friend and someone I could talk to about this who would tell me sense and not what I wanted to hear. Mark was my friend, not Allan's.

I hugged him, in the cold autumn night and we lingered in each other's arms. I said I wanted to walk a while by myself and he let me go. He was supposed to meet a friend for a recital at the Royal Festival Hall. He had to cross over the pedestrian bridge that spans the north and south banks of the river.

He stood on that bridge for a long time. As I walked away towards Westminster, I felt his sad gaze hover all around me like a cloud of tears.

He called and he called, he sent texts:

Come to Chinatown and eat rice with me. I need to talk to you.

I ignored the first few calls and messages but they became more imploring. I loved Allan, I didn't want to hurt him and I certainly wasn't shutting him out, not purposely but subconsciously but this was what he expected, from his programming.

He was expecting rejection when he wanted to give love and I was not able to let him in any more. We fulfilled each other's sickness. In all of his life as a man, Henry has been the only woman who has stuck around. She put her own dreams of becoming an architect on hold, and shelved her life to support him so he could go through his journalism degree. She brought up his two daughters by an earlier marriage as if they were her own.

The unanswered calls continued, now he thought I was abandoning him. Finally I called him and excused myself from Andy Vama and Mark, chatting at the table.

"Look, I can't do this right now. I am going home after here, to sleep. I feel sick."

"No, come to me. I want to buy you a poem." A favourite pastime of Allan was to buy scroll poems from a Soho street poet, they serendipitously seemed to always know where he was at and gave coded advice on the situation he was in.

"I can't my darling, I need to finish up here and go home." The text message that followed a few minutes later shook me.

There is only one right way for you, for us, for everyone my darling. Can't wait to see you. Need you in my life.

Then another:

OK, I'll come to you. I need to talk about this. We need to see where we go from here.

I wish, on all the full moons that have passed between now and then, more than half a hundred moons ago that I had gone to him, to talk about it because then maybe what happened later might never have happened at all.

India Shining

The version of India that is paraded for the five star Taj tourist is the one I enjoyed during the first few trips. The Taj Hotel group belongs to the wily Ratan Tata, and they have a slick marketing operation in St James' in London, attached to one of their UK hotels. I was invited to go to India as their guest. I had wanted to do for a long time, and the first trip was in 2002. Many trips followed in succession and they had some ostensible purpose attached to them, such as distribution of Indobrit or unearthing a viable outfit to sell advertising to local businesses, yet I longed to slip away to see something else of India.

She doesn't offer herself up like a twelve course taster menu at a five star hotel. No, the Mother country is hard work, maybe more so for the prodigal lost children who forsook her for other continents. She doesn't forget and forgiveness is hard won. My grandfather's generation held a particular disdain for all things sub-continental, they didn't look back for fear of being turned into the proverbial pillar of salt.

We, however, the spiritually and emotionally disenfranchised, wanted something more than to live under Liberty's towering statue, we needed shelter from the less than comforting ragged white cliffs of Dover. We had been disemboweled of our nationhood and the countries, which promised status and security, had turned their backs once they had cashed in the IMF and Aga Khan grants and made all the right outward gestures of acceptance.

More and more, I felt I could never belong to England. There was nothing I aspired to wrap myself in, no comfortable moral blanket that made me feel as if I was home. My European featured and white-skinned children presented more questions than they voiced answered and , issues of identity began to percolate through the image of the life I had constructed around me. The things I had wanted and achieved, the house in the country and the new Mercedes every year, the subtle snobbery of a new Chanel coat every spring, all of it was a blur and a mess from the view atop my Jimmy Choo's.

I had a lot and I craved more and more, as if the acquisition of things and people might make me feel "whole." My father had realised it was all a fraud, this hunt for more, long ago, when he left for South Africa in 1994. He didn't feign nostalgia for the quarter century he had spent building a life in London.

He was able to shake it off and move on. The property market had collapsed but he clung onto his substantial English property portfolio, and, with a loan from his bank manager, he took off, back to Africa. He still has the bug.

For me, Africa was too complicated, I had gone back, had tried to find a home in her heart but it isn't a place for a single mother. I couldn't forget or ignore the hatred in the eyes of native Kenyans, whose country was still ruled by a chasm of Us and Them. I don't have Karen Blixen's obtuse obduracy but she didn't have the sick and twisted Fazal brothers living just a Jeep ride away.

India had been a place in my imagination, somewhere that I came to know through the books of people such as Naipaul, whose own complicated relationship as a son once removed comes through in his writing. But suddenly, like a forgotten flower in the corner of the garden, a hibiscus in the mid-morning sun, she had come into full bloom.

It was the moment India came to be a force, not just in terms of numbers because of the burgeoning population, but because finally, after the struggle of half a century of post-partition blues, the pantheon of deities seemed to be smiling luck and success on her.

I did the India Tourist Board's version of India Shining. I went to the luxurious spas, Neemrana, Devi Ghar and Angsana. Farookh Chotia, who was finding success through the lens with *Vogue* in the US shot, an exquisite fashion editorial based on *White Mughals* at Neemrana. That storyline had to be changed at the last minute when William and his dithering overly exasperated me. Thankfully, another book, a much better book, came out, called *One Last Look Back* by Susanna Moore and Allan gave me a preview copy, so I could change the story led text boxes. William was there and he oversaw the shoot, I had decided to return to Delhi, having set it up. Being around him for too long made me lose my centre of gravity, he is like a psychic black hole, he sucks the blood and life out of everyone around him.

India is not the filmy fantasy represented in tourist-guides which pose as books such as Dalrymple's. He can't ever understand India because he is too preoccupied with himself and running away from his own shadow. India is an extreme experience; she expunges all trace of ego, is scabrous in her evaluation of all that you thought was important. India is about erasing, taking away preconceptions.

Just the stark juxtaposition of wealth and scarcity – the tuk-tuk ride from Malabar Hill mansions to the slum dog hovels, though a short one, is hard to grasp. Yet there is dignity and honesty in this poverty, no one can capture the real experience of India, if you really open yourself up to her. She is like a detoxification spa for the soul.

The people I met, the wealthy landowners, from the new Mughal princes who owned half of Bangalore or cultivated vineyards in the intemperate Indian climate, to the lowliest bell-boy or those scruffy dirty kids, who sell tuberose garlands in the street, they were all savvy and generous. Indian people are born hosts. They love to show you their country, their cultures and traditions but still, it is with the deference offered to an outsider.

The closest I have ever felt to India, and also to some sense of where I came from, was in the hills in Rajasthan, at an old castle fort that had been turned into a five star hotel.

It wasn't about the luxury or the thoughtfulness that had gone into every aspect of designing the space. It wasn't even the empty bottles of Perrier Jouet that seemed to blend naturally in this Orientalised version of eastern hospitality, it was the way the sky opened up to me up that night, like a prayer. The stars seemed to sing out and were reflected in the cascading streetlights, which lit up in the village below in the valley. Fragments of sounds – laughter and life and singing floated up, barely discernable but affirming of other lives, very different from my own – resonated in the deep black darkness which was punctuated only by candle-light.

There is an ancient Sanskrit mantra, which was on one of Pathaan's early compilations when they were still great, the Gayatri Mantra, and slowly the song rose from the stereo behind the table where I sat, alone, with my thoughts. I had started to realise that India wasn't the white sahib's playground of elephant polo and puppet Maharajahs with no power. Through the soul of the song came through a sense of connectedness, through the ancient tones of the music, a strand of who I was and what that meant, had hooked me. I could see reflections of myself in the Northern Indians, the women with their high foreheads and almond-shaped eyes the colour of midnight and dreams, but it was more than this obvious physical identification.

Gayatri is an incarnation of Saraswati, the Goddess of beauty and the consort of Lord Brahma who represents strength. This sense of India, of unity, replaced the fragmentation of the cold continent which I now called home. I knew there was more to me than the emptiness of Europe.

I wanted desperately to know more about her, so I could understand more about myself. I knew writer-intellectuals and ambassadors, actresses and tycoons; all of them represented one facet of the multi-headed Hydra, but none could lay claim to the definitive version of what India was. To me, the answer lay not only in the unscrambling of so many characters and interpretations but it was also about unlearning the prejudices of old and wiping the slate of the mind clean of the Western dogma that I had learned from television and stupid books that pervert the truth of literature and history.

I had found an old friend whose essence had stayed the same but whose physical appearance had changed. Rediscovering her, accepting that my experience of her had been pure illusion, was the first step in understanding myself. In order to find out the truth about something, we must first embrace the lies. I want to know more and more of India, the more I learn about her, the less I know, but the journey is a progressive one, it is like taking baby steps into the core of myself that has lain vast and empty for so long. Half a life.

Not One but Two

There's a Linda Rondstadt song about being *Torn Between Two Lovers*. It isn't a fun place to be. Willie's fake domesticity was coming undone. Olivia had uncovered years of shenanigans, such as the Indian assistants who had done more than confirm Willie's obscure research. He needed to cheat like a fish needs water. Every woman, every next conquest, filled the void inside him, he needed to be admired and flattered.

Olivia was no beauty to Willie, no English rose, more like a prickly Scottish thistle, she was the gaunt embodiment of the opposite of the women he picked, with soft skin and dark eyes, he liked Indian takeaway, preferably posh British Asian Islamototty.

He caved in as she vented. More and more colourful e-mails hit the gossip columnists' in-boxes about my exploits with William and Allan, which he had kindly told her about, as if in defence of his own behaviour. They came from an e-mail address with her name on it, although we were never able to trace who was really sending them, I am still sure she had something to do with it. Allan said to ignore it all. The strength I had previously seen in him drained away, like the tide going out.

These men's wives were not my problem. The way I saw it, their home situation couldn't have been great or they wouldn't have been sniffing around like dogs sniff bitches on heat. As much as they professed to love their wives and to want to protect their families, that was how little I believed them.

Allan called me at the office the next day. He sounded tired, the e-mails had been sent to colleagues of his at *The Observer* and at *The Guardian*. Behind the scenes, I know second-class surrogates such as Justine Hardy were mixing the pot, making the rumour go further.

"I want to talk to you about this. Henry can't find out, it would kill her."

He had never worried about hurting her before, had the hole in their open relationship been shut closed again?

"What do you want to talk about? I told you what I am going to do," I was tired too, and irritable. I hated the pregnant feeling, sore breasts, feeling heavy and
236

hormonal. I had booked an appointment with my gynaecologist for the next day to have the screening interview before the abortion.

"I want you to know that I would love you to have my children. That in the scheme of life, in my Boho-Buddhist nihilistic Hindu way, I think this was meant to happen to us. And I want to come with you and hold your hand when you wake up, and tell you I love you and it's all ok, that you did the right thing."

The right thing for who, I wondered. But I bit my tongue to stop the venom.

"Go and see Claire. This happened to another friend of mine…"

"I thought you said you had never…"

"No, no, not by me, Clarkey. She had to go and see this woman. Go and see her I'm going to text you her number right now."

"Will you come with me?" I was afraid to ask, for all these protestations of being there and the *Golden Pond* love, it didn't feel real.

"Oh darling, you know Wednesday is deadline day. I'll try but…"

"Don't worry about it."

Something in me was stewing. These men, fantastic, brilliant, seemingly strong and capable, both were crumbling. I was angry that I was the one being made to look like the marriage-breaking husband-stealing harpy. I wasn't, stuff happens, and it happened to us. I didn't set out to cause pain, though in Olivia's case when I saw the agony she put herself through by staying with a serial and unreconstructed philanderer such as Willie, it was easy to turn the knife a few times.

I went to see Claire. He had given her his real name, Peter Drabble but she knew who he was. She was very concerned and asked how I felt about the situation. She sent me off to have a scan.

The texts messages couldn't have come through at a worse time: *Waiting to hear from you. Too quiet.*

Then he called and he told me that he would be different, that he would always be my friend and that he would always stand by me.

Maybe if it had been just one baby and not the double bubble of two, maybe I wouldn't have panicked so badly. There is something about ending one life, it is careless but in this situation, it might be considered the necessary evil. But two felt more than a little careless and sure enough, two tiny embryos showed up on the scan. The radiologists' face lit up and I almost fell off the examination table.

"Oh my, you are lucky, you have two bundles of joy," she beamed at me.

That would make me a serial murderess and an adulteress then, I thought. The thoughts that were going through my head were not rational. I dressed fast and made my way back to the doctor's office. It didn't help that my phone rang with Willie's number flashing on the screen. I was barely dressed and his nasal high pitched squeal came at me, I hadn't said a word.

"Yasmin, Yasmin it's Willie, you'll never believe what you niece has done now…"

I cut him off. Was this a deliberate mistake or had he called me for another mind fuck, to let me know that he was communicating with the enemy?

"It's not Yasmin it's Farah. Don't ever call me again."

I hung up and my heart turned to stone. All was not well in my world; I could feel that something much bigger than I knew and was party to was going on behind the scenes.

After that, I didn't trust Allan. As much as he said he hated Willie, as much as he despised his writing and his pretensions (Allan was a much better writer, hands down), I started to think that they were teaming up. He had joked about it before, that when we ended, he would call up Willie and go out for a Glenmorangie to commiserate.

He wouldn't speak to me, after that. I got into his office voice mails by tricking someone at *The Guardian* reception and saying that I was his PA and that he was unable to access his messages from outside. They obliging reset the pin number, which I said I would relay to him. Again, it felt as if something cold and dark passed over my heart when I heard Yasmin's shrill phony voice on his messages.

"Allan, it's Yasmin, Yasmin Alibhai Brown…I am Farah's aunt and I *must* speak to you…It's very urgent, you are in a lot of danger and I have to tell you so much about her."

Her tone was part seductress, part headmistress, he had told me he was worried that she wanted to sleep with him, he had kept her at a great distance. Of course now they all had something in common: Farah, the great she-demon.

My head spun, I felt sick in my stomach, as if I had been punched in the stomach. I delivered the scan to *The Guardian* offices, marked in an envelope for his attention and I sent him the bill for the consultation with his girlfriend's gynaecologist. I was going to deal with this with my own doctors and friends. I didn't trust anyone or anything to do with him. Then I called his wife at the Natural History Museum, where she had a port-a-cabin office for the architectural firm, which was carrying out the extension and building work for their new wing. I cut and pasted all the e-mails and transcribed all the texts he had ever sent me and I faxed the lot of them to her. I told her that we had been seeing each other for months, that I was pregnant and that all I really wanted was for him to stay away.

Telling the truth is the mistress' best revenge. She was polite and thanked me for telling her. He had sent me poems, I sent them to her.

***

Maybe you were exactly what I needed then. You said you were the white knight. You would be around till you were 70 and I was bored and fed up with you, and I told people to get that old man away from me. We would pick armfuls of bluebells and mushrooms and kick leaves in the Fall together. You said you would make me great fires and sit and read me John Donne poems. That we would wear big baggy sweaters and you would cook for me. And I believed you. From white knight to Don Quixote to black hole that I sometimes just can't see a way out of, I've fallen so far. I walk around carrying your babies, twins, two black dots on a scan and I am more scared for my future than I have ever been.

And you don't want to know. I know he has called you, tainted us with his version of Farah. I know you are plotting some strange revenge to sanctify your weakness and the pain you have shed on me. I know the aunty-ji has been on her crusade against everything I am and will ever represent to her. And yet still, part of me refuses to believe that you have turned your back in a week on a future we talked about together.

Trying to see a future for us as friends or whatever but cant, baby fear.

You text. There *doesn't have to be a future, all we have is now.*

I reply. *Tired. Bored by your fears.*

I know I said I never wanted to talk to you again, called you a liar, a coward and a cheat. I tore up your poem and your cards and shoved them all back in your own envelope and biked it back to you. I know I said you were so damaging I was dying inside. But I did love you, and you? I don't know anymore, can't see clearly for the tears that blind me, day and night.

People say you wanted my youth and my energy but I have neither of those left in me. That you were flattered by the Indian bird babe on your arm, liked the turning heads and the Gucci boots. Wanted something different, kicking, not sickly like the cancer ridden wife at home. Can't think straight I am so tired.

And I wonder how I will explain their father to the two lives growing inside me, which I feel like stabs of energy every now and then? How will I do this with all the anger and the hatred and the sadness you have brought into my life? You

239

drank deep of me Allan and you've taken the last fading rays of the light and the youth I had left me and left in me with your soulless darkness which pervades and disables me, every way I turn. And everywhere I turn, I fall because you, he, she the poison has filled my lungs and I can't breathe anymore.

Yet everyday away from you, removed from the circles of lies and the deceit and words feels like a day reclaimed to my own story and back in my own life. I now know that you don't have to know the difference between Glenmorangie and Glenfiddich to have class. That style is more than being "Left Bank" enough. I don't want your life of plastic people and fake words, endless openings, too much to drink, this fake power you think you dispense like salt in a loose shaker. You don't have that over me anymore. It takes a bigger person than you can be, my poor darling, to face up to what's yours, and own it.

***

After the abortion, I found it hard to reconcile what I had done. This was when I started to step into the twilight zone, the space between what I knew was happening around me and what was going on unspoken but still tangible. The e-mail campaign didn't stop, the papers had caught hold of the story and were threatening to print long and gory pieces, with or without my participation.

I went to see the media lawyer, David Price, about it. He suggested we get an injunction to stop whoever was doing it and serve it on Olivia, Yasmin and William. We did, it cost thousands of pounds but it contained a very watertight gagging order, by HH Justice Eady which prevented any newspapers writing about any of our children so at least they would be protected. It also banned Olivia from sending me or anyone else anymore e-mails.

They all denied that it had anything to do with them. They maintained that I was meant to be sending out these salacious e-mails about myself in an attempt to mar their lives.

The Daily Mail's Fe-mail had wanted to profile me for an article for a while and through Richard Kay who was someone I knew slightly, I wrote a long piece about what had happened, telling it all as it had really happened. I had been promised that they wouldn't change names or details and leave it as it was, the press had closed ranks around Allan, they felt sorry for Allan's wife, she had only recently recovered from the cancer but almost every week for a few weeks there was something in Ephraim Hardcastle or Spy alluding to who it might have been, this other party in this terrible triangle with the "Frisky Eastern Beauty." He was described as a senior Guardian Executive, Guy went as far as to describe him as an editor of a Guardian group magazine. William was named and shamed.

The article came out but not at all as I had written it and of course, in an attempt to save his own and the affected sensibilities of middle England over their poached eggs, Paul Dacre changed the names of the people, calling William Walter and Allan Adrian. Through the references in the piece it was obvious who they were. No one came out of it well at all, but there was a Pyrrhic sense of justice, if I was going to go down in flames I had decided that I would take them all with me.

Angella Johnson, a reporter for *The Mail on Sunday* contacted me after *The Daily Mail* piece came out. She had heard that I was disgruntled with the way the story had been printed and offered me the chance to tell it as it really was. I played along with her, and in spite of promises that she wouldn't do a stitch up, that she would be fair and portray the story sympathetically, the headline in the next week's edition blurted out "Prison Past of Sex Avenger," in true *Mail on Sunday* style.

I can't say I wasn't warned, so many friends told me to stay away from the tabloids. I felt as if my truth didn't matter anymore, that I didn't exist.

These women and their wretched husbands were doing whatever they could, which was a lot, to destroy any remaining vestige of me and I felt I wanted to get my version of the truth out. The tabloids are not a place for truth or stories, they are all fiction and fast-news. The fee promised by *The Daily Mail,* which had never been the motivation for the article, didn't came through because I didn't have it in writing and the sycophantic editor told me that it offended Paul Dacre's sensibilities to pay someone for such a tawdry story. I had become a household name. Add to this the weekly poison that came from a certain unimportant Asian web site that kept on and on about me, I felt as if I was living in an episode of Crimewatch dubbed Farahwatch. Life was out of control.

Then I had the police come and take away my computers in order to investigate allegations that I had been harassing William and Allan or hacking into their e-mails.

Nothing ever came of those allegations and the senior officer investigating the case told me he felt Allan had been dragged in to make a statement reluctantly by his wife. His statement which was shown to me by the police, made him out to be the injured and abused party in our affair, even though he had started and continued it. Do cuckolded wives think they will get sympathy or redress from the blunt-edged instrument that is the law? It made my life difficult for a while, I had to report to Hounslow CID and Holborn, to extend comply to my bail conditions while the police "investigated" this mucky media story. They found it all captivating, titillating, a lot more interesting than the regular beat crime they had to cover.

Here I was. Seemingly I had it all. The house in the country, two beautiful and bright children, the new flashy car every year, columns in an important regional paper and comment pieces in most of the broadsheets at one time or another. On the surface it all looked good. But underneath it all, the magazine was driving me deeper and deeper into debt. I stole a credit card from a temporary nanny in order to buy office equipment because the computers had been seized. I was falling behind on mortgage payments on all of my properties and on more than one occasion my father coughed up arrears of more than £10 000 to ward off potential evictions. I was living on the knife-edge.

The court case regarding the word Indobrit came and went. I didn't understand IP law and I already owed the solicitors I had retained £40 000 before we had even gone to court. I fired them and thought I could do it on my own.

On the day of the case, I went into court and told the Judge that I needed time to either retain a new solicitor. Then I left. Anjoom was given a default judgment, which stated that she alone owned the trademark for the word Indobrit. She lied and thus instigated the downfall of something that was so good for so many people. Ego in an ugly academic is a wicked thing. Maybe she wanted to start her own magazine; maybe she wanted me to welcome her back into the fold. I wasn't going to. The Judge made a costs order against me which I couldn't possibly pay.

I had borrowed money through a bridging loan when I had closed the deal on the house in Hampshire. It was a temporary measure through a so-called friend. He decided I should pay £8 000 in legal fees and interest when I had borrowed the money for about two months. The principle amount had only been £30 000. I refused. He asked for a bankruptcy order against me, which I tried to defend but at the time, everything was closing in on me. The flats were all financially precarious. I was losing my temper and no amount of sedatives and anti-depressants could take the edge off the anxiety and fear I felt all the time.

Marina has always been small for her age, and very slight. She wasn't three yet and was running round the flat which had wooden floors throughout. Imran put his foot out and deliberately tripped her up. I lost it with him, I grabbed him by the scruff of his collar and put him outside the front door. When he cried and begged that he was sorry I let him in and he started to tease her and make her fall over again. I just couldn't stand it. I had fired the long-term au-pair who had forgotten his place and that he was not a part of the family, just paid-for help, and he had been deported back to Hungary. We tried a succession of temporary nannies, without any success. I picked him up again and I threw him on his bed. He hit his cheek hard against the bedside table and immediately the bloom of a bruise started to show up on his cheek.

The next day, the school phoned me and asked if I would go in for a meeting. I had told him to say that he fell over and hurt himself but they either didn't believe me or wanted to verify the story. I stuck to my version of the truth but I felt awful making him lie about what happened.

Marina's school also asked for a meeting to ensure that she was all right. Eaton House had reported the situation to Social Services. They didn't take any action, but I knew I was losing control. I had never taken my short temper or my anger out on my children before.

My mother was in London for the summer. They had been pressuring me for a long time to send Imran and Marina to Cape Town for school, just for a year, so I could deal with all the legal mess and put my life back on track. They were close to both kids and I thought no harm would come of it although I was reluctant to let them go.

They behaved very differently as grandparents than they had as parents; I suppose old age had made them want to redress the imbalance old grievances that their own children had displayed. They scored no points when they tried it first time round.

When my father sent the prospectus for the International School in Cape Town, with its green grass campus and rainbow faculty, I was sold. A year was not a long time and I did need the time to try and clear my head.

Marina didn't want to go but when I said goodbye at the airport I must admit I was relieved. Imran was used to being a jet-set kid. My children were the last ties to my sanity. They were the control I needed to keep me in check, they demanded a routine, regular mealtimes, school runs and homework. Letting them go left me undone.

I could tell you all the things I did, every gory detail but it doesn't matter anymore. I stole a succession of credit cards to keep the magazine going, I didn't care about the lifestyle, it was slipping away. And what was so heartbreaking was that on the surface, it still looked so good. *Foreign Policy Magazine* wrote a review about the Bollystan issue and the screen goddess, Aishwarya Rai, beautiful but forgettable, graced the cover of that issue, in a photo taken by Jamie Hughes, specifically for the magazine.

Jamie is a one-man charm offensive. Aish surrounded herself with her predominantly gay male entourage, her makeup artist and hairstylist had been flown out to London with her, as part of Miramax's promotion of Gurindher Chadha's film, *Bride and Prejudice*, a modern Bolly playback of the much-loved Jane Austin classic.

Curry kings and steel magnates offered to inject money into it, but they came with their own agendas. They wanted to use the magazine as a political platform for their own aspirations. We would lose full editorial control. I started talking to a business accountant in Birmingham about raising some finance but in the Byzantine corrupt and convoluted world of government funding, those that know their way around and how to access the pots of gold want to be paid handsomely for their services, both in up front fees, to enable them to act, a sort of retainer,and then again on a percentage, when the funding came through.

I desperately wanted the magazine to work and there was no reason it shouldn't. I let a lot of people who had invested a lot of trust and faith in me down, but I didn't do it to hurt anyone or because I wanted to buy shiny, pretty things. It was done because I couldn't see a way out of it. Printers and writers were screaming to get paid, everyone seemed to have their own agenda as to what they wanted and expected from me. Don't believe them when they cry "victim" from the top of a hill, they were all party to the sickness. Ambarina Hassan and Jessica Hines were managing editors and had come on board to give me some room to breathe and try and do other things.

Parag and I had worked on an outline for a TV program based on the idea of Bollystan, showing off and showcasing her best and most brilliant denizens. SKY TV were about to commission it, as a series, and we were looking at options for presenters, the charming Jon Snow was an obvious choice.

Richard Brock had worked on *Sharia TV,* a series for Channel 4 and we had become close, he was another in the list of married, unavailable men who came into my life, promising nothing and alluding to everything. He was going to direct the series and we had a good working relationship.

I had retained Imran Khan from the onset, when I started to be bullied by the police about Allan and William. Really that was a civil matter and should have been dealt with by the county courts. The stress of the stupid, baseless allegations of e-mail hacking and other nonsense made me careless. I was being watched but I didn't care anymore if I was caught, I had had enough. Imran was solid. Subtly, he tried to coax the truth out of me, but I had started to believe my own lies.

No one and nothing could reach me anymore. I had moved down to the house in Hampshire because I was fed up with almost weekly early morning visits and searches from DC Sophie Cockroach and the gang from Fulham Police Station. I had deliberately missed a court appearance, in spite of Imran's pleas to make sure that I attended but I knew the game was up.

Judge John Samuels had had enough. He had let me out on bail, he had treated me with only respect, yet almost every time I appeared in front of him, there were more crimes that I had committed added to the CPS' ever-growing list of indictments. I told Imran that I would surrender but that I needed to tie up some loose ends. I never did finish what I had started, in the end it all imploded.

When I was finally arrested in Hampshire, it wasn't with sniffer dogs and screaming sirens. It was a quiet Sunday afternoon. I had decided to turn myself in that week, there was no hope of bail, I had accepted that I had made an ass out of Judge Samuel's trust and respect for me. Judges don't like it when defendants continue to commit crimes, even alleged crimes while they are out on bail; it makes the system look farcical. The police came, and saw me putting some stuff away in the kitchen, I was standing on a chair. I had locked the door to the front of the house but they came round the back and saw me through the glass in the French doors which lead out onto a patio and then the garden. I refused to answer the door. It was a Tom and Jerry moment.

They went back to the car to get something to force the door open and I hid behind a pile of laundry. When they came in they couldn't see me so they went upstairs and I ran out of the house into the garden, behind the shed.

They searched the house high and low, they came out to the shed a couple of times but they didn't look behind it. I did my best foxhole praying, that PC Plod wouldn't venture into the long grass where I had staked my position. He didn't.

Then just as they had given up, one of the young officers decided to take a last look, behind the shed, and there I was.

Prison Pastimes

I was in prison for twenty-one months. That amount of time has to change even the hardest core serial criminal, which is how I was portrayed in the press. There was extensive coverage dedicated to my arrest, guilty pleas and eventual sentencing. I was held on remand from May 18 to October 13 2005, and in that time, we made a deal with the investigating officer who was bullying the prosecutor and seemed to have taken the lead role in this courtroom drama. I agreed to plea to some indictments, some fell away.

Imran Khan came to see me in Holloway soon after I was held on remand. We made several bail applications, but the barrister who was representing me described his position as reminiscent of King Canute, trying to hold back the sea as the tide went out. The Judge, HH John Samuels, was inclined to agree. The CPS piled more and more illusion onto the actual extent of my criminality, the latest was an allegation that I had committed mortgage fraud amounting to hundreds of thousands of pounds.

Marina was in London with my mother, she was meant to be returning to live with me again and we pleaded to the Court that I should be allowed out pending the trail, as she would have to be put into care. Samuels sternly stated that as my mother had previously looked after her, he saw no reason why she should not continue to do so. Everything else we said fell on similarly deaf ears.

Imran felt that if there was something deeply wrong in me that if we could find a psychiatrist that could give it a name, perhaps Samuels would look at the case less severely. At best, I could hope for a long probation period. Imran, in all the time he defended me, never judged me. He was always on my side and he was someone I trusted completely. Perhaps he wasn't harsh enough with me. We needed a pre-sentencing report and Dr Tony Nayani was someone that Imran trusted and worked with often. But it was the summer holidays. First Imran was away then Dr Nayani was away so by the time the pre-sentencing reports had been done, we were already in mid-September, then we had to find an open date for sentencing.

The barrister I had was competent, he must have been, he had been selected to be a tenant at the exclusive Tooks Court, Michael Mansfield's chambers. I had known and grown to trust Imran through Bobby Sayed, the founder of the controversial EMMA Awards. Now we sat down in the gloom of Holloway's visiting room, where solicitors met their clients, in supposed privacy, although there are strange cases when confidential information told to solicitors somehow managed to find its way into the CPS' notes. Holloway was investigated conclusively for bugging legally privileged conversations.

We had started to chart out my story for the Judge. It's called a proof. It's so that the sentencing Judge can glean some insight into the state of mind and the situation that the defendant was in, when they committed the crimes for which they are before him. In Italy, the magistrate has to visit the defendant's home, and meet their family and friends; it humanizes the criminal and puts the judge back into the real world, out of his ermine and robes.

The lack of scrutiny of the police and the prosecutor in the court room, the laxity of rules when it comes to what they can do and say to a defendant to try and gain a conviction, none of it could survive the public gaze or the oxygen of truth once the blustering and rhetoric are removed. Judges see through a lot of the shenanigans but in the end they are all players on the same team. The alliances that justice makes in the name of the law in the UK court system proves that she is at best, myopic.

The court ordered a Probation Officer's Report. Arik Yacobi from London Probation fitted me in along with several other women he had been told to evaluate one afternoon at HMP Holloway. There were a remarkable number of us to be seen in a short space of time, seven women in two hours. I was the last.

He was fat and had the worn look of a leftover hippy. He looked dirty, in his khaki trousers, which were stained with coffee and filth and his t-shirt, which depicted some long defunct peace movement or band, was hanging over his trousers, covering up a huge stomach. He wore NHS glasses and fidgeted as he spoke to me. I tried to overlook the ugliness and the squalor that emanated from him but I knew the minute I saw that, my fate was doomed and sealed by this man. I would hang.

In the twenty minutes he met with me, he was more concerned about having lost the keys to his prison locker where he had to leave everything when he entered the prison's boundaries. He had left them in another room, where he had done the previous interview, but this didn't stop him from searching high and low while he was meant to be listening to what I was saying.

He asked the perfunctory questions, and as soon as he heard that I had been a journalist and an editor, he launched into a personal diatribe about how much he hated media. When I tried to point out that I worked in ethnic media, this Jew-hating Jew launched in again about how pointless ethnic media was and how it lead to divisions within mainstream society and was the cause for the a lack of motivation for new immigrants to assimilate.

I was shocked by this overtly racist view but tried to steer him back to the subject, which was me and my probation report. The Judge lays a lot of importance to the report and it was essential that this hater grasped that I was sorry for what I had done. A little contrition could go a long way, I had been advised. He dutifully sat and listened and while I make no excuses for what I did, or tried to justify it in any way, other than madness and desperation, when he started moving restlessly again to indicate that my twenty minutes were up, I was worried.

My goose was cooked. He told me that Judge Samuels barely took notice of the reports submitted to him, that it was all a penitent's waste of time. He also told me that Samuels was a stern judge and that I was probably looking at a prison sentence. In fact Judge Samuels had a reputation as being a reformer. He didn't send people to jail if he felt it is going to break apart families or cause other long-term harm. He had previously told my legal team that he was going to give me a community service sentence, albeit a harsh one, but that I had tested him too far, which was true enough. I also found out later that Samuels puts a lot of stock into what goes into the Probation Services report.

To cover myself, I wrote a letter of complaint to London Probation. In the long-term we didn't need it, but it was the beginning of a long and tedious relationship with some of the pedantic and lazy civil servants installed in comfy union-protected jobs around the business of punishment and control. Being a probation officer is like having tenure at a university. It is almost impossible to lose that place; they have to practically commit murder most foul to be considered for the slightest relegation. My complaint was passed around from pillar to post and no one took the slightest initiative as to how to respond to it or to investigate it. I went back to the landing and phoned Imran straight away. He was shocked and promised to write a letter to London Probation asking that we should have another Probation Report, but he suggested that we wait till Yacobi's report came through.

The Asian media had taken the story with glee and run with it, I had stopped caring. A lot of what was printed was true but a lot of it was exaggeration and hyperbole. It read better to make me into a brown-skinned Bonnie and Clyde. I didn't see much of the press in prison but friends who came to visit told me about it.

My mother brought Marina to visit me a few days after I was held on remand in May 2005. She was meant to be coming back to live with me, but now she would have to go to Canada and Cuba and spend time with my mothers' witch-like sisters. I dreaded the thought of my beautiful, fragile little princess having to be around them, they were rough and loud, even old age hadn't infused any sense into them. Of course she didn't understand what was going on, she wanted to stay and she sobbed as if her heart was being torn out of her chest when it was time to go. We both cried. I have always found it difficult to say goodbye to her, I am sure she has big abandonment issues.

We tried to go in front of Samuels and make the case that Marina needed me and that I should be let out on bail, he refused. Instead he rescinded the £10 000 bail money that my parents had to pay, as I had failed to make a court appearance. My mother was more angry and upset about the loss of her money than anything else but in a twist of fate, and a manner quite symbolic of the way the UK's Criminal Justice System operates, it was returned to her in error. She didn't say a word and she cashed the cheque.

The courts, the Judges, the prisons don't care about the effect that the separation from her family has on a woman, or even worse on her children. You become a criminal, number one and everything else after that. They try to make provisions for children's visiting days and she came to a couple of those, if my mother was in the country but saying goodbye was too awful, I almost didn't want her to come. Communicating with them was even worse.

The prison runs a monopoly on its telephone system with BT. The charges are astronomical and the excuse given is the extra manpower needed to monitor the phone calls made by inmates. For a £5 weekly phone card, I could speak to them both for five minutes in total. There are limits as to how much we can spend in prison when we are sentenced, so it was hard to buy more than a couple of these phone cards in a week. I would try and call on a Sunday when I knew they would be at home but they both did a lot of growing up in that time that I missed out on, and that is something I can never make up to either of them.

The agreement with my parents was always that they would be returned to me as soon as I was out of prison.

What made it harder for me was the proof, which I had now completed and lay, firmly closed, in an A4 notebook. It made it very clear, in black and white and my neat but illegible handwriting that my parents were the most dysfunctional and neurotic caregivers. Now I had repeated the cycle of history and ensured that the scars would extend their reach over another generation by handing my children over to them, like a human sacrifice. I had filled over two hundred handwritten pages, which had been typed up and given to the Judge.

Samuels was perfunctory but detailed. He told me that I had held a position of great responsibility, that I had lived an affluent lifestyle and that I had used other people's money to pay for it. He said I was manipulative and he sentenced me to the longest period he could, in order to make an example of me, he said, to deter any one else from my position and background. The sentencing seemed to run on for an hour, he sentenced me individually for the charges of theft, for a total of two years. For two counts of perverting the pourse of justice, I was handed another eighteen months. The sentences were to run consecutively. I would have to do half of that.

Imran came down with Nick Wrack and he looked as shocked as I felt. He felt the Judge had been too harsh and he promised to start the process of appeal straight away. He told me to keep my head down and to stay in touch. We should speak on Monday.

.

I was taken back to the North London prison, on that Friday afternoon. Life in prison goes on, in spite of whatever shocks a prisoner might have been dealt by the Judicial System. I was told I still had to go to education. The evening's *Metro* carried a front page story about me, the socialite's downfall from great heights. The prison managed to keep it away, in a moment of uncommon sensitivity.

Shellshocked, I entered Stevie's class. She was cool, a Boho Notting Hill style hippy who was the textile teacher. She had encouraged me earlier to do paintings on textiles and had given me some of the art room's fabric paints in empty vitamin bottles to take back to the cell, on the wing. Learning to paint and sew was something I had always wanted to do but had never had the time for. Now I had all the time on the world, maybe nearly another two years.

"Right, so what do you want to do?" She was carefully watching over me. She knew about the sentence, the news had been forwarded back to the prison and the education department, everyone was stunned but tried not to show it. I had been put on a suicide watch earlier that week as I had been tearful. In prison I learned to cut myself with razor blades. It was the last thing I could measure and therefore control, as I slashed small and then larger cuts into both arms, making a filigree of red lace where the blood seeped through. It was just a temporary release, it let out some of the physical pain but the itchiness as the scars started to form and skin grew back was unbearable and made me forget the initial discharge of anxiety or pain.

"I don't know." I felt very small, as if I had been reduced to being a child again, but the textile class was a place I could be myself, she was endearing and encouraging. There are a few shining souls in the prison system and Stevie is definitely one of them.

Then Sandra looked over at me, from where she was sewing hems and edges on do-rags. She stood up tall, all six feet of her, shining, black like an Amazon. She came over to me and put her arms out. I hugged her and she held me close, the way she might have done one of her daughters. She was a lifer, in for murder,

250

she had beaten a man who had raped her daughter and even though she was over fifty and a Rastafarian and therefore non-violent, her sinewy muscles and strength knocked him flat in one blow. I admired her; it is something any mother would do.

"Look," she said as she caressed my hair and let me cry into her overalls, "The worst is over, you know what you have to do now. You just have to get on and do it."

I looked up at her, all bleary-eyed and broken and I felt so grateful that this Nubian goddess, who until now, had always been polite, but not warm, had reached out to me. I could never repay that kindness no matter how many riches I may ever gain. It took someone who had been at that point of despair to tell me that it could only get better from then.

"You said you wanted to learn how to use a sewing machine," said Stevie, "And you wanted to make something for your daughter, so let's make a bag for her."

And completely matter-of-factly, with her pixie face set into her unnaturally blond cropped hair, Stevie was threading the sewing machine for me. She opened the door to learning something new and I went through.

From time to time, Sandra looked over, to see how I was and the three of us were soon absorbed in this woman's work, in the most unlikely setting.

Fame has its advantages. In the life I had left behind, there were a lot of hangers on, who leeched off my notoriety and clung on, as if some of the attention in the spotlight might pass through to them. They were burnt, like errant moths to the flame. I did what I did to survive. I thought I was acting rationally, but you can't tell a crazy person that she is crazy. Here, I was left alone.

Most of the female prison population is on sedatives or anti-depressants. As in any institution, where there is an abundance of females, many of us ovulated and had our periods at the same time of the month, which lead to some bitchy days, as regular and monotonously predictable as the rest of the prison schedule.

What kills is the drip-drip attrition, the way the system is designed to wear down women. I had Imran on my side and there were more than a few dozen frantic phone calls I made to him, at the office and on his mobile, to ask him to send a letter or advise about a problem with a guard or a governor. He was an angel; he sent letters by fax to the governor and was always calm and efficient. I wish I could say the same about some of the assistants he had around him. My relationship with him suffered because in that open-heartedness that defines him, he employed students fresh out of law school with little or no experience.

One of these, a fresh faced Asian girl who couldn't have been more than twenty-five came to Holloway to finish the proof which was taking a lot longer than I had imagined it would. It was the first time I had examined every significant event in my life in detail, to try and understand what made me tick, or not, as it transpired. She was efficient but when she left she dispensed some trite bit of advice about how I should look at my life and not make the same mistakes again, that this was the chance for a new slate. I was too shocked to react to her, but later I called Imran and asked how she dared to judge or question me. He reprimanded her. I had enough to contend with, survival was the main preoccupation for the time being.

I had come across Counselling in Prison, a charity, which is run by volunteer counselors. Some of the murky monsters that were coming up from the pages of the proof were proving to be more than I could manage myself. This was the first time I had acknowledged and given a name to the sexual abuse and the rape from decades ago. Annette, a sympathetic and street smart counselor found me and we sat for hours on the bench in the rose garden, she just listened as I talked and I tried to make sense of it all.

All I needed was the validation of being heard. I didn't need an audience of millions or hundreds of thousands, who knows, papers all lie about their readership figures, from *The Daily Mail*, I needed another woman to just hear me out. Judgment without mercy is cruel punishment and although I still thought that Judge Samuels dealt with me harshly, this period gave me the time I had craved all my life to think and to write. The proof was the skeleton of this book. I have never had time, for anything. My life has been a helter-skelter of noise camera and action to keep the ghosts at bay. I thought if I could create enough distractions and fitinas that I could somehow stay in control and not give in to the fears, which haunted my waking. Addiction helped too.

As soon as I was sentenced, I was transferred from Holloway to leafy Downview, in Surrey. The surroundings were more pleasant but the new governor was still unsure of his position and the place needed a radical overhaul. The Prison Officer's Union was very strong in there and abuse of inmates by officers went largely unreported and unpunished. Prison is a place to keep your head down and say nothing. Just do what you are told and get on with it. But I couldn't close my eyes to the daily injustices, not everyone had an Imran Khan to fight their corner and protect their rights from a marauding establishment, hell-bent on depriving us from the most basic human rights. I wrote complaints and letters for women who couldn't manage to, for themselves.

I wrote a lot of complaints which were not satisfactorily dealt with and with the notable exception of one complaint that was upheld and dealt with admirably by the Ombudsman's office, about access to calls and phone cards at HMP Foston Hall, I realised how awful the complaints system was, even the Ombudsman's

Office knew which prisons were the worst offenders but they were stymied by governors who had too much power and clanned together to ignore any rulings made against them. A governor's prison is his own personal fiefdom.

In December 2005, while I was still at Downview, a probation officer came to see me from the resettlement department. I isolated pretty much all the time, unless I was on the wing for dinner or trying to get something administrative sorted out. They were worried that I seemed sad and upset depressed. My parents, in all their wisdom, had decided not to tell my children that I was in prison. They said that I was traveling. My mother stood over them so that they couldn't speak to me freely and they were not being given my weekly letters. I wanted them to know why I couldn't call them all the time, everyday. They were used to me traveling, especially to India for magazine-related work, and calling them all the time. I wanted them to understand that I couldn't call.

My parents sent money to my friend Sandra, who sent it to the prison in postal orders so I could buy phone cards to call overseas on the prison phones but it was invariably never enough.

The probation officer said that there was a charity that could help to ascertain whether the children were all right, if I would consent to them making inquiries. I signed the necessary forms so International Social Services could begin the procedure, and I agreed to pay the £400 fee. I needed reassurance, from someone on the outside that the children were cared for and in good spirits; the calls on the phone had become more terse and unbearable. In May, when the ISS finally got round to initiating the situation, my concerns had died down. Other mothers inside had explained that my children were displaying natural reactions of feeling rejected.

They were settling into their new South African lives and enjoying the International School. The headmistress there assured me that she would look out for both of them. At that time, my parents were good at sending me sheaves of Marina's attempts at colouring, or colour photos of the children printed on sheets of A4 copy paper, so I could see how they were growing. Occasionally I would get a school report. They seemed to understand how important the link was between me and my kids and that my concerns were real.

I asked the ISS investigation to stop, but the Probation Department told me that it had to be completed now. I said that was fine but I would no longer be paying the £400 fee they required. Not once, in all that time, did the ISS make contact with me to ascertain what my fears were. The case drifted from London to Johannesburg to Cape Town, with all the vigour and enthusiasm that civil servants and charity workers can muster up. Barely nothing.

The weekends dragged, there were never enough prison staff, so the wings took it in turns to lock in the women for extra hours. I didn't mind, as I had the basic comforts; a television, a shower in my room, a toilet, and sink. I had put up my own paintings and photos of the children on the bulletin board and I had made a patchwork curtain, of images that represented different faiths and spirituality. There was a peacock, a Buddha, a *hamsa* and other symbols of universal faiths.

The cell was cozy, in as much as a prison cell could be, but behind the canvas tapestry which acted as a curtain, the shadows of the prison bars presented themselves, silent centurions of my solitude.

I complained a lot. Sometimes I think it was the only thing that reminded me I was still alive. I had plenty of causes for complaints. The prison system has a mind-numbingly stupid system of white, pink and blue forms, with varying degrees of confidentiality. The pink forms were supposed to go straight to the governor in a brown envelope.

When they were not dealt with satisfactorily, the Independent Monitoring Board, which is a charity set up by a group of volunteers, got involved. They have a mandate from the Home Office to go into any part of a prison to investigate a complaint. That's the theory. The reality is that only once, at Downview, where the IMB and the Prison Officers are in each other's pockets, did I receive a response stating the nature of my complaint was far too sensitive for them to deal with.

The next port of call was the Area Manager, who inevitably sided with the governor so there was little point in seeking any kind of redress there. Sometimes, I would write to my MP, Sir Malcolm Rifkind, to make the prison services see that I wasn't going to roll over and play dead dog. As far as I was concerned, I was serving out my punishment and they were not there to make it any worse or inflict any further misery, which sometimes it felt they thought it was within their mandate to do. Sir Malcolm's office were of enormous help and although the ex-Home Secretary, one of Maggie's trusted right hand henchman, isn't known for his liberal views on prison reform, he was fair and generous with his time and correspondence with me. I suppose there can't be many residents of Chelsea and Kensington who are banged up and need his help as their parliamentary representative.

I saw my children a little bit. That summer they came to London. It was in June 2006. I had been trying to apply for home leave to spend some time with them, but this was falling on deaf ears and the long-winded security procedure in the prison. In the early summer of 2006, Sir Malcolm's office took up my cause and wrote to the governor asking him to look at my request application for home leave and to consider the children.

Downview's Probation and Security department were being characteristically slow about granting the licence which would allow me to spend any time with them, and they were in London only for a few short weeks.

The new governor was still learning his way around what he could and couldn't do; he had been at Head Office prior to being a prison governor and was not having an easy time of it.

Downview is meant to be fairly proactive and reformist in its outlook, there are family days and provisions in place to accommodate different religions, if their administrators could get past the gluttonous eye of Rosie, the chaplain. She wanted to save our souls exclusively for Christianity. Maybe she thought it meant more brownie points for her in heaven later. I saw a lay Buddhist teacher who came in every six weeks, or as much as her busy schedule allowed. We chanted and prayed together and she brought in endless folders of photocopied notes, about the different tenets of Buddhism and the precepts. She was small and sweet, I think she might have been Chinese. She brought in incense and prayer beads and laminated cards with Buddhist doctrines on them such as, "I am responsible."

I believe in karma. It has always caught up with me in my life and now with light speed technology, it travels faster than ever and all the transgressions committed here and now are to be accounted for in the present, and surely in this life.

But something else had caught my eye, Kabbalah. I had found books about it in Holloway's library. From the salubrious surroundings of leafy Surrey, Holloway seemed a thousand miles away. They had a few books on Kabbalah in the prison library. The noise and the smell of Holloway, which is a condemned building and has been deemed unfit for purpose by Anne Owers the prisons inspector, all seemed distant.

In March of 2006 Jena died. There were a couple of decent governors at Downview, one of whom pulled out all the stops so that I could go to the *Jamat Khanna* the night they announced her death. I didn't want to go to the funeral, although I was asked if I would like to attend, by the same governor. Two prison officers escorted me in a taxi, there and back to the little community hall in Acton.

My father was there and for the first time, he appeared really old. He was thin and seemed much shorter than I recalled, he was playing patriarch, as the oldest man and the first born son in the family, he lived up to what he had to do.

Various aunts and cousins I hadn't seen in years made a fuss over me and the guards loosened their hold; they undid the handcuffs which bound me to the pretty female officer, Abby, who was out of uniform. They were happy, they were getting paid overtime, and it was a Friday evening. The other guard was the

PE instructor, Ron, who was always straightforward and fair. There were some guards at Downview who were human and realised that they could get more out of female inmates, who could be an unruly lot, with honey rather than vinegar.

Yasmin was there, giving the best performance of her life in the part of the sorrow-filled daughter. Her eyes were puffy from crying and for a moment, I felt sorry for her. She had thrown Jena out of her house when her live-in babysitting duties were no longer needed and Jena had fallen on her knees to beg housing from the state. I was glad she was free of her awful children, who only ever loved her when they wanted something from her. She had brought up three generations of the Damji family and she deserved some space and a home of her own. None of them helped her.

My mother is malicious. She had always hated Jena because Jena attracted love and admiration wherever
she went; she was truly loved and had many friends. In the early years before my father's mind was poisoned with alcohol and my mother's vitriol, he had always taken Jena's side, in the arguments between her and my mother. She wanted to die. She had started to suffer from dementia and she stopped eating. It was as if the will to live had been sucked out of her. I don't know how much she knew about me or about my situation, but Yasmin, snotty and tearful, blurted out, as she sobbed into my navy Chanel boucle coat, "She always loved you the most, she talked about you all the time."

My own relationship with her had become a little strained, in the year before Imran and Marina went to Cape Town. Whenever I went to see her, her fridge was filled with moldy, uneaten food, yet she paid someone to cook for her. She didn't like the woman's food. Jena was a consummate cook, and no one could make a *pilaf* or a mutton curry like she could. She used to love to cook, it made her feel like a mother and a caregiver. Not eating was the first sign from her frail little body that something was terribly wrong.

Still she assumed that same pose, like a chubby white Buddha, perched cross-legged on her green velvet sofa. Face turned, eyes cast downwards, skinny, wrinkled fingers worrying away at the prayer beads on a worn silk string. Her flat was always dusty and although it was meticulously tidy, she couldn't muster the effort to clean it. A carer was meant to do that twice a week, but given the layer of white dust that covered everything, it was clear she wasn't doing it anything and still being paid for it.

Jena wouldn't complain to those who were inflicting the pain and the discomfort on her. She would moan, generally about everything when we went to visit and Marina was both scared and fascinated by her.

"Jena smells old," she said one day in the infinite and some wisdom of a two-year-old.

"Really? What do you mean?" My daughter's mind fascinates me, every time.

"I don't know," she said and she skipped away, "She just smells old and bit dying."

I didn't know what to say and muttered something about not saying nasty things, but she turned her head and she looked at me with the pure honesty of her hazel eyes and said nothing else. I had seen her squirm as Jena tried to cuddle her, she is not a tactile or affectionate child until she knows a person, and then she is all kisses and smiles. She alternated between Jena's lap and her spot on the floor. I often picked up a Nando's takeaway to feed the children if we were going to her in West Ealing, and Jena didn't approve of that.

She didn't see how hard it was to be a single mother in London, with two small kids and that sometimes it was better to feed them Nando's, because at least I knew that they would eat it, than to fight with them about food they weren't going to eat. My life must have looked like a breeze to her, she had really suffered to bring up her brood. There are shortcuts every mother learns to take, modern motherhood is a maze of timesaving, energy conserving methods, we learn to do and make do, in the minimum amount of time that we have available.

She was the closest thing I ever had to a mother, which isn't unusual in extended Asian families. But I hated what they did to her; there was no respect, in spite of all the propaganda that we put out, about loving and looking after the elders in the community. She lived off her state pension and she was denied dignity, even in death with her vulture-like children trying to steal the halo of grief, in abject outpourings of emotions.

I think they cried so much because they felt guilty. Yasmin, the great media commentator used my Jena, in her inane *Independent* columns, half the things she attributed to my grandma, Jena would never have said, but I suppose she has to make her weekly word count with something, and crazy ethnic family sells. Everything is "material" in Yasmin's hollow shell of a life; she gave up on reality a long time ago, maybe when Sky left her.

It was hard not to be cynical about Jena's death. Yasmin said she died all alone, which was what she was most afraid of in the world, but my father said she died surrounded by people that loved her. She had a wide circle of friends of all ages, teenagers, young mums and other great grandmas often came to visit her in her cramped flat in West London, everyone wanted to stop her from feeling lonely, but hers wasn't the loneliness that can be fixed with company and a good laugh.

Hers was fed by regrets and recriminations, of a life only half-lived. She could have been and done anything, but life didn't give her half a chance, only problem children who lived muddled and truthless lives.

In July 2006, the children came and visited me at Downview, which was ghastly. At the exact same time, the ISS finally contacted Cape Town Social Services to enquire about the children's wellbeing, although I had asked for the investigation to be stopped. They had still never asked for input from me at all. When they returned to their beach house, back in South Africa, my father was furious and he started to use my son as the messenger of his hate.

Imran was angry and upset when my father told him that I wanted to have him put into foster care. I tried to explain that this was old, that I had asked for it to be stopped but my father enjoys playing the hero. He lives by creating divisions, because he thinks it gives him power. When they returned to Cape Town, they were advised that they had to make an appointment for the social worker to come out to the house and ensure that the children were healthy and safe.

I was still trying to get home leave to be able to spend a few days with them but my pleas were going nowhere.

The governor I had liked, who saw the stupidity of some prison rules, such as not being allowed to have beads and sequins sent into the prison for hobby-work, and who facilitated access to these with a signature and a smile, had been moved to the resettlement unit, so I didn't see much of him. Joyti de Laurey had come to Downview, amidst allegations that she had tried to bribe the Hindu priest who was visiting her at HMP Send, in a blaze of notoriety. She was ghosted which means that no one, including the prisoner is given any notice that she is about to be moved, or where to. A guard simply comes into your cell and says:

"Pack up. You're leaving."

And that is it. One way the prison authorities manage to contain so many women, in overcrowded and inhuman conditions is by constantly undermining them. Our friendships are called into question when guards try and play childish mind games; with allegations that such-and-such is a snitch. Fights and arguments flare up over property being lost or stolen, inmates run the prison laundry and even faintly nice garments can disappear. The prison keeps property cards and cells are searched randomly and without notice, so the thief is caught before long.

Downview had rules for this and rules for that. I understood the necessity of rules for safety and security but some of their diktats seemed petty and unnecessary. All the while the new governor was still finding his feet and appeared powerless. Life behind a desk at HQ and the reality on the front line, on active prison duty are two very different worlds.

I thought the rule about not being allowed to have papers or notes over the edge of the bulletin board was a particularly stupid one. I wanted to cover up as much of the ugly, old magnolia painted wall as I could with pretty pictures, as it was stained and cracked. The education department at Downview helped me to find a course I wanted to do on Crime and Social Justice. It was run by the Open University and funded by the Prisoners' Education Trust, of which Judge Samuels had become the chairman.

The course allowed me to use my mind, I enjoyed the arduous homework assignments and I learned there was a whole science of the nature of Criminology, the course touched on many aspects of crime, and the causes of crime. The more time I spent in prison, and the more into the coursework I delved, I realised that I was not the average white-collar criminal. Looking at the crimes I had committed with a clear and clinical eye, through the analysis of Criminology, enabled me to be more dispassionate about my situation. I had come from a privileged background, I had everything I could have ever wanted, yet still at the very pit of me, where the first foundations of where this entity I knew as me, started, there was a hole.

I have read a lot of pop psychology in my time, I have been analyzed and reanalyzed by the best in every school of psychological thought, but the mind cannot look at itself. It's like fire trying to understand the concept of heat. I had not been able to separate my mind from my ego; I thought it all came as part of a whole, messy package. The Buddhist chanting and invocations really helped to quiet my mind.

Finally, I received the long awaited books about Kabbalah from the centre on Stratford Place. These seemed to make sense in a way that other philosophies and religions did not. I had rejected Islam and Ismailism wholesale, at it was the doctrine of the family and I wanted to distance myself as fast and as far as I could from anything to do with them. Buddhism seemed too nihilistic, I didn't like the idea of having no control in my destiny and I found it hard to believe that everything was already written, anyway. What was the purpose of my life if it was just to go through some set of objectives, pitfalls and experiences already prescribed to me? I also couldn't believe, as in the Buddhist's doctrine that I could have chosen the parents I had.

Finally the application for home leave came through. It was initially a tentative three days. Imran had returned to Cape Town with my father. It came with a lot of conditions and I was released to go back to my flat in Chelsea. The bankruptcy proceedings against me had wiped out all of my assets and whatever remained was left in a trust I had set up, years ago, to benefit the children. All the flats and houses in my own name were gone, except for this tiny studio flat by the river, which I had always rented out to tenants.

259

We had an amazing three days. On the last day I called the prison and spoke to the resettlement Senior Officer. I asked if he would extend my licence for one day, as Marina was really upset and they were going to stay in London for an extra day if he agreed. He did, with the friendly warning, "If you don't come back, I will come and find you."

It was as if I was getting to know my child for the first time, she was four at that time and when she had left London, she had been two-and-a-half. The snatched time together, dispensed at Her Majesty's pleasure, wasn't enough to see the changes in her. One morning, we were locked in the flat because the lock had jammed and fear flooded her tiny face,

"Mum, don't call the police."

"Why not?"

"Because they will come and take you away from me," she said.

I wondered if I would ever be able to heal the damage done to her by the rift that I had caused. We passed the key through the letterbox and a neighbour let us out. She was full of questions about prison life. What was the food like? What happened during the day? It was difficult to explain the mind-killing futility or how this was meant to be punishing me, at a cost to the taxpayer of £40 000 a year.

When it was time to say goodbye, I had to drop her at the station to hand her back to my mother, as part of the terms of my licence specified that I could not go to the airport. She kicked and she screamed, she resisted and I had to fight to hand her back to my mother as I turned my back and took the train back into London. I have never cried to leave my mother. I have never even looked back, away from her, I can live my life, close to her, she kills. I watched her face contort as she saw that Marina would rather stay with me, in spite of the luxury and physical objects they dumped on her. She knew she was loved absolutely, unconditionally.

I had asked for a subsequent home leave to attend a day conference in preparation for the exam for the Open University course. I asked if I could stay out the night but they refused and only granted a one-day licence. I had also asked to attend a week long course at ARTS London on making handmade bags, by a leading designer.

The day I was going out to attend on licence for the Open University conference, my licence was nowhere to be found. One of the conditions of the terms of the licence was that I had to sign a copy of it and carry it with me everywhere. And I wasn't allowed to leave until we found it. Jackie, the Senior Officer on duty that Saturday morning couldn't understand it. I could. This was the paper pusher's revenge in the back office, I had complained about her, Brenda, losing my applications and so she had shunted my licence under a pile of papers, which she thought we would never find. The SO was determined.

"I'm going to get you out of here today," she said.

We went up to the admin office and we both searched high and low for the darned essential piece of paper and its three copies. While we were looking, I found something in a file that said my licence for the bag-making course had been denied. The prison didn't deem it was requisite for my resettlement, it said. I didn't say anything but while we looked, I steamed. Finally we found it and Jackie was astonished.

"I wonder why it was left here? Everyone else's was down at the gate. That Brenda."

That Brenda had almost succeeded in putting the kibosh on my day out. The more I thought about it, the more I stewed. I stewed all the way to London. I stewed all day during the revision seminar and I continued to stew over it at around the time I should have been leaving London to head back for Surrey. Fuck them. I hated Downview, I hated the namby-pamby governor who was too frightened to face up to his own staff, I had come to severely dislike the education department who had tried to make me into their new prodigy.

At forty I was felt a tad a bit too old to play the ingénue. I appreciated what they taught me, but the talent was mine and I went along with entering pieces into local art exhibitions and fairs and the annual Koestler Awards, but then they became proprietary about my work. Items which I had made using the prison's materials were deemed to "belong" to the prison. I was having none of it. I demanded my pieces back and asked for the entries into the Koestler to be returned forthwith, which was a shame because a scrapbook I had compiled for my children *The Buddha Wuddha Dharma Rama* had won a merit. I decided I wasn't going back to Downview.

That night, I appealed to Sir Malcolm to help, laying out the case as to why I needed to do this course at Arts London and I wrote an e-mail to the governor and the deputy governor stating that they were causing a lot of distress by ignoring the fact that I had no means to make a living when I came out of prison. I couldn't go back into media, and the magazine had folded. I needed them to take my request seriously. The e-mails bounced back as the e-mails listed for them on the Prison Services website were not correct. Surrey police came to the flat to see if I was there, I didn't answer the door and they left. A lot has already been written about "blogging on the run." I had some things I needed to take care of, then I was going to surrender myself, which I knew I had to, there were as still seven months to run on my sentence, and that was if

I didn't get any extra time added for "absconding," although they knew all the time exactly where I was.

The Daily Mail contacted me via a blog I started on MySpace, and said that they wanted to meet and interview me about prisoners' rights and why I had not returned to prison. I didn't trust the smarmy reporter, Neal Sears, at all. I asked Guy Adams what he thought of him and he told me to go back to prison and not to get involved with *The Daily Mail* that I would only end up hurting myself. Then they offered to pay the fee, which had been outstanding since the article I wrote about Allan and Willie.

I knew it was a sting because they are about as capable of subterfuge as Basil Fawlty. I saw it as a quick and convenient way to get back to prison, which is where I needed to get. I finished the outstanding business I still had, which included securing my flat by letting it out and sending off some documents so that the bankruptcy could be lifted. It was well over three years since the whole fiasco had started.

I had gone to Devon, because I had never been there and because if I were caught I would not be returned to Downview, it was out of their "catchment" area.

I met Neil Sears' correspondent colleague Paul Bracchi at a hotel in Plymouth. It was obvious from the way they were all behaving like spies from a bad Austin Powers film that there was subterfuge involved. Trying so hard not be obvious, they stood out like sore thumbs.

As soon as I arrived, I asked him for some money to pay the minicab driver who had brought me from where I was staying in Devon. I could see him anxiously watching me from the glass door in the hotel lobby, was I going to run away? They had kept the location of the meeting secret till I arrived in Plymouth and I was told to call Paul Bracchi or the photographer when I arrived at a certain roundabout. During these last six days, I was in constant contact with a Sergeant at the local police station to Downview Prison. They made a big deal of checking us into the room for the interview and setting up the recorder, they had hired a photographer who I think might have been an undercover policeman. At the end of the interview, after enough tears and contrition for the reckless way I had behaved in the past, he handed me an envelope stuffed full of £50 notes. He said he would see me down to my taxi, which was waiting.

He took me down another bank of elevators and there, lo and behold and much to my non-surprise were two Plymouth plain-clothes detectives waiting to arrest me. I was held in the local police station and then sent to a prison in Gloucestershire, HMP Eastwood Park, which was the closest one.

It was a busy, urban prison, which had been set up more for people held on

262

remand than for people serving out sentences. The guards were extremely nice and the governor who adjudicated my "absconding," listened to the reasons I did not want to go back to Downview. I had with me the copies of my e-mails to my MP and the governors, explaining why I was unhappy. She respected my point of view although in no way did she condone it and she gave me one week's loss of canteen and one week's loss of earnings.

These punishments were suspended, which meant if I stayed out of trouble within the prison system for thirty days, they would not come into effect. This was the lightest form of reprimand that she could do; I had been expecting at least an extra three months tacked onto the end of my sentence. I thanked God and Kabbalah and decided to put my head down and get on with it.

Now the chaos and unsuitability of this new prison hit me. I wrote to the governor of Downview, stating that I was sorry and that I wanted to come back, I got a terse reply from his deputy, Collin Harnett, that this would not be possible. By the time I got the reply, I was more settled and saw that the staff genuinely cared about the female inmates; they did everything they could to help.

My experience with Governor Memory made me realize that there were still some people within the prison system who hadn't had the humanity eviscerated out of them, but they were few and far between. I was about to enter the innermost circle of hell and experience the other spectrum of prison life. I was told I had to pack up, I was being shipped to HMP Foston Hall in Derbyshire.

Costa del Foston

I was shipped along with another woman, who had recent court appearances near HMP Eastwood Park, to Foston Hall in a Securicor van. Human Rights campaigners and indeed elements within the present administration deem these cattle trucks as unfit for human use. You are locked in a small cubicle, within the metal van, which is airless and has no window. No light is able to enter the dismal cage because the windows are tinted out, either black or red, which makes the passing vista look like something from Mars. Everything that is green is turned a blistery red hue.

This other girl, a pretty Asian Pakistani girl in her late twenties, was returning to Foston Hall and told me that I would like it. She had been caught up in the collapse of her husband's criminal empire, which was financed by importing heroin from Pakistan and Afghanistan. She was beautiful, in a filmy Bollywood way. She had four children who were with his mother and she was relieved to be returning to Foston Hall, she was in the privileged wing, which had more "freedom" than the rest of the prisoners and it was easier to get shipped out into an open or semi-open prison from there. Her children could resume their visits again. She also had applied for a visit to go and see her husband who was in a men's prison only two miles away. The application had gone in nine months ago, she still hadn't heard anything.

It was situations such as these that infuriated me. I asked her how she felt about being in prison for some hideous length of time, she had already been in for two years and had another four years left to go. The Judge had handed her a heavier sentence than the one he gave her husband, as he deemed that she was really the mastermind behind it all. She was resigned to it but said she would never forgive him. I asked if she would leave him. She looked at me as if I had grown another head suddenly,

"And where would I go? I have four children; no other man's family would accept me."

She told me how they had been married very young, she was a lot younger than he was, by about ten years, and she had been in awe of his glamorous lifestyle and all the things he could buy. But didn't she have any inkling of how he was getting the money? She must have known, he bought properties over the Midlands and was considered one of Birmingham's big suppliers. Didn't it bother her that drugs ruined lives?

"Our boys don't take them, it's only the white *gorah* that take drugs, and good, look how they are, and they don't deserve to live."

"That's rubbish, Asian boys take lots of drugs…"

She interrupted with a steely look in her eye, "No, they are too smart for that. They pretend to do it, but really they sell. The Q'uran says they are meant for hell anyway."

Then I knew she must have had an inkling as to what was happening in her husband's life and was not quite the innocent with the latest Chloe handbag she might have had me believe. She had been programmed very well, by the dogma he fed her to partake in a scheme so hideous that it would ruin young people's lives forever, and to justify it with this kind of prattle, that what she and her husband were doing was just a short circuit to the final solution to which urban white kids were destined anyway. I liked her, I felt sorry for her, but I didn't understand her. Prison is a good place for the suspension of judgment.

I had started to correspond regularly with the Kabbalah Centre in London. They had a prison outreach program, which sent me books and CDs. I wrote to the administrator of that program and I was amazed that he wrote back and that his letters were filled with light and compassion. He was matter-of-fact about it and spoke about Kabbalah in a way that I could respond to, not with the esoteric mumbo-jumbo that some of the older books espouse. I tried it, the practice of restraint and non-reactivity and it worked. The essence of it is that there is darkness and there is light and every moment of my life I have a choice, to grow to the light or to react to something in anger or violence or malicious words, which will compound the darkness in my life. I made a conscious effort to try and do positive actions, to help and create a space around myself, which was first of all neutral.

Then from that space, I could build the sort of life I wanted. It was hardest to change my thinking. The clamouring self-doubts and my ego, the length and width of the Great Wall of China, wrestled in me, to tell me that it was a cult, I couldn't possibly change. Who did I think I was kidding to pretend I could?

But I was persistent. Change happened quietly, I noticed it myself, as I grew less angry about the situation at Foston Hall and governor Paddy Scriven's ineptness. I decided I could best effect change once I was out. I received ignorant letters from Tony McNulty and Gerry Sutcliffe who were both Home Office Ministers then, which they had written to my MP, in response to my complaints. These men showed how little they knew about what really happened inside a women's prison by the way they couldn't address any of the issues raised in my letters and complaints.

I had been banned from using the computers at Foston Hall. They were all networked but it was impossible to get on the internet. However, just in case, 266 it was deemed, in another life, I might have been a hacker, which was a natural progression from having once been a journalist and so I was barred from the computer room. Friends wrote letters for me on the Word program, which wasn't easy given my illegible hand. There's always a way around a stupid imposition, a favour owed or some small gift, that can easily bypass what had been decreed for no sensible reason. It's the small deals that are made over a bar of chocolate or a letter written home, that made life bearable inside.

Foston Hall used to be a country estate. Then it was a children's home and then the Government requisitioned it to make it a Borstal. It has had several incarnations, in the last fifty years, as an institution for the insane, as a men's prison and now, under the alcoholic tremor of Paddy Scriven's hands, it was considered the worst run female prison in the entire estate. It had the highest rate of self-harm and suicide and the least understandable system of administration. She wants to govern everything micro-cosmically. But she is inherently lazy and would much rather sit in her wood-paneled office which looks out onto the rose beds and acre-long field that prisoners are not allowed to access. The only time we could walk around it was when we were supervised, during an exercise break, on Saturday mornings, notably when Paddy was away. She teetered around in four-inch fake Prada heels and ageing department store suits, the kind young women wear when they are starting out and can't afford proper clothes. She must have been close to sixty yet still she believed she looked thirty. Once upon a time she might have been quite attractive but now she was a poor replica of that long forgotten beauty, though she was trying to hold onto it, this faded remnant of something she might have had for a moment, at best.

The gossip was that she also liked a tipple, before noon, if possible and she was blotto after lunch. Paddy ate her lunch off china plates and with silver cutlery, not for her, the plastic plates we prisoners were given. Her food was catered from the local village, not cooked in the prison kitchen.

She circled me like a shark almost as soon as I arrived. It was a game, she had heard about my complaints and frequent redress to Ombudsman and Imran Khan. She needed a rabble rouser in her sylvain retreat like she needed a hole in the head. Maxine Carr was an ex-élève of Costa del Foston and had been close to Paddy Scriven.

She had been released back out into the world from there and Paddy had supported all her applications for a new identity, and a new home and the taxpayer had paid for it.

I wanted to apply for Home Detention Curfew to serve out the last four months of my sentence and every single obstacle that was possible was put in my way. When I tried to get the appointed outside probation officer to check my address he could not gain access. That was it, as far as he was concerned he had tried, he had ticked his box, and gone to inspect the flat. There was nothing more he was obliged to do. He totally ignored the human face of this problem. I tried to get the locks changed from inside but again, everything proved more than difficult. Friends tried to help but locksmiths were curious as to why a person in prison would want to have access to her flat if she wasn't going to be in it for months.

My skanky tenant, Rachel Swank, who claimed to be a TV presenter turned out to be a glorified stripper and was running a dubious escort agency from the flat. She stopped paying any rent and I was paying the mortgage from money *The Daily Mail* had paid and some savings I had managed to keep untouched.

I wrote to her to evict her, so I could use the flat as the address for HDC and she wrote to the prison's security department stating that I was harassing her, politely omitting the fact that she was in the flat illegally. When I tried to evict her, she called the police and they told my friend who was there to change the locks that he had to go back with the right papers. He had all the documentation he needed but the tenant played the innocent blonde and he happened to be six feet tall and black.

She paid one month's rent and stayed there for seven months. It wasn't the loss of money that hurt, although that was painful it was that I could see this being the course the rest of my life might take. I was a criminal; I would always be doubted, second-guessed and treated unfairly. I was told I could no longer communicate with her and although the Senior Officer from Security saw through her machinations he was powerless to stop her. The police came to see me at Foston Hall, to investigate complaints from her that I had let the flat to her illegally and that it wasn't mine to rent. I was hauled out of the prison to the local cop shop and thanks to a lot of paperwork and a copy of the title deeds from an entry in Land Registry that line of enquiry was NFA'd.

The library was meant to be a resource for us in prison, to try and sort out our resettlement needs. There was a prisoner who I had met at another prison, Sherelle, who had a long sulky face and a nasty attitude. I wasn't clear what she was in for, it seemed to change on a weekly basis and she had difficulty in keeping her story straight.

The Resettlement Governor was Amanda Dobbs, a openly lesbian woman who had worked her way up through the ranks from being a lowly officer just a couple of years ago, to this position of power by sleeping her way up the pay grade. I didn't like her at all. I tried to talk to her and she addressed me as "the lass who absconded from Downview." I told her in a formal complaint that I was not a lass and considerably older than she was and that it was the strangest abscondment, as I was in constant contact with local Surrey police station. I am not sure what they made of me; they went from being super careful in their dealings to being downright useless and neglectful. The resettlement team at Foston is pathetic, they seem to want to do everything possible to stop an inmate's progress and resettlement plans that they can. And in the scheme of things, in the Queen of Hearts dispensation of power in the Alice in Wonderland of Foston Hall, they held all the trump cards. I got nowhere and Christmas 2006 was probably the lowest point of my life.

I had maintained a blog, with the help of a friend who was a journalist. I would read it out to her over the prison's monitored phone calls and she would upload it on my MySpace page. If I couldn't reach her by phone, I would send it under Rule 39, which was reserved for privileged correspondence between a solicitor and a prisoner and left the prison sealed and not security checked. It took a while for them to catch on to that and only when one of the officers saw that I had written about him on the blog, did they figure out how to stop these entries.

The message was delivered though, word came back that the Home Office was investigating lapses in Scriven's paranoid but porous security. It became harder and harder to talk to my children, my parents took them to India for the holiday and although they promised to take a mobile phone, I couldn't contact them. That was the first time my father made mention of the children's social worker and when I questioned him about it he shut up like a clam in cold water and I could get nothing else out of him. I asked Imran, who said something vague about Mrs Adonis and that she was nice. I wasn't concerned about it, I wish I had been. My parents had taken the opportunity to recreate themselves as perfect carers – at least in their eyes – only this time, with my children. They told me there was a court order keeping the children in South Africa and that they had been made wards of the court.

If I wanted them back, I would have to apply through the Cape Town Family Court. It was impossible to sort out the simplest problem in prison, all our phone numbers had to be security vetted, and the money we were allowed to put onto our telephone accounts from our personal accounts was too little to allow any kind of administration of this volume or intricacy. I had to sit on my hands and wait it out.

Power is a strange thing when it is put into the hands of small people. It can be perverting and used for pure evil. I remember Val, a fat and frumpy, but generally kind officer from Downview telling me how she reacted when someone had pushed in front of her, to get the last parking space in the superstore car park. "I just thought to myself, you wait till I see you in my prison, you bitch, because then you'll see who gets the last laugh."

I wondered if it was normal but she was one of the officers I got along with well and I didn't question the logic. They are all failed somethings. No one starts out in life at the tender age of five or six and looks with dreamy, faraway eyes to that distant place when they can achieve their chosen career as prison officer. Prison officers have to take the most basic tests and evaluations to ensure they are suitable and they don't earn much more than a supermarket clerk.

The Official Secrets Act binds them, so they aren't going to retire in style on the royalties of that tell-all autobiography either. Day in, day out, they are tied to the same routine as the prisoners whom they are guarding: they eat, sleep and shit when they are told, although they can leave it all at the gate at the end of their grueling eight-hour shift, there is still the gloomy prospect of having to do it all over again. The gray prison pallor overcomes their complexions too, from too many hours spent inside. There is a new and enlightened breed. Helen, the pretty blonde on my wing at Foston Hall really wanted to help and chose it as a career option. She wanted to help people change but having been an officer for about two years now in the horrible stifling atmosphere of Foston Hall, she had seen too many people leave and come back.

The statistics were damning, Foston Hall had the highest number of recalls from probation and parole than any other prison in the UK. There was no way to address the problems that made us end up here in the first place, it was purely about survival.

The staff survived on snitching on each other, on inmates and the heavily gay quotient of officers and the bitchiness that existed when these femme on femme relationships ended, added to the general air of paranoia and nastiness.

January was the cruelest month, in 2007, never mind TS Elliot. When February 16th finally came round, I was unleashed on the world, with little ceremony. The prison handed me my belongings, which I had left in the B+B in Devon and had been kindly sent on by the Devonshire Constabulary, and I was allowed to call a taxi, but I had to wait outside the gate. I had been told there was a lot of media interest in my release and I half expected a flash of paparazzi at the gate. But the flesh-eating tabloid public has a short attention span, and Imran Khan claimed to not know my exact release date and fobbed enquirers off with something a little later in February. Maybe Foston Hall in deepest Derbyshire was just a train ride too far to justify capturing my wobbly new legs, on which I ventured into my new life.

Standing in the drizzle of a February morning, with too much stuff and sheaves of papers, complaints, letters and examples of how the Prison Service treated women unfairly, I waited for the cab. I was intent on doing something with the rest of my life. Something good. No doubt some of the injustices poured on the incarcerated population were, in the eyes of the poached egg eating *Daily Mail* readers, nothing they should care about. But change comes from inside, from having the courage to know you can.

It takes a massive effort and a lot of support. Instead of spending money on rosebushes and catered lunches daily, called in from outside, if governors such as Paddy Scriven had the slightest inkling of how much good they could do, and what positive changes they could bring about in the lives of women who had turned to crime, surely they would step up to it.

The cab arrived. It was driven by a woman who couldn't have been less than sixty, and her friend who accompanied her on this Thelma and Louise journey of adventure, transporting an ex-con back to London.

The first stop was my probation officer in Dorset Close, off Marylebone Road. I was given an allocated time to be there and I couldn't face trains with so much luggage. It is amazing how much I gathered in those twenty-one months. I was like a magpie, collecting things around me, almost in an obsessive or manic way,
to weigh me down and prove I still existed. He was sprightly and kind, Alaistair Wood. He was a senior probation officer. I had no idea where I was going to go after the Probation interview. I didn't know if the tenant had left the flat, or anything in it.

I picked up my keys, the last keys to have worked which I had sent out when I was still trying to get the HDC, from the friend that had tried to secure the flat for me. It was Sandra, who had introduced me to Allan, years ago. She was all hugs and smiles and a blaze of colour, in her Soho media office, and it was like coming home for real, seeing her outside of prison visiting rooms.

"So now you are out what are you going to do?" She asked.

"Get into my flat and have a proper bath with real soap."

My life had become a lot smaller, my needs a lot simpler. But finally it was a life which I could call my own. I had set off on the journey to create my own definition of who I was and who I could become. There's nothing like freedom after enforced isolation, to focus the mind and reset priorities.

The last almost two years had been about unlearning old behaviour and discarding expectations, mine but mostly other people's of how I should be in this world. That included letting go of any deviancy such as crime. Anything self-destructive or dishonest was no longer an option and though I knew this in my head, the test would be whether I could live by these principles, in this new life. I knew I had a lot to prove and the burden was immense but it didn't weigh me down. I wasn't stepping into this new vision for anyone or with anyone's blessing. I was, for the first time doing what really mattered *to me*. I didn't know what that was or even which way to turn, but a small voice, the one I had always ignored, was urgent and audible and I felt this time, if I was going to make a success of the potential I could feel in myself, I had to listen.

I had created a life that fitted who I am, not what anyone thought I should be.

The next forty years is going to be about being me. There's nothing left to tell, there's no more left to write about it.

Another half a life to live it.